To Graeme
with all my love,

Anne xxx

Beyond the Highland Line

Kilchurn Castle, at the north end of Loch Awe;
'fast falling to decay, having lately been struck by lightning'

BEYOND THE
HIGHLAND LINE

Three Journals of Travel in
Eighteenth Century
Scotland

Burt, Pennant, Thornton

A.J. YOUNGSON

COLLINS
St James's Place, London
1974

William Collins Sons & Co Ltd
London · Glasgow · Sydney · Auckland
Toronto · Johannesburg

First published 1974
© A. J. Youngson 1974

ISBN 0 00 216051 X

Set in Monotype Baskerville
Made and printed in Great Britain by
William Collins Sons & Co Ltd Glasgow

CONTENTS

ILLUSTRATIONS

———◄►———

INTRODUCTION

I hope that this book will prove of some interest to those who enjoy accounts of travel, or who wish to obtain some understanding of what the Highlands were like two hundred years ago, and more. Johnson's *Journey* is the most famous and in many ways the best book about the Highlands in the eighteenth century; but it is readily accessible. What is re-printed here is not to be found in every home or library, yet Burt, Pennant and Thornton are all, at least in parts, informative and very readable.

The selections have been made with an eye chiefly to the light they throw on the manners and customs of the people, and on how they earned their livelihood. Thus the geological, archaeological and antiquarian passages in Pennant are omitted, as are most of the details of Thornton's fishing and shooting exploits.

The introductory essay gives a brief sketch of the Highlands and of how life was changing there in the eighteenth century. The reader who wishes to know more may consult my *After the Forty-Five*.

Edinburgh,
October, 1972

NOTES ON THE EXTRACTS

In extracting the several passages and paragraphs included in this book, I have tried to make up an abbreviated but continuously interesting version of each author's work which would seem as little discontinuous as possible. Sometimes a succession of pages are reproduced as they were originally printed, but sometimes single paragraphs follow one another with something omitted between each. Wherever there is an omission, and a fresh start has been made, this is indicated by a double stroke || at the beginning of the paragraph. In the few cases where a paragraph has not been included entire, this is indicated by an aposiopesis. Authors' footnotes have sometimes been omitted without indication, but some are included. Where footnotes are my own – and these have been kept to a minimum – they are followed by my initials.

The reader who wishes to refer back to the original should have no difficulty in doing so. Burt's letters are all numbered, which makes reference easy. And in the cases of Pennant and Thornton, the narrative is in the form of a journal with dates in the margin, and these dates are included in what is printed here.

The authors' own spelling and punctuation are given unaltered.

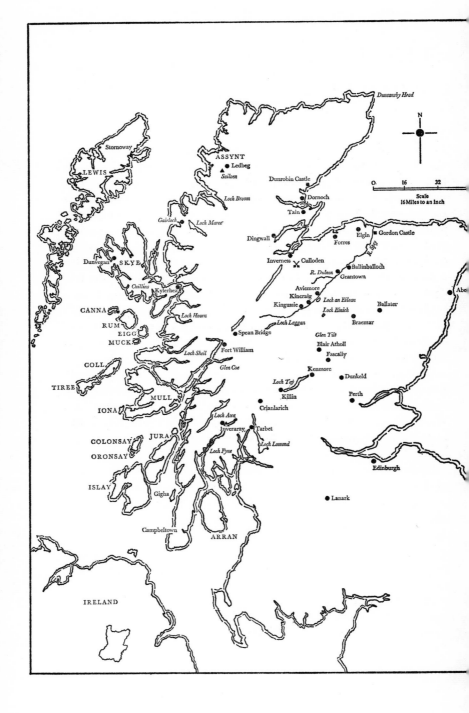

THE HIGHLANDS IN THE
EIGHTEENTH CENTURY

Until towards the very end of the eighteenth century, visitors to the Highlands did not report what they saw in romantic terms. Little inclined to go into raptures over Highland scenery, they tended to speak of the country almost with horror, as a black howling wilderness, full of bogs and boulders, mostly treeless, and nearly unfit for human habitation. To some extent, this was the result of their prejudices, for they were accustomed to life in the fertile, undulating, populated country further south. On the other hand, their attitude was sometimes detached and could be scientific. Pennant, for example, was a Fellow of the Royal Society, and it is significant that he dedicated his 1772 *Tour* to Sir Joseph Banks, who had with Captain Cook carried out what Pennant described as 'a circumnavigation, founded on the most liberal and scientific principles,' and who contributed the 'Account of Staffa' which Pennant included in his *Tour*.

In the first half of the century no one visited the Highlands for pleasure, or out of a sense of scientific curiosity. Roads were few and very bad, even south of the Great Glen; the loyalty of many of the clans was suspect; over large areas the law could not be enforced, unless exceptional efforts were made; and everyone spoke Gaelic. This, indeed, provided the most intelligible definition of the Highlands; they were the region where Gaelic – 'that nervous expressive tongue'[1] – was the only language of the great majority of the inhabitants. This area contracted during the eighteenth century, but only a little. It reached up the whole west coast from Campbeltown to Cape Wrath; it included the Outer Hebrides as well as the eastern slopes of the Grampians to within forty miles of Aberdeen; it extended as far south as Callander; and in addition, the

[1] J. L. Buchanan, *Travels in the Western Hebrides* (London 1793), p. 112.

Highlands were usually taken to include all the east coast north of Inverness, although Caithness was – and is – Scandinavian rather than Celtic in social origin and language.

The region thus defined is about one fifth of the area of England, Scotland and Wales, or approximately equivalent to the whole of England south of a line drawn from Ipswich to Hereford. In character, it varies immensely, being one sort of country south of the Great Glen and another north of that natural division, the east coast being quite different from the west coast, and the islands different again. It is not easy to appreciate the complexity of Highland geography, and in the eighteenth century, when travel was so much more difficult, the diversity of the region was even harder to grasp than it is today. Brief accounts are bound to oversimplify. But James Watt, who visited the Highlands in 1776 in order to survey the proposed route of the Caledonian Canal, wrote a description which is not easily improved upon:

The Highland mountains, which commence at the Firth of Clyde, extend upon the west side of the Country to the Northernmost Parts of Scotland; in general they begin close at the Sea Shore; they are intersected by deep but narrow Vallies; the Quantity of Arable Land is exceeding small, and its Produce greatly lessened by the prodigious rains that fall upon that Coast. The Tops of the Mountains are craggy, and their Sides are steep, but they produce a Grass very proper for breeding small Black Cattle, and in some Places for feeding Sheep.

The Sea Coast is exceedingly rugged and rocky, and abounds with great Inlets, which are excellent Harbours. It is sheltered by many Islands, which like the Main Land, are generally mountainous and rocky, but rather more fertile.

The Salt Water Loughs or Arms of the Sea, are Nurseries for Fish, of which many Kinds are found in Plenty in the Seas upon these Coasts. The Herrings, the Cod, and Ling, are those which are taken in greatest Quantities, and exported to Foreign Parts; but there are other Species, which may perhaps become Subjects of Trade.

The Shores produce in abundance the *Alga Marina,* or Sea Weed, which being burnt, makes the Alkaline Salt called Kelp. The Quantities of the Commodity made and consumed of late Years are immense, and the Rents paid for the Kelp of some Shores, have borne a great proportion to that of the Land they surrounded.

Kelp

There are in many parts of the Country considerable Coppice Woods of Oak and other Timbers. The Oak Woods have been greatly hurt by the destructive Practice of cutting them for their Bark, the Timber being often left to rot upon the Spot.

Timber -

The East Coast of *Scotland* exhibits a very different Prospect. The high Mountains are several Miles distant from the Sea Coast, the intermediate Space consists of Arable Lands intermixed with Hills of a moderate Size and Height. In many Places, great Tracts of level Ground are in a very advanced State of Cultivation, but the Country in general will admit Improvements and the Spirit of making them seems to be daily increasing. Although the Sea Ports are in general inconvenient, and the Coast no Way sheltered, yet [south of Inverness] it is lined with Towns, the Inhabitants of which are industrious. In many Places they subsist by fishing, though the fish upon that Coast are not to be compared, either for Plenty or Size, to those upon the West Side of the Country.[1]

It should be added that several of the islands on the west coast – Lewis, Skye, Mull and Islay – are quite large, and that the Outer Hebrides are a considerable distance from the mainland; Stornoway, on the east coast of Lewis, is about forty miles west of Loch Broom.

By the standards of the day, the Highlands were not very thinly peopled in the eighteenth century. Around 1750 there seem to have been about 300,000 inhabitants, of whom some 50,000 lived on the islands. This means that about a quarter of the whole population of Scotland was living in about one

[1] In 'Third Report of the Committee appointed to enquire into the State of the British Fisheries' (1785) App. 22.

half of the land area.[1] But the people were distributed very
unevenly over that area, living mostly in little groups of eight
or ten houses in the glens and straths or along the edge of
inland or sea lochs, or on the more congenial and cultivable
land near the sea shore. There were no concentrations of
population, very few villages, few sizeable regions even, where
large numbers of people lived within easy reach of one another.

This fragmentation of the population was largely a consequence of Highland geography, for communities were divided
from one another by extensive moorland, high mountains, or
the sea. But it was developed and perpetuated by prevailing
agricultural practices and by the clan system.

The origins of the clan system are obscure, but its functioning
for many generations before 1750 is clear enough. The Highlands constituted an area of mountainous country so broken up
and difficult to traverse that unified military control, and thence
unified government, could not be established. Small, largely iso-
lated communities therefore organised themselves in each district under the leadership of a chief, made their own laws and
conducted their own affairs. The chief settled all disputes and
regulated matters at his discretion; from his judgment there
was no appeal. His habitation was the centre of the life of the
clan, a number of whom constantly attended him both at home
and away from home. The larger clans consisted of several
'tribes' with a chieftain at the head of each, representative of a
family descended from that of the chief. Some of the sons of
these chieftains might live for most of the year at the chief's
house, being brought up with his children.

Every chief surrounded himself with as large a number of
followers as possible; his importance and capacity for self-
defence – as well as for injuring others – was not according to
his annual income but according to the number and fidelity of
his vassals and tenants. This mattered, because between the

[1] The Highland population increased to almost half a million by the middle
of the nineteenth century, but is now not very much larger than it was in
1750. The population as a percentage of that of Scotland is now only about
7%.

clans mutual rivalry and suspicion predominated, and each was so ready to take advantage of another's weakness that almost the only security which a chief could have lay in the command of a small army of followers, who would fight for him and his property; and the principal safety and means of livelihood that was within the reach of the ordinary Highlander was to place himself under the protection and among the adherents of some powerful chief. The land was the chief's; but the glory of the chief was the glory of all his kindred and followers. The clan regarded the chief as the father of his people, and themselves as his children; they believed him bound to protect and maintain them, while they were bound to regard his will as law, and to lay down their lives at his command. 'The most sacred oath to a Highlander, was to swear by the hand of his chief. The constant exclamation, upon any sudden accident, was, may God be with the chief, or, may the chief be uppermost.'[1]

These communities were poor, conservative, and in a sense barbarian; that is to say, their ambitions were concentrated on hunting, military exploits, and what has been called 'rude conviviality'. But they had to have a means of livelihood, and accordingly each was settled on its own territories in a system of economic as well as military subordination. It is no doubt true that the clansmen were little interested in improving their lot by commercial enterprise, and it is certainly true that at any rate prior to 1750 most of the produce of the land – cattle, corn, fish and game – was consumed by the clansmen themselves, a good proportion of it at the habitations of the chief and chieftains, in generous hospitality. But produce there had to be, either for direct consumption or for exchange in the lowlands, and in this respect land tenure and the organisation of agriculture were of the greatest importance. These determined, almost completely, the material well-being of the clan. And they were also responsible, after the 'Forty-five, for much of the confusion and misery which ensued when efforts were made to adapt a feudal or patriarchal system to the requirements of life in an increasingly commercial world.

[1] John Home, *The History of the Rebellion* (London 1802), p. 9.

The lands of the chief were let to his relations upon easy terms in larger or smaller farms according to the importance of the individuals concerned; and were by them parcelled out in turn to their friends and relations, on the same kind of terms. These principal tenants, or tacksmen as they were called, were the cadets of the family, or gentlemen of the clan, and they acted both as military officers and as managers of land. In general, they seem to have considered themselves to have as much right to the land as the chief himself, and to have regarded their farms as hereditary possessions; and when, after 1746, many of them were deprived of their farms they, along with large numbers of the ordinary Highlanders, regarded it as a piece of gross and unfeeling injustice. Next to the tacksmen were the tenants, who held land either directly from the chief, or, more commonly, from a tacksman; and below the tenants were the sub-tenants or cottars.

Thus every man was, to a greater or lesser extent, a cultivator or renter of land. In return, the tacksmen provided the chief, when he required it, with as many fighting men as they were able, and gave also a certain share of the produce of the land which they held from him. The system encouraged the subdivision of land into lots as small as possible, for the more the land was subdivided, the larger would be the number of men at the chief's command. As a result, the number of tenants and cottars settled on the farms was large, and their plots of land were very small, in the case of the cottars scarcely sufficient to afford a livelihood even to a small family: they had, as a rule, 'grass for a cow or two, and as much land as will sow about a boll of oats'. Their obligations, besides that of serving the chief in war, were to pay a very small sum of money as part of the rent, to pay the remainder in kind (butter, oatmeal, a fraction of a sheep), and to assist the tacksman or tenant to farm such land as he retained in his own hands.

The nineteenth century thought very poorly of these arrangements:

with the land so much subdivided, with no leases, and with tenures so uncertain, with so many oppressive exactions, with no incitement to industry or improvement, but with every encouragement to idleness and inglorious self-contentment, it is not to be supposed that agriculture or any other industry would make any great progress. For centuries previous to 1745, and indeed for long after, agriculture appears to have remained at a stand-still.[1]

There is a good deal of truth in this, although it over-simplifies a complicated situation. The principal crops were oats and barley, sometimes a little flax. Vegetables were scarcely grown until towards the end of the eighteenth century; even potatoes were uncommon before the 1770s, although in the next decade or two they became the staple food of most Highlanders. In the first half of the century and in several districts throughout most of the second half of the century also, the rotation of crops was unknown. Instead, the land was divided into infield and outfield; the former was constantly cropped, either with oats or bear, along with an occasional ridge of flax where the ground was thought suitable, and the latter, commonly, was plowed three years for oats, and then for the next six years left at 'pasture' for horses, black cattle and sheep. The instruments of cultivation were the cas-chrome or crooked spade, which consisted of a strong piece of wood about six feet long, bent near the lower end, with a thick flat wooden head, shod with an iron tip; and the old Scots plow. This latter was a crude, simple and antique instrument which could scarcely do more than scratch the surface of the ground; even so, plowing required the labour of five or six men, assisted by an equal if not a larger number of horses or cattle. There were no carts, so all bulky commodities had to be transported on horse-back, on sledges, or on the backs of men or women. In rough country where horses could not go, it was hard work to carry sea-weed, used as a manure, up to the small pockets of good soil which were worked among the rocks:

> One must be a hard-hearted taskmaster that will not pity a poor woman with her petticoats tucked up to her knees, and a heavy load of dung, or wet sea-tangle, on her back, mounting those rugged declivities and steep hills, to the

[1] J. S. Keltie, *A History of the Scottish Highlands* (Edinburgh 1879), p. 8.

distance of a compleat mile from the sea before they lay the burdens on the ground.[1]

Clumps of brushwood and heaps of stones everywhere interrupted and disfigured the fields. Until almost the end of the century many Highlanders adhered to the immemorial practice of beginning to plow on Old Candlemass Day, and sometimes did not finish sowing until June. Nothing was then done in the fields until September, when the crops were harvested. But due to poor soil and an unreliable climate, failure of the harvest was not infrequent, causing scarcity or even famine. According to one authority, the inhabitants of some of the Western Isles looked for a failure once in every four years.

But grain crops were not the sole or perhaps even the most important produce of highland agriculture. It was in the raising of livestock, particularly cattle, that the Highlanders found their chief advantage. Horses, of course, they had to have, and they kept surprisingly large numbers; this was because so many were needed for plowing, and for transporting peat, sea-weed, shell-sand, and other items. From some districts these garrons, as they were called, were sent for sale to the lowlands. Active and hardy, they seem to have resembled a modern Shetland pony,

> so small that a middle-sized man must keep his legs almost in lines parallel to their sides when carried over the stony ways; and it is almost incredible . . . how nimbly they skip with a heavy rider among the rocks and large moor-stone, turning zig-zag to such places as are passable.[2]

For most of the year these horses were allowed to run wild among the hills; but in the severest weather they were some-times brought down and fed, if there was food to spare. Sheep were far less important, and were kept simply to provide a little wool and to supplement the Highlander's meagre diet. They were housed a good deal of the time, partly because they did not have the stamina to withstand the winters out of doors, and partly because, in the hills, foxes and eagles would be sure

[1] Buchanan, *op cit* , pp. 148–9.
[2] Burt, *Letters*, Letter xx.

to pick off a proportion of them. There were flocks of goats, kept for their milk, and for the skins which were sold at the little towns on the Highland frontier, like Crieff or Blairgowrie. But what really mattered were the small shaggy black cattle, much the most important and often the only money-producing item on a farm. Money rents were paid from the sale of cattle, and this also provided most of the income which enabled the Highlanders to buy metal goods, salt, tobacco and occasional articles of dress in the lowlands. Not surprisingly, there was a tendency to overstock the farms with cattle. During summer and autumn the beasts were kept on the hills so as to prevent them from injuring the crops, which were unprotected by walls of any kind. After the harvest the animals were brought back and allowed to roam freely across the farms or even whole districts, being given little or nothing to eat except what they could pick up for themselves in the fields. There was an idea that the housing of cattle tended to enfeeble them; this, coupled with the almost complete absence of winter fodder, meant that many died of cold and starvation every winter, and that those which survived were mere skeletons, scarcely able to stand when the warmer days returned and the grass began to grow again. In many districts the movement from the *baile geamhraidh* or winter 'toun' set in the midst of the cultivated land, to the summer pastures in the hills was an annual migration which, although on a small scale, had epic qualities:

As there were extensive shealings or grasings attached to this country, in the neighbourhood of the lordship of Badenoch, the inhabitants in the beginning of summer removed to these shealings with their whole cattle, man, woman, and child; and it was no uncommon thing, to observe an infant in one creel, and a stone on the other side of the horse, to keep up an equilibrium; and when the grass became scarce in the shealings, they returned again to their principal farms, where they remained while they had sufficiency of pasture, and then, in the same manner, went back to their shealings, and observed this ambulatory course during the seasons of vegetation; and the only operations attended to during the summer season was their peats or fuel, and repairing their rustic habitations. When their small crops were fit for it, all hands descended from the hills, and continued on the farms till the same was cut and secured in barns, the walls of which were generally made of dry stone, or wreathed with branches or boughs of trees; and it was no singular custom, after harvest for the whole inhabitants to return to their shealings, and to abide there until driven thence by the snow . . . The cultivation of the country was all performed in spring, the inhabitants having no taste for following green crops or other modern improvements.[1]

About the end of August or the beginning of September, when the animals were in peak condition – the beef 'extremely sweet and succulent' – the drovers collected their herds, and drove them along the winding roads or tracks through the glens and over the hills to the fairs and markets at Crieff, Perth, Falkirk, or in the north of England.

Agriculture was the principal occupation and the sale of cattle was the main trade of the Highlanders. In other respects they were almost entirely self-sufficient. Men were quite commonly their own tailors, shoe-makers, stocking-weavers, coopers, and carpenters. They made nets and hooks for fishing, brooches, and rings 'for their favourite females'. Plows, sledges, cas-chrome and rakes (when used) were made on the farm. Salt was a shilling the bushel; little soap was used; they had no candles, but instead split the roots of fir trees. There was no tea or sugar consumed, and only a little whisky, ale being the common drink. The women, as well as the men, were weavers, and it was they who waulked the cloth on a wicker instrument, about ten feet by three, called *cleadh luaidh*, sitting on either side and working the cloth to and fro with their hands or feet. They made the short tartan coats, breeches, plaids and long or short gowns which were everyday wear throughout the Highlands; and also a little linen, sometimes for sale further south.

Prior to 1750 or thereabouts, if anything was needed which

---

[1] *Old Statistical Account* (1798), Vol. xx, pp. 24–5, Boleskine and Abertarf (Inverness).

could not be produced locally, it was not easy to obtain. The only town of any importance was Inverness. Campbeltown was no more than a small fishing port, and Stornoway was scarcely even that. Fort Augustus, Inveraray, Crieff and Dunkeld were very small places indeed, and there were no others worth a mention. As a result, there were few central stores where salt, iron, tobacco or corn could be purchased even when there was money to pay for them. If such goods were wanted, a long journey had probably to be undertaken to the nearest town, ideally when a fair was being held and itinerant merchants offered a wider than usual choice.

It is well known, of course, that clansmen ventured outside their own territory for other reasons than those of honest trade. Clan wars, or at least sporadic skirmishes between clans, were at one time an established part of life. These might or might not be connected with what was euphemistically described as 'cattle lifting'. In wild country, thinly inhabited and full of places of concealment, there was an obvious temptation to drive away someone else's cattle roaming in the hills. By the middle of the eighteenth century those who took part in such expeditions seem generally to have been 'broken' men, belonging to no particular clan and possibly regarded simply as outlaws. They operated particularly successfully near the lowlands, where there was less danger of retaliation. Rannoch, for example, according to the Old Statistical Account, was prior to 1745 'in an uncivilised barbarous state, under no check, or retraint of laws'. Gangs from Rannoch

> laid the whole country, from Stirling to Coupar of Angus, under contribution, obliging the inhabitants to pay them Black Meal, as it is called, to save their property from being plundered. This was the centre of this kind of traffic. In the months of September and October they gathered to the number of about 300, built temporary huts, drank whisky all the time, settled accounts for stolen cattle, and received balances. It would have required a regiment to have brought a thief from that country.[1]

The victims tried to protect themselves by organising armed

[1] *Old Statistical Account* (1792), Vol. II, p. 457, Fortingal.

bands to fight off the raiders; but the honesty of these in turn came into question, and it was alleged that they sometimes used their position to travel about the country under the pretence of enquiring after stolen cattle but actually preparing for depredations of their own. Suspicion, conflict and occasional warfare were thus the order of the day.

Thrice during the eighteenth century the military valour of the Highlander was turned against the government. In the autumn of 1715 the Jacobite chiefs raised the standard for King James, the Old Pretender, in western Aberdeenshire. Many clans responded, either from loyalty to their chiefs or out of a love of war or hope of plunder; and in a short time 12,000 men were assembled under arms, coming mostly from the central and west Highlands. This affair, which was pursued on the Jacobite side with little skill or effective enterprise, lasted only a short while and had small result. Some prisoners, mostly taken at the battle of Preston, were hanged, and a rather feeble attempt was subsequently made to disarm the clans. More important, the government strengthened its defensive arrangements by sending General Wade to the Highlands in 1724, charged with the task of building roads to facilitate the movement of troops and supplies south of the Great Glen; and it organised some of the loyal clansmen into the so-called 'independent companies', later the Black Watch, whose duty it was to patrol the frontier and provide intelligence of what was happening in the remoter Highlands. A minor and totally abortive rising took place in 1719. Then, a quarter of a century later, in July, 1745, the Young Pretender landed with a handful of followers at Eriskay in the Outer Hebrides. His hope seemed a forlorn one.

A few days after his arrival, some Highlanders (not a very considerable number) joined him, and descending from their mountains, undisciplined, and ill armed, without cavalry, without artillery, without one place of strength in their possession, attempted to dethrone the king, and subvert the government of Britain.[1]

The attempt failed, but its failure was not complete until almost

[1] Home, *op. cit.*, pp. 1–2.

nine months after Charles's landing, and there were times when it seemed very near success; and all this despite the facts that Inverness and the north Highlands were held for the government by loyal clans such as the Mackays and the Rosses, and that the army which Charles led into England late in the autumn of 1745 was only about half the size of the forces which the Earl of Mar had been able to command in 1715.

As the Highlanders advanced south, it became clear that the vast majority of the population in the lowlands of Scotland and in England were indifferent or actively hostile to the rising. In the absence of general support within the country, or of effective help from France, the rebellion was almost bound to fail; yet so incompetent was the handling of the government troops, so brave and often skilful were the rebels, that the issue remained for some months in doubt. Charles reached as far south as Derby, and the clansmen loyally marched with him although far from home in a strange and hostile country. But two armies were in the field against the Prince, each larger than his own, and he had to retreat. In April 1746 was fought the murderous, disastrous Battle of Culloden, and the rebellion was over.

The Battle of Culloden ended much more than the 'Forty-five. Drastic steps were taken both to 'pacify' the Highlands and to destroy for good the military power of the chiefs and the clans. Government troops 'scoured' the glens in the summer of 1746, and little mercy was shown to those who had been involved in the rebellion. The operation of disarming the Highlanders was begun again, and this time pursued with thoroughness. Their pride and identification with their fellow-clansmen were struck at by an Act which proscribed the wearing of tartan – 'the garb of sedition'.[1] No fewer than eleven Highland estates belonging to rebellious chiefs were seized and transferred to the Crown, to be managed for the better part of thirty years by a group of Commissioners dedicated to improving, modernising and 'civilising' the Highlands. At the same time, those chiefs and nobles who remained in possession of their lands found their legal powers and status reduced by the

[1] G. S. Prye, *Scotland from 1603 to the Present Day* (Edinburgh 1962), p. 66. This Act remained in force until 1782.

abolition of their hereditary rights of jurisdiction over those living within their territories.

Yet these assaults by government on the clan system were less effective in destroying it than the insidious operation of commercial forces. These forces had been felt before the 'Forty-five in some districts, notably in lowland Perthshire and in the south-west; but they obtained new scope after the rebellion for two reasons. First, the military power of the chiefs was shattered, evidently beyond repair; and at the same time they were brought into increasing contact with the 'modern' lowland world – a world where landowners enjoyed more of the good things of life than in the Highlands partly because they made their estates pay. Men, so long the pride of the Highland chief, no longer supported his position. In order to live well, to emulate his richer neighbours further south, to enjoy the material pleasures of Edinburgh and London, what he needed was money. And so the Highland proprietors began to take advantage of the legal power, which they undoubtedly possessed but had never exercised, of doing with their land as they pleased, renting it to whom they pleased, regardless of the feelings, the protests and the customary rights of the old tacksmen and tenants. It was this breaking up of established social and economic relations which destroyed the old pattern of feudal or patriarchal life in the Highlands and which brought about the state of confusion which existed there, in varying degrees of intensity, for at least a hundred years after 1750.

By almost any standard, the changes which took place were rapid, and to the members of a conserving society[1] they seemed extremely, overwhelmingly rapid. Moreover, one followed another, so that change was persistent, spreading from the frontier districts northward and westward into Sutherland and the Outer Hebrides. Strong passions were aroused by the new search for profitability. Tacksmen, asked for a higher rent or removed from the land in favour of a stranger who offered more,

appear to have resented this procedure as they would a

[1] The idea of conserving and innovating societies is discussed in Stuart Piggott, *Ancient Europe*, Ch. 1 (Edinburgh 1965).

personal injury from their dearest friends. It was not that the addition to the rents was excessive, or that the rents were already as high as the land could bear ... What seems to have hurt these gentlemen was the idea that the *tacksmen* laird, the father of his people, should ever think of anything so mercenary as rent, or should ever by any exercise of his authority indicate that he had it in his power to give or let his farms to the highest bidders.[1]

Many proprietors were loath to change, either from attachment to their people, or from a love of feudal show. But as the Highlands were gradually absorbed into a world dominated by technological change and all the progressive ideas of the Enlightenment, it became increasingly difficult – and in the end it became increasingly costly – to swim against the tide.

The new landlordism had in the first place the devastating effect of reducing the chiefs, as Dr Johnson put it, to mere 'traffickers in land'. It also had its own unattractive aspects. Under the old system tacksmen, tenants and sub-tenants had been, in important ways, equal before the chief, and chiefs had treated their people with kindness or at least consideration. Now the tacksmen either disappeared altogether, or, like the new lessees, were left free to do as they chose, and some of them oppressed and exploited the tenantry without scruple. This was all the harder to bear when the oppressors were those who had once been the tenants' own equals, but in the Outer Hebrides, at least, it seems to have been newcomers who caused most trouble:

> There is a great difference between that mild treatment which is shown to subtenants and even scallags, by the old lessees, descended of ancient and honourable families, and the outrageous rapacity of those necessitous strangers, who have obtained leases from absent proprietors, who treat the natives as if they were a conquered, and inferior race of mortals.[3]

[1] Keltie, *op. cit.*, p. 34.
[2] These were almost landless dependants whose time was devoted almost wholly to serving a subtenant, tacksman or laird.
[3] Buchanan, *op. cit.*, p. 50.

Probably the worst conditions existed where, in remote areas, the remains of feudal power lingered on. This did not always happen, for many estates continued to be directed by landlords who did not allow the search for profit to take precedence over all other considerations.

Nevertheless, the material advantages of life in the Highlands decidedly shifted in favour of the landlords and their immediate subordinates during the second half of the eighteenth century. The miserable standard of living of the ordinary people, subsisting almost entirely on potatoes and oatmeal, possibly declined a little. Their liability to food shortage may have increased, and their liability to dispossession certainly did. 'Life at the top', on the other hand, improved. The sale of produce expanded, and rents rose faster than prices. Some tacksmen, and some proprietors, began to unite the business of grazing and agriculture with that of trade, coupled occasionally with smuggling. Dr Johnson, on his visit to the Hebrides, found wine, polite conversation, and books in several languages in the houses of the proprietors. The tacksmen were no less prosperous. Renting large and often advantageous farms, able to employ labour for nothing or almost nothing, having the necessaries of life cheap and many of its luxuries smuggled to their doorsteps, they rolled, it was said, in ease and affluence.

These far-reaching changes were based in the first place on agricultural innovation. The old system of run-rig, sometimes coupled with the annual redistribution of land, began to disappear. Land began to be enclosed, and rotations to be practised. Lime was increasingly used on the fields, and more modern farm implements came slowly into use. In this last respect one of the most striking innovations seems to have been the use of farm carts. Wheeled vehicles in the Highlands before 1750 were exceedingly uncommon, and in the remoter districts farm carts were virtually or completely unknown. It was said that no cart was seen even in the burgh of Campbeltown until 1756; and that there was none in North Uist, South Uist or Benbecula as late as the end of the century. But by the 'seventies and 'eighties they were in use in most parishes, at least in the central and eastern Highlands. As a result of such innovations

28

more manure could be used, better crops were grown, and this made it easier to provide winter feed for the animals. Also, the old idea that the cattle would be enfeebled if they were housed in winter began to pass away. Thus the herds were strengthened, the soil was not continually depleted and worn out, and further improvements in husbandry became possible.

These changes, however, were not what dominated Highland agriculture. Improvements in tillage or in the management of cattle were less important than the spread of sheep farming. Before 1760 or thereabouts every household in the Highlands kept a few sheep; but there were no sheep farms, for the sheep grazed with the cattle, and were a subordinate item in the general scheme of agriculture. In the 1760s, however, experienced sheep farmers from the south began to rent farms in Argyll, Dunbartonshire and Perthshire, and to work them simply as sheep farms. Gradually sheep-farming spread north, and by the end of the century it was important in much of Argyll, in western Perthshire, and in parts of Inverness-shire as far north as Fort Augustus. The rents which the sheep farmers could offer exceeded what could be afforded by the old modes of agriculture, and so land formerly occupied by a number of tenants was often converted into sheep farms. Where once there had been many families, now there was only a shepherd, his flock and his dogs. The sheep-masters commonly came from the lowlands, bringing their sheep and their shepherds with them. This was not always the case – many of the tacksmen and even sub-tenants, seeing how much more profitable the new system could be than the old, wisely took a lesson in time, and rented land to stock it with sheep, reducing the arable to a minimum. But in general sheep-farming was an activity best performed on a large scale, and the opportunities for the sub-tenants were not good. Unable, on the whole, to adopt this new system of agriculture, they were swept aside by it; and by the 1780s the great and growing grievance of the Highlands was one familiar in England in the sixteenth century, 'that sheep do eat up men'.

Those who were removed had to find – or be found – somewhere else to live. Considerable numbers left the Highlands altogether. But in some cases the landlords settled them on waste land never before cultivated, giving them some small encouragements such as a few sticks of timber to build a house, or a boll of meal, or a little seed; or they might be settled near the coast and encouraged to become fishermen as well as farmers. The idea that fishing was to be the salvation of the Highlands, or at least of the ordinary Highlanders, attained remarkable popularity in the 'eighties and 'nineties. It was founded on the unquestionable fact that the seas off the west coast teemed with fish. There were white fish such as ling and cod ('esteemed superior to the Newfoundland'), haddock and whiting, flat fish, mackerel 'in mighty shoals' and salmon, besides lobsters, oysters and crabs, which brought no price and excited no attention. But above all there were herring. Great shoals of herring passed down the west coast from June onwards, some remaining in the Minch, but enormous numbers crowding into the narrow channels and the sea lochs along the coast, and in the Hebrides. Their arrival was marked by a rippling of the water, and by the large numbers of solan geese or gannets which attended them.

Fleets of herring busses awaited the arrival of the shoals. The largest numbers of these ships were Dutch – Holland had for long dominated the herring trade of western Europe; but the British fleet was growing, and by the 'seventies and 'eighties anything from a few dozen to a couple of hundred vessels would be found during the season concentrated initially at Campbeltown or in Shetland. Most of the fishing was not done directly from the busses, but by means of open boats, manned by four or five men, fishing at night. The Dutch fished out to sea, but the British busses remained on or near the coast, where the shoals were often very dense although their appearance in any particular loch or bay could never be relied upon. Loch Hourn, Loch Broom and the Long Island were particularly celebrated for herring, although Loch Fyne and the Firth of Clyde were the centre of the general west coast fishery, working for the rising industrial and commercial city of Glasgow, as well as for exportation to south-west Europe and the West Indies.

The native Highlanders had little part in all this activity. They were too poor to own busses, although some of them had small open boats which were usually fairly safe inshore. Their operations were limited, because it was illegal to sell to the herring busses, and salt for preserving fish, which would have made exportation possible, was very difficult to obtain because of the oppressive salt laws. This made it difficult for them even to preserve fish for their own use, and as a result they were only occasional fishers on a very small scale.

Efforts were made in the 'eighties and 'nineties to alter this state of affairs, and a number of little fishing villages were established by landlords or by the British Fisheries Society. Ullapool, begun in the late 1780s, was a modest success, at least to begin with, and Tobermory slowly developed into a little fishing and trading port. But these were very small places, struggling for survival, and they were of no importance before the 1790s. Before that, there were only four settlements worth a mention on the entire west coast. At Bowmore, on Islay, there was a handful of houses. Campbeltown, on the other hand, was the largest town in the Highlands after Inverness, and had been not unimportant even in 1750. It had an excellent harbour, a population already of several thousand when Pennant visited there in 1772, and was the principal port on the west coast for the herring busses. Stornoway, approximately 200 miles north of Campbeltown by the shortest possible sea route, hardly existed in 1750, but grew rapidly in the following decades. It too depended principally on the herring fishery, and a small fleet of about two dozen decked vessels was based there in the 1780s. The harbour was almost unimproved – there was no pier – but the little town boasted over forty slated houses, and the Earl of Seaforth, whose creation it partly was, might sometimes be met at the inn – 'the good woman of the house rushed into the room, calling out, "Seaforth, Seaforth!" and before we could utter a word, Seaforth, who was at her heels, appeared'.[1] Stornoway was in the far north-west and saw few visitors; but every traveller in the Highlands visited Inveraray.

[1] J. Knox, *Tour through the Highlands of Scotland and the Hebride Isles* (London 1787), p 183.

This beautiful little town was being built by the Dukes of Argyll from about the middle of the century. Thornton thought it 'hardly worth notice, being a small, inconsiderable fishing place, and chiefly dependent upon the castle',[1] but it was a singular example of stylish town-building, in a romantic situation, according to the best eighteenth century taste. There was a harbour, and half a dozen small vessels took out wood, oak-bark, and timber, and brought back meal, porter and coals. But at the end of the century Inveraray contained fewer than a thousand inhabitants.

Efforts to turn the Highlanders into fishermen did not meet with much success, for they clung to their little pieces of land as offering at least some apparent security in an insecure world; and it was difficult both to fish and to farm. Non-agricultural activity of any kind, except for strictly local consumption, was indeed unusual even towards the end of the century. To this there were, in the second half of the century, two principal exceptions; the making of whisky and the making of kelp.

The first of these was of course bound up with agriculture. Barley was grown throughout the Highlands, and distillation was carried on in every district, legally and illegally, openly and in places of concealment, in small stills and in moderately large stills, for private consumption and for public sale. Consumption seems to have increased considerably after about 1760 – claret and brandy were previously the drink of gentlemen – and government did its best to make whisky a source of revenue. There resulted a prolonged struggle between the illicit distillers and the excisemen, in the course of which hundreds – in one year alone over a thousand – illegal stills were seized and condemned. Strings of small Highland horses carried the produce along remote tracks and drove roads to the final purchasers, and some good grain districts, such as Islay, became established suppliers for other parts of the country. The illegal section of all this activity was a gamble rather than an industry, and observers usually condemned it as demoralising: but to some extent it perhaps took the place of

[1] Thornton, *Tour*, p. 251.

View in Glen Coe;
'infamous for the massacre of its inhabitants in 1691'

Benledi, a few miles west of Callander

Rumbling brig over the Brahan, near Dunkeld

cattle-lifting, which had been 'looked on as a sort of sport, or test of prowess',[1] something in which the Highlander saw little wrong.

Kelp-making, in which after 1750 increasing numbers of people, young and old, male and female, were engaged for two or three months a year, was confined to the coastal districts in the west. Kelp was made from several kinds of seaweed. It was used principally in the manufacture of soap and glass, and its price was rising in the later decades of the century. The landowners soon realised that money was to be made in marketing kelp, and they therefore employed their tenants in cutting, drying and burning the ware. The season was short, so it paid to hire as many people as possible. By the 'eighties thousands of Highlanders were thus engaged in the summer, earning two or three pounds in the course of three months – a very noticeable addition to their cash income, although the work was hard, especially in watching and occasionally stirring the boiling liquid. The Long Island was the great scene of kelp-making, but it was also carried on in Skye, Mull and on the mainland. It may be questioned by how much the ordinary Highlanders really benefited. Their incomes rose but so, sometimes, did their rents. Because kelp-making took so much time, agriculture was neglected; fields were more over-run with weeds than ever, and animals were sometimes lost because the boys who should have been attending them were busy on the sea-shore. Also, the supply of sea-weed for use as a manure – one of the few manures the people used – was diminished.

The kelp, reduced to a hard, rock-like substance, was loaded on board ship and taken south. Most commodities transported in the Highlands – meal was probably the most important – were moved in this way. Small items might be carried about by pedlars, who were welcome for the news they brought, as well as the goods, to remote glens and straths. Occasional fairs provided an important opportunity for trade. Where there were roads, strings of garrons might be seen wending their way through the hills, each horse with a pair of 'cassies' or panniers

[1] Sir Iain Moncrieffe of that Ilk and David Hicks, *The Highland Clans* (London 1967), p. 13.

slung across its back. No other means of transport was practicable, for the vast majority of Highland roads were bad almost beyond belief; indeed, they would not now be recognised as roads at all. Between 1725 and 1736 General Wade built about 250 miles of road and a number of important bridges. But all of this was south of the Great Glen, the line of many of the roads was not well chosen, and they were seldom properly maintained. For the Highlands, however, these roads set a new standard. Wade's successors extended the system, both north and south of the Great Glen, and by the 1780s there were almost 1,000 miles of military road in the Highlands. But even these roads were more nearly what we would call tracks, often remarkably rough, stony, steep and winding, and large stretches of them soon fell into disrepair.

Proprietors made some efforts to build roads of their own. Soon after 1760, for example, a road was begun from Inverness to Fort William along the north shore of the loch, and in the 1790s it was pronounced an 'excellent' road; but it was impassable for carriage beyond Drumnadrochit. The cost of road building was alarmingly high because the difficulties were so formidable – rock had often to be blasted out of the way, and innumerable bridges had to be built, even although most of these were no more than crude wooden structures; and whatever was built had to withstand, if it could, the Highland climate – immense quantities of water pouring down hillsides, washing away soil and small stones and destroying flimsy bridges. Little wonder that even by the end of the century most districts complained not of bad roads but simply of 'want of roads'.

Yet what was done made a great difference between 1750 and 1800. Some districts, at least, became accessible to strangers. In the 1720s Burt seems to have been unable to move more than a mile or two out of Inverness without a guide; but fifty years later it was a simple matter at least to ride over scores of miles of road even north of the Great Glen. Commercially the roads were not of much importance. But men and ideas travelled along them, bringing the Highlanders into increasing contact with a world other than their own, further weakening their local attachments to old ways and old superiors. Easier travel, instead of improving matters, tended to intensify dissatisfaction and unsettlement in the Highlands. And as time passed, people left in increasing numbers. *emigration*

Emigration was nothing new, but it seems to have entered a new phase after about 1765 or 1770. Just before 1775 quite a number of ships sailed from Fort William, Skye, Stornoway, Islay and other places, many of them to the Carolinas; and contemporaries reckoned that in the twenty years from 1763 'above 30,000 persons' went to America. Checked by the American war, emigration rose again in the 'eighties; in June 1768 for example,

> 550 persons embarked in one ship for America, of whom 500 were from one estate only. A gentleman who happened to be present at the embarkation, declared, that the parting scene between the emigrants and their friends who remained behind, was too moving for human nature to behold.[1]

Not all who left the Highlands crossed the Atlantic. Many drifted down into the nearby lowland towns, especially Glasgow, to be absorbed into the rising urban and industrial population.

The causes of this emigration were several. Much of it was led by tacksmen, resentful of being asked to compete with others for farms which they deemed their own, fearing, perhaps, that their situation could never be satisfactory in a land dominated by the increasing value of money and the decreasing value of men. The tacksmen were accustomed to take a lead in clan affairs, and they were men of substance, able to charter vessels and to pay for their own, their family's and their dependants' removal. Others followed them, or followed their example, who were the victims of the spread of sheep farming – itself often the cause of that raising of rents which dislodged some tacksmen. Others, again, may have removed because starvation first put them on the road. Local shortages were common, but there had been a severe general scarcity just three years before the 'Forty-five. In 1770, due to unusually severe weather, there was another remarkable scarcity, and in 1782 the potatoes

[1] Knox, *op. cit.*, p. lxxxix.

35

were frost-bitten as early as October, and there ensued one of the worst famines recorded in the Highlands, requiring private and public intervention to prevent widespread mortality.

These calamities, and the flow of people southward and across the Atlantic which they helped to bring about, drew attention to the Highlands. The eighteenth century believed that men were wealth, and to see them leaving the country in large numbers was most disturbing. Moreover, these were people who now fought for the Crown instead of against it, whose great fighting qualities had been shown at Fontenoy, Brandywine, on the Heights of Abraham, and in innumerable other battles. Interest in the Highlands sharply increased, and yet, as Dr Johnson remarked, to those in the south 'the state of the mountains, and the islands, is equally unknown with that of Borneo or Sumatra'. They were an undiscovered country, and those who set out to discover them, and to recount their wildness, their strangeness, and their remoteness, were pioneers. The best known is Dr Johnson himself, who made his tour to the west coast with Boswell in 1773. Pennant had been there the previous year, and a few years earlier had made his first tour, principally of the central and south-west Highlands. John Knox, a retired London bookseller, had interested himself in the subject in the 1760s, and in the next twenty years made numerous visits, resulting in several books, notably his *View of the British Empire* and *Tour of the Highlands*. Also, the Reverend John Walker had travelled through a great deal of the Highlands between 1760 and 1786, making two particularly prolonged journeys of several months, one in 1764 'to enquire into the state of religion in the Highland counties' on behalf of the General Assembly of the Kirk, and the other in 1771 in order to examine 'the natural history of these counties, their population, and the state of their agriculture, manufactures, and fisheries'.

Almost all these early visitors had a serious scientific or economic or religious-educational interest in the country. Dr Johnson was the least serious of them, more like a modern tourist who travels for his entertainment or general instruction; but Johnson was a profound student of human nature, and he came because he hoped to see 'a people of peculiar appearance, and a system of antiquated life'. In his *Journey* he declares himself disappointed; yet the evidence is overwhelming that although the Highlands in the 1770s and 1780s were in many places very different from what they had been fifty years before, when Burt saw a part of them, they retained not only their natural grandeur, but also a good deal of the primitive simplicity of an ancient way of life.

EDWARD BURT

Very little is known for sure about the author of *Letters from a Gentleman in the North of Scotland*. According to the *Dictionary of National Biography*, he has been 'variously described as an engineer officer who served with General Wade in Scotland in 1724–28, as an army contractor, and as an illiterate hack-writer, who ended his days in dire distress.' There was an Edward or Edmund Burt with Wade in Scotland in the 1720s who seems to have had some responsibilities in relation to the collection of rents and the maintenance of the 'highland galley' which Burt refers to in the last of his letters – 'a vessel of about five-and-twenty or thirty tons burthen ... employed to transport men, provisions, and baggage to Fort Augustus, at the other end of the lake.'

Burt's death was announced in the *Scots Magazine* for 1755 in the following terms: '4 January 1755. At London, Edmund Burt Esq., late agent to General Wade, Chief surveyor during the making of roads through the Highlands, and author of *Letters concerning Scotland*.'

Written in the mid-1720s, the *Letters* were not published until 1754. They were re-published in 1755 and 1759, and there were several re-prints during the nineteenth century. Internal evidence suggests that Burt lived for some time in or near Inverness, and that he made a number of journeys along the Great Glen and into some of the adjacent high country. As a record of manners and conditions in these regions fifty years before 'travelling' there came or could come into fashion, the *Letters* are both unique and entertaining.

Burt : 1726

LETTER III

|| Inverness is one of the royal boroughs of Scotland, and jointly with Nairne, Forres, and Channery, sends a member to parliament.

|| It is not only the head borough or county-town of the shire of Inverness, which is of large extent, but generally esteemed to be the capital of the Highlands; but the natives do not call themselves Highlanders, not so much on account of their low situation, as because they speak English.

This rule whereby to denominate themselves, they borrow from the Kirk, which, in all its acts and ordinances, distinguishes the Lowlands from the Highlands by the language generally spoken by the inhabitants, whether the parish or district lies in the high or low country.

Yet although they speak English, there are scarce any who do not understand the Irish tongue; and it is necessary they should do so, to carry on their dealings with the neighbouring country people; for within less than a mile of the town, there are few who speak any English at all.

What I am saying must be understood only of the ordinary people; for the gentry, for the most part, speak our language in the remotest parts of Scotland.

The town principally consists of four streets, of which three center at the cross, and the other is something irregular.

The castle stands upon a little steep hill closely adjoining to the town, on the south side, built with unhewn stone: it was lately in ruins, but is now completely repaired, to serve as a part of the citadel of Fort George, whereof the first foundation stone was laid in summer 1726, and is to consist of barracks for six companies. This castle, whereof the duke of Gordon is hereditary keeper, was formerly a royal palace, where Mary, the mother of our king James the First, resided, at such times

41

when she thought it her interest to oblige the Highlanders with her presence and expense, or that her safety required it.

You will think it was a very scanty palace, when I have told you, that before it was repaired, it consisted of only six lodging-rooms, the offices below, and the gallery above; which last being taken down, and the rooms divided each into two, there are now twelve apartments for officers' lodgings.

While this building was in repairing, three soldiers, who were employed in digging up a piece of ground very near the door, discovered a dead body, which was supposed to be the corps of a man; I say supposed, because a part of it was defaced before they were aware.

This was believed to have lain there a great number of years, because when it was touched it fell to dust. At this unexpected sight, the soldiers most valiantly ran away, and the accident, you will believe, soon brought a good number of spectators to the place.

As I was talking with one of the townsmen, and took notice how strange it was that a body should be buried so near the door of the house; "Troth,' says he, 'I dinno doubt but this was ane of Mary's lovers.'

I verily believe this man had been afterwards rebuked for this unguarded expression to me, an Englishman; because, when I happened to meet him in the street the day following, he officiously endeavoured to give his words another turn, which made the impression I had received, much stronger than it had been before.

But this I have observed of many, (myself not excepted), who, by endeavouring to excuse a blunder, like a spirited horse in one of our bogs, the more he struggles to get out, the deeper he plunges himself in the mire.

|| The bridge is about eighty yards over, and a piece of good workmanship, consisting of seven arches, built with stone, and maintained by a toll of a *bodle*, or the sixth part of a penny, for each foot-passenger with goods; a penny for a loaded horse, etc.

And here I cannot forbear to give you an instance of the extreme indigence of some of the country people, by assuring you, I have seen women with heavy loads, at a distance from the bridge (the water being low), wade over the large stones, which are made slippery by the sulphur, almost up to the middle, at the hazard of their lives, being desirous to save, or unable to pay, one single bodle.

From the bridge we have often the diversion to see the seals pursue the salmon as they come up the river: they are some-times within fifty yards of us; and one of them came so near the shore, that a salmon leaped out of the water for its safety, and the seal, being shot at, dived; but before any body could come near, the fish had thrown itself back again into the river.

|| Before I leave the bridge, I shall take notice of one thing more, which is commonly to be seen by the sides of the river, (and not only here, but in all the parts of Scotland where I have been,) that is, women with their coats tucked up, stamping, in tubs, upon linen by way of washing; and this not only in summer, but in the hardest frosty weather, when their legs and feet are almost literally as red as blood with the cold; and often two of these wenches stamp in one tub, supporting themselves by their arms thrown over each other's shoulders.

But what seems to me yet stranger is, as I have been assured by an English gentlewoman, that they have insisted with her to have the liberty of washing at the river; and, as people pass by, they divert themselves by talking very freely to them, like our codders,[1] and other women, employed in the fields and gardens about London.

What I have said above, relating to their washing at the river in a hard frost, may require an explanation, viz. the river Ness, like the lake from whence it comes, never freezes, from the great quantity of sulphur with which it is impregnated; but, on the contrary, will dissolve the icicles, contracted from other waters, at the horses' heels, in a very short space of time.

From the Talbooth, or county gaol, the greatest part of the murderers and other notorious villains, that have been com-mitted since I have been here, have made their escape; and I think this has manifestly proceeded from the furtherance or connivance of the keepers, or rather their keepers.

Codder: one who gathers peascods. A.J.Y.

43

When this evil has been complained of, the excuse was, the prison is a weak old building, and the town is not in condition to keep it in repair; but, for my own part, I cannot help concluding, from many circumstances, that the greatest part of these escapes have been the consequence, either of clan-interest or clannish terror. As for example; if one of the magistrates were a Cameron (for the purpose) the criminal (Cameron) must not suffer, if the clan be desirous he should be saved. In short, they have several other ties or attachments one to another, which occasion (like money in the south) this partiality.

|| The town-hall is a plain building of rubble; and there is one room in it, where the magistrates meet upon the town business, which would be tolerably handsome, but the walls are rough, not white-washed, or so much as plastered; and no furniture in it but a table, some bad chairs, and altogether immoderately dirty.

The market-cross is the exchange of the merchants and other men of business.

There they stand in the middle of the dirty street, and are frequently interrupted in their negotiations by horses and carts, which often separate them one from another in the midst of their bargains or other affairs. But this is nothing extraordinary in Scotland; for it is the same in other towns, and even at the Cross of Edinburgh.

Over-against the cross is the coffee-house. A gentleman who loves company and play, keeps it for his diversion, for so I am told by the people of the town; but he has condescended to complain to me of the little he gets by his countrymen.

As to a description of the coffee-room, the furniture, and utensils, I must be excused in that particular, for it would not be a very decent one; but I shall venture to tell you in general, that the room appears as if it had never been cleaned since the building of the house; and, in frost and snow, you might cover the peat-fire with your hands.

Near the extreme part of the town, towards the north, there are two churches, one for the English and the other for the Irish tongue, both out of repair, and much as clean as the other churches I have seen.

Edward Burt

This puts me in mind of a story I was told by an English lady, wife of a certain lieutenant-colonel, who dwelt near a church in the low-country on your side Edinburgh. At first coming to the place, she received a visit from the minister's wife, who, after some time spent in ordinary discourse, invited her to come to kirk the Sunday following. To this the lady agreed, and kept her word, which produced a second visit; and the minister's wife then asking her how she liked their way of worship, she answered – Very well, but she had found two great inconveniences there, viz. that she had dirtied her clothes, and had been pestered with a great number of fleas. 'Now,' says the lady, 'if your husband will give me leave to line the pew, and will let my servant clean it against every Sunday, I shall go constantly to church.'

'Line the pew!' says the minister's wife; 'troth, madam, I cannot promise for that, for my husband will think it *rank papery*.'

‖ The houses are for the most part low, because of the violent flurries of wind which often pour upon the town from the openings of the adjacent mountains, and are built with rubble-stone, as are all the houses in every other town of Scotland that I have seen, except Edinburgh, Glasgow, Perth, Sterling, and Aberdeen; where some of them are faced with Ashler stone; but the four streets of Glasgow, as I have said before, are so from one end to the other.

The rubble walls of these houses are composed of stones of different shapes and sizes; and many of them, being pebbles, are almost round, which, in laying them, leave large gaps, and on the outside they fill up those interstices by driving in flat stones of a small size; and, in the end, face the work all over with mortar thrown against it with a trowel, which they call *harling*.

This rough-casting is apt to be damaged by the weather, and must be sometimes renewed, otherwise some of the stones will drop out.

It is true this is not much unlike the way of building in some remote parts of England; only there, the stones are squarer, and more nearly proportioned one to another: but I have been thus particular, because I have often heard it said by some of the Scots in London, before I knew anything of Scotland, that the houses were all built with stone, as despising our bricks, and concealing the manner and appearance of their buildings.

This gave me a false idea of magnificence, both as to beauty and expense, by comparing them in my thoughts with our stone buildings in the south, which are costly, scarce, and agreeable to the eye.

The chasms in the inside and middle of these walls, and the disproportionate quantity of mortar, by comparison, with the stone, render them receptacles for prodigious numbers of rats, which scratch their way from the inside of the house half through the wall, where they burrow and breed securely, and by that means abound every-where in the small Scots towns, especially near the sea. But among the inner parts of the mountaints I never saw or heard of any such thing, except, upon recollection, in a part called Coulnakyle in Strath-spey, to which place I have been told they were brought, in the year 1723, from a ship among some London goods.

‖ The houses of this town were neither sashed nor slated before the union, as I have been informed by several old people; and to this day the ceilings are rarely plastered: nothing but the single boards serve for floor and ceiling, and the partitions being often composed of upright boards only, they are sometimes shrunk, and any body may not only hear, but see, what passes in the room adjoining.

When first I came to this country, I observed in the floors of several houses a good number of circles of about an inch diameter, and likewise some round holes of the same size, the meaning of which I did not then understand; but not long after, I discovered the cause of those inconvenient apertures.

These, in great measure, lay the family below open to those that are above, who, on their part, are incommoded with the voices of the others.

The boards, when taken from the saw-mill, are bored at a good distance from one end of them, for the conveniency of their way of carriage.

They put a cord (or a *woodie* as they call it) through the holes of several of them, to keep them flat to the horses' sides, and the corners of the other end drag upon the ground; but before these boards are laid in the floor, the holes are filled up with plugs, which they cut away even with the surface on each side; and when these stop-gaps shrink, they drop out, and are seldom supplied.

Those houses that are not sashed, have two shutters that turn upon hinges for the lower half of the window, and only the upper part is glazed; so that there is no seeing any thing in the street, in bad weather, without great inconvenience.

Asking the reason of this, I was told that these people still continue those shutters as an old custom which was at first occasioned by danger; for that formerly, in their clan-quarrels, several had been shot from the opposite side of the way, when they were in their chambers, and by these shutters they were concealed and in safety; but I believe the true reason is, the saving the expense of glass, for it is the same in the out-parts of all the towns and cities in the low-country.

LETTER IV

|| What I have hitherto said, with respect to the buildings of this town, relates only to the principal part of the streets; the middling sort of houses, as in other towns, are very low, and have generally a close wooden stair-case before the front. By one end of this you ascend, and in it above are small round or oval holes, just big enough for the head to go through; and in summer, or when any thing extraordinary happens in the street to excite the curiosity of the inhabitants, they look like so many people with their heads in the pillory.

But the extreme parts of the town are made up of most miserably low dirty hovels, faced and covered with turf, with a bottomless tub or basket in the roof for a chimney.

The pavement here is very good; but, as in other small towns where the streets are narrow, it is so much rounded, that when it is dry, it is dangerous to ride, insomuch that horses, which are shod, are often falling; and when it is dirty, and beginning to dry, it is slippery to the feet, for in Scotland you walk generally in the middle of the streets.

I asked the magistrates one day, when the dirt was almost above one's shoes, why they suffered the town to be so excessively dirty, and did not employ people to cleanse the street? The answer was, 'It will not be long before we have a shower.'

‖ Here is a melancholy appearance of objects in the streets; – in one part the poor women, maid-servants and children, in the coldest weather, in the dirt or in snow, either walking or standing to talk with one another without stockings or shoes. In another place, you see a man dragging along a half-starved horse little bigger than an ass, in a cart about the size of a wheel-barrow. One part of his plaid is wrapt round his body, and the rest is thrown over his left shoulder; and every now and then he turns himself about, either to adjust his mantle, when blown off by the wind or fallen by his stooping; or to thump the poor little horse with a great stick. The load in his cart, if compact, might be carried under his arm; but he must not bear any burthen himself, though his wife has, perhaps, at the same time a greater load on her loins than he has in his cart: I say on her loins; for the women carry fish, and other heavy burthens, in the same manner as the Scots pedlars carry their packs in England.

The poor men are seldom barefoot in the town, but wear brogues, a sort of pumps without heels, which keep them little more from the wet and dirt than if they had none, but they serve to defend their feet from the gravel and stones.

They have three several sorts of carts, of which that species wherein they carry their peats (being a light kind of loading) is the largest; but as they too are very small, their numbers are sometimes so great, that they fill up one of the streets (which is the market for that fuel) in such manner, it is impossible to pass by them on horseback, and difficult on foot.

It is really provoking to see the idleness and inhumanity of some of the leaders of this sort of carts; for as they are something higher than the horse's tail, in the motion they keep rubbing against it till the hair is worn off and the dock quite raw, without any care taken to prevent it, or to ease the hurt when discovered.

Some of these carts are led by women, who are generally bare-foot, with a blanket for the covering of their bodies, and in cold or wet weather they bring it quite over them.

At other times they wear a piece of linen upon their heads, made up like a napkin cap in an inn, only not tied at top, but hanging down behind.

Instead of ropes for halters and harness, they generally make use of sticks of birch twisted and knotted together; these are called *woodies;* but some few have ropes made of the manes and tails of their horses, which are shorn in the spring for that purpose.

The horse-collar and crupper are made of strawbands; and to save the horse's back, they put under the cart-saddle a parcel of old rags.

Their horses are never dressed or shod, and appear, as we say, as ragged as colts. In short, if you were to see the whole equipage, you would not think it possible for any droll-painter to invent so perfect a picture of misery.

If the horse carries a burthen upon his back, a stick of a yard long goes across under his tail for a crupper; but this I have seen in prints of the loaded mules in Italy.

When the carter has had occasion to turn about one sort of these carts in a narrow place, I have seen him take up the cart, wheels and all, and walk round with it, while the poor little horse has been struggling to keep himself from being thrown.

The wheels, when new, are about a foot and half high, but are soon worn very small: they are made of three pieces of plank, pinned together at the edges like the head of a butter-firkin, and the axle-tree goes round with the wheel; which having some part of the circumference with the grain, and other parts not, it wears unequally, and in a little time is rather an-gular than round, which causes a disagreeable noise as it moves upon the stones.

I have mentioned these carts, horses, and drivers, or rather draggers of them, not as immediately relating to the town, but as they increase, in great measure, the wretched appearance in the streets; for these carters, for the most part, live in huts dispersed in the adjacent country. There is little need of carts for the business of the town; and when a hogshead of wine has been to be carried to any part not very far distant, it has been placed upon a kind of frame among four horses, two on a side, following each other; for not far off, except along the sea-coast and some new road, the ways are so rough and rocky that no wheel ever turned upon them since the formation of this globe; and therefore if the townsmen were furnished with sufficient wheel-carriages for goods of great weight, they would be seldom useful.

The description of these puny vehicles brings to my memory how I was entertained with the surprise and amusement of the common people in this town, when, in the year 1725, a chariot with six monstrous great horses arrived here, by way of the sea-coast. An elephant, publicly exposed in one of the streets of London, could not have excited greater admiration. One asked what the chariot was: another, who had seen the gentleman alight, told the first, with a sneer at his ignorance, it was a great cart to carry people in, and such like. But since the making of the roads, I have passed through them with a friend, and was greatly delighted to see the Highlanders run from their huts close to the chariot, and looking up, bow with their bonnets to the coachman, little regarding us that were within.

‖ It is a common thing for the poorest sort hereabouts to lead their horses out in summer, when they have done their work, and attend them while they graze by the sides of the roads and edges of the cornfields, where there is any little grass to be had without a trespass; and generally they hold them all the while by the halter, for they are certainly punished if it be known they encroached ever so little upon a field, of which none are enclosed. In like manner you may see a man tending a single cow for the greatest part of the day. In winter the horse is allowed no more provender than will barely keep him alive, and sometimes not even that; for I have known almost two hundred of them, near the town, to die of mere want, within a small compass of time. You will find in another letter how I came to know their numbers.

Certainly nothing can be more disagreeable than to see them pass the streets before this mortality, hanging down their heads, reeling with weakness; and having spots of their skins of a foot diameter appearing without hair, the effect of their exceeding poverty; but the mares in particular are yet a more unseemly sight.

When the grass in the season is pretty well grown, the country-people cut it and bring it green to the town for sale, to feed the horses that are kept in it; as others likewise do to Edinburgh, where there is a spacious street, known by the name of the Grass-market; and this is customary in all the parts of the low country where I have been, at the time of the year for that kind of marketing.

Hay is here a rare commodity indeed; sometimes there is none at all; and I have had it brought me forty miles by sea, at the rate of half-a-crown or three shillings a truss. I have given twenty-pence for a bundle of straw, not more than one of our trusses, and oats have cost me at the rate of four shillings a bushel, otherwise I must have seen as we say, my horses' skins stripped over their ears. But this is not always the case; for sometimes, after the harvest, oats and straw have been pretty reasonable.

A certain officer, soon after his arrival at this town, observing in what a miserable state the horses were, and finding his own would cost him more in keeping than was well consistent with his pay, shot them. And being asked why he did not rather choose to sell them, though but for a small matter; his answer was, they were old servants, and his compassion for them would not suffer him to let them fall into the hands of such keepers. And indeed the town-horses are but sparingly fed, as you may believe, especially when their provender is at such an extravagant price.

Here are four or five fairs in the year, when the Highlanders bring their commodities to market: but, good God! you could not conceive there was such misery in this island.

One has under his arm a small roll of linen, another a piece of coarse plaiding: these are considerable dealers. But the merchandise of the greatest part of them is of a most contemptible value, such as these, *viz.* Two or three cheeses, of about three or four pound weight a-piece; a kid, sold for six-pence or eight-pence at the most; a small quantity of butter in something that looks like a bladder, and is sometimes set down upon the dirt in the street; three or four goat-skins; a piece of wood for an axle-tree to one of the little carts, etc. With the produce of what each of them sells, they generally buy some-thing, *viz.* a horn, or wooden spoon or two, a knife, a wooden platter, and such-like necessaries for their huts, and carry home with them little or no money.

LETTER V

|| If you would conceive rightly of it, you must imagine you see two or three hundred half-naked, half-starved creatures of both sexes, without so much as a smile or any cheerfulness among them, stalking about with goods, such as I have described, up to their ancles in dirt; and at night numbers of them lying together in stables, or other outhouse hovels that are hardly any defence against the weather. I am speaking of a winter fair, for in summer the greatest part of them lie about in the open country.

The gentlemen, magistrates, merchants, and shop-keepers, are dressed after the English manner, and make a good appearance enough, according to their several ranks, and the working tradesmen are not very ill clothed; and now and then, to relieve your eyes yet more from these frequent scenes of misery, you see some of their women of fashion: I say sometimes, for they go seldom abroad; but when they appear, they are generally well dressed in the English mode.

As I have touched upon the dress of the men, I shall give you a notable instance of precaution used by some of them against the tailor's purloining.

This is to buy everything that goes to the making of a suit of clothes, even to the stay-tape and thread; and when they are to be delivered out, they are, all together, weighed before the tailor's face.

And when he brings home the suit, it is again put into the

scale with the shreds of every sort, and it is expected the whole shall answer the original weight. But I was told in Edinburgh of the same kind of circumspection, but not as a common practice.

The plaid is the undress of the ladies; and to a genteel woman, who adjusts it with a good air, is a becoming veil. But as I am pretty sure you never saw one of them in England, I shall employ a few words to describe it to you. It is made of silk or fine worsted, chequered with various lively colours, two breadths wide, and three yards in length; it is brought over the head, and may hide or discover the face, according to the wearer's fancy or occasion: it reaches to the waist behind; one corner falls as low as the ancle on one side; and the other part, in folds, hangs down from the opposite arm.

I have been told in Edinburgh that the ladies distinguish their political principles, whether Whig or Tory, by the manner of wearing their plaids; that is, one of the parties reverses the old fashion, but which of them it is, I do not remember, nor is it material.

|| My next subject is to be the servants. I know little remarkable of the men, only that they are generally great lovers of ale: but my poor maids, if I may judge of others by what passes in my own quarters, have not had the best of chances, when their lots fell to be born in this country. It is true they have not a great deal of household work to do; but when that little is done, they are kept to spinning, by which some of their mistresses are chiefly maintained. Sometimes there are two or three of them in a house of no greater number of rooms, at the wages of three half crowns a year each, a peck of oatmeal for a week's diet; and happy she, that can get the skimming of a pot to mix with her oatmeal for better commons.

To this allowance is added a pair of shoes or two, for Sundays, when they go to kirk.

These are such as are kept at board-wages. In larger families, I suppose, their standing-wages is not much more, because they make no better appearance than the others. But if any one of them happens, by the encouragement of some English family, or one more reasonable than ordinary among the natives, to get clothes something better than the rest, it is ten to one but envy excites them to tell her to her face, 'she must have been a *heure*, or she cou'd n'ere ha getten sic a bonny *geer*.'

All these generally lie in the kitchen, a very improper place one would think for a lodging, especially of such who have not wherewithal to keep themselves clean.

‖ I have seen women by the river's side washing parsnips, turnips, and herbs, in tubs with their feet. An English lieutenant-colonel told me, that about a mile from the town, he saw, at some little distance, a wench turning and twisting herself about as she stood in a little tub; and as he could perceive, being on horseback, that there was no water in it, he rode up close to her, and found she was grinding off the beards and hulls of barley with her naked feet, which barley, she said, was to make broth withal: and, since that, upon inquiry, I have been told it is a common thing.

They hardly ever wear shoes, as I said before, but on a Sunday; and then, being unused to them, when they go to church they walk very awkwardly; or, as we say, like a cat shod with walnut-shells.

I have seen some of them come out of doors, early in a morning, with their legs covered up to the calf with dried dirt, the remains of what they contracted in the streets the day before; in short, a stranger might think there was but little occasion for strict laws against low fornication.

When they go abroad, they wear a blanket over their heads, as the poor women do, something like the pictures you may have seen of some bare-footed order among the Romish priests.

And the same blanket that serves them for a mantle by day, is made a part of their bedding at night, which is generally spread upon the floor: this I think they call a *shakedown*.

‖ Let those who deride the dirtiness and idleness of these poor creatures, which my countrymen are too apt to do, as I observed before; let them, I say, consider, what inclination they can have to recommend themselves? What emulation can there proceed from mere despair? Cleanliness is too expensive for their small wages; and what inducement can they have, in such a station, to be diligent and obliging to those who use them more like negroes than natives of Britain? Besides, it is not anything in nature that renders them more idle and uncleanly than others, as some would inconsiderately suggest; because many of them, when they happen to be transplanted into a richer soil, grow as good servants as any whatever; and this I have known by experience.

It is a happiness to infancy, especially here, that it cannot reflect and make comparisons of its condition; otherwise how miserable would be the children of the poor that one sees continually in the streets! Their wretched food makes them look pot-bellied; they are seldom washed; and many of them have their hair clipped, all but a lock that hangs down over the forehead, like the representation of old Time in a picture: the boys have nothing but a coarse kind of vest, buttoned down the back, as if they were idiots, and that their coats were so made, to prevent their often stripping themselves quite naked.

The girls have a piece of a blanket wrapped about their shoulders, and are bare-headed like the boys; and both without stockings and shoes in the hardest of seasons. But what seems to me the worst of all, is, they are over-run with the itch, which continues upon them from year to year, without any care taken to free them from that loathsome distemper. Nor indeed is it possible to keep them long from it, except all could agree, it is so universal among them. And as the children of people in better circumstances are not nice in the choice of their companions and play-fellows, they are most of them likewise infected with this disease; insomuch that upon entering a room, where there was a pretty boy or girl that I should have been pleased to have caressed and played with (besides the compliment of it to the father and mother), it has been a great disappointment to me to discover it could not be done with safety to myself. And though the children of the upper classes wear shoes and stockings in winter-time, yet nothing is more common than to see them bare-foot in the summer.

LETTER VI

One day, when I was in Edinburgh, I walked out with three

married women, whose husbands, some time after dinner, retired to their respective avocations or diversions, and left them to my conduct. As we approached the fields, we happened to meet a woman with cherries: this gave me an opportunity to treat the ladies with some of that fruit; and as we were walking along, says one of them to me, 'Mr – , there is a good deal of difference between a married woman in Scotland and one in England. Here are now three of us, and I believe I may venture to say, we could not, all of us together, purchase one single pound of cherries.' You may be sure I thought their credit very low at that time, and I endeavoured to turn it off as an accident; but she told me that such kind of vacuities were pretty general among the married women in Scotland; and, upon her appeal to the other two, it was confirmed.

|| The working tradesmen, for the most part, are indolent; and no wonder, since they have so little incitement to industry, or profitable employment to encourage them to it.

If a bolt for a door be wanted, the dweller often supplies it with one of wood; and so of many other things, insomuch that the poor smith is sometimes hardly enabled to maintain himself in oatmeal.

The neatness of a carpenter's work is little regarded. If it will just answer the occasion, and come very cheap, it is enough. I shall not trouble you with further instances. But to show you what they might be, if they had encouragement, I shall mention a passage that related to myself. I sent one day for a *wright* (they have no such distinction as *joiner*) to make me an engine to chop straw withall for my horses; and told him it must be neatly made, and I would pay him accordingly; otherwise, when it was done, it would be his own. The young man, instead of being discouraged by the danger of losing his time and materials, was overjoyed at the conditions; and told me, at the same time, that he should be quite undone, if he was long about work which he did for his countrymen, for in that case they would not pay him for his time. In fine, he made me the machine, which was more like the work of one of your cabinet-makers in London, than that of an Inverness carpenter;

and he brought it home in as little time as I could reasonably expect.

Here I may observe, that when a young fellow finds he has a genius for his trade or business, and has any thing of spirit, he generally lays hold of the first occasion to remove to England, or some other country, where he hopes for better encouragement. Hence, I take it, arose a kind of proverb, That there never came a fool out of Scotland. Some, perhaps, would be giving this a different interpretation; but what I mean is, that the cleverest and most sprightly among them leave the narrow way of their own country: and from this may come, for aught I know, another saying, That they seldom desire to return home.

This very man of whom I have been speaking took occasion to tell me, that in two or three months he should go to seek employment in London.

The fishermen would not be mentioned, but for their remarkable laziness; for they might find a sale for much more sea-fish than they do; but so long as any money remains of the last marketing, and until they are driven out by the last necessity, they will not meddle with salt water.

At low ebb, when their boats lie off at a considerable distance from the shore, for want of depth of water, the women tuck up their garments to an indecent height, and wade to the vessels, where they receive their loads of fish for the market; where whole cargo is brought to land, they take the fishermen upon their backs, and bring them on shore in the same manner.

There is here none of that emulation among the ordinary people or any of that pride which the meanest cottagers in England generally take in the cleanliness and little ornaments of their hovels; yet, at the same time, these poor wretches entertain a kind of pride which is, I think, peculiar to themselves.

The officers of a certain regiment kept here a pack of beagles; and suspecting some of them to be in danger of the mange, they sent to the boatmen to take them out a little way to sea, and throw them overboard, imagining their swimming in salt water would cure them of the distemper, if they were infected. The servant offered them good hire for their trouble; but they gave him bad language, and told him they would not do it. Upon this, some of the officers went themselves, and, in hopes to prevail, offered them a double reward; but they said they would not, for any money, do a thing so scandalous as to *freight their boats with dogs;* and absolutely refused it.

‖ The lodgings of the ordinary people are indeed most miserable ones; and even those of some who make a tolerable appearance in the streets are not much better.

Going along with some company towards one of the out-parts of the town, I was shown the apartment of a young woman, who looks pretty smart when abroad, and affects to adorn her face with a good many patches, but is of no ill fame.

The door of the house, or rather hut, being open, and nobody within, I was prevailed with to enter and observe so great a curiosity. Her bed was in one corner of the room upon the ground, made up with straw, and even that in small quantity, and upon it lay a couple of blankets, which were her covering and that of two children that lay with her. In the opposite corner was just such another bed for two young fellows, who lay in the same room.

At another time I happened to be of a party who had agreed to go five or six and twenty miles into the Highlands, a small part by land the rest by water; but a person who was not agreeable to any of us, having, as we say, pinned himself upon us, and being gone home, it was resolved that, to avoid him, we should set out at ten o'clock the same night, instead of the next morning, as was at first intended. About twelve we arrived at the end of Loch Ness, where we were to wait for news from the vessel. We were soon conducted to a house where lives a brother to the Pretender's famous brigadier;[1] and upon entering a large room, by the candle, we discovered, on different parts of the floor, nine persons, including children, all laid in the manner above described; and among the rest, a young woman, as near as I could guess about seventeen or eighteen, who, being surprised at the light, and the bustle we made, between sleeping and waking, threw off part of the blankets,

[1] Presumably MacIntosh of Borlum, the most skilful and active of the Jacobite commanders in the 'Fifteen. A.J.Y.

started up, stared at us earnestly, and, being stark naked, scratched herself in several parts till thoroughly wakened.

After all this, I think I need not say any thing about the lodgings of the meanest sort of people.

I shall not go about to deny, because I would not willingly be laughed at, that the English luxury is in every thing carried to an exorbitant height; but if there was here a little of that vice, it would be well for the lower order of people, who, by that means, would likewise mend their *commons* in proportion to it.

|| Our principal diet, then, consists of such things as you in London esteem to be the greatest rarities, viz. salmon and trout just taken out of the river, and both very good in their kind; partridge, grouse, hare, duck, and mallard, woodcocks, snipes, etc. each in its proper season. And yet for the greatest part of the year, like the Israelites who longed for the garlic and onions of Egypt, we are hankering after beef, mutton, veal, lamb etc.

It is not only me, but every one that comes hither, is soon disgusted with these kinds of food, when obliged to eat them often for want of other fare, which is not seldom our case.

There is hardly any such thing as mutton to be had till August, or beef till September; that is to say, in quality fit to be eaten; and both go out about Christmas. And therefore at or about Martinmas (the 11th of November), such of the inhabitants who are any thing beforehand with the world, salt up a quantity of beef, as if they were going a voyage. And this is common in all parts of Scotland where I have been.

It would be tedious to set down the price of every species of provision. I shall only say, that mutton and beef are about a penny a pound; salmon, which was at the same price, is, by a late regulation of the magistrates, raised to twopence a pound, which is thought by many to be an exorbitant price. A fowl, which they in general call a hen, may be had at market for twopence or twopence-halfpenny, but so lean they are good for little. It would be too ludicrous to say that one of them might almost be cut up with the breast of another, but they are so poor that some used to say they believed the oats were given them out by tale.

|| The little Highland mutton, when fat, is delicious, and certainly the greatest of luxuries. And the small beef, when fresh, is very sweet and succulent, but it wants that substance which should preserve it long when salted. I am speaking of these two sorts of provision when they are well fed; but the general run of the market here, and in other places too, is such as would not be suffered in any part of England that I know of.

We (the English) have the conveniency of a public-house (or tavern if you please) kept by a countrywoman of ours, where everything is dressed our own way; but sometimes it has been difficult for our landlady to get anything for us to eat, except some sort of food, so often reiterated, as almost to create a loathing. And one day I remember she told us there was nothing at all to be had in the town. This you may believe was a melancholy declaration to a parcel of *poke puddings;* but, for some relief, a Highlander soon after happened to bring to town some of the moor-game to sell, which (in looking out sharp) she secured for our dinner.

Hares and the several kinds of birds abovementioned, abound in the neighbouring country near the town, even to exuberance: rather too much, I think, for the sportsman's diversion, who generally likes a little more expectation; so that we never need to want that sort of provision of what we may kill ourselves; and besides we often make presents of them to such of the inhabitants who are in our esteem; for none of them, that I know of, will bestow powder and shot upon any of the game.

It is true they may sometimes buy a partridge for a penny, or less, and the others in proportion: – I say sometimes, for there are not very many brought to market, except in time of snow, and then indeed I have seen sacks-full of them.

I remember that the first hard weather after I came, I asked the magistrates why such poaching was suffered within their district; and their answer was, that there was enough of them, and if they were not brought to market, they should get none themselves.

The river is not less plentiful in fish. I have often seen above a hundred large salmon brought to shore at one haul. Trout is as plenty, and a small fish the people call a little trout, but of nother species, which is exceedingly good, called in the north of England a *branlin*. These are so like the salmon fry, that they are hardly to be distinguished; only the scales come off the fry n handling, the others have none.

It is by law no less than transportation to take the salmon ry; but in the season the river is so full of them that nobody minds it, and those young fish are so simple the children catch hem with a crooked pin. Yet the townsmen are of opinion that ll such of them as are bred in the river, and are not devoured t sea by larger fish, return thither at the proper season; and as proof, they affirm they have taken many of them; and, by vay of experiment, clipped their tails into a forked figure like hat of a swallow, and found them with that mark when full-grown and taken out of the *cruives*.

‖ The meanest servants, who are not at board wages, will not make a meal upon salmon, if they can get anything else to eat. have been told it here, as a very good jest, that the Highland gentleman, who went to London by sea, soon after his landing passed by a tavern, where the larder appeared to the street, and operated so strongly upon his appetite that he went in; that here were among other things a rump of beef and some almon. Of the beef he ordered a steak for himself; but, says he, et Duncan have some salmon. To be short; the cook who ttended him humoured the jest; and the master's eating was ightpence, and Duncan's came to almost as many shillings.

‖ I shall conclude this letter with an incident, which, I confess, is quite foreign to my present purpose, but may contribute to my main design.

‖ Since my last, as I was passing along the street, I saw a woman sitting with a young child lying upon her lap, over which she was crying and lamenting, as in the utmost despair concerning it. At first I thought it was want, but found she was ome from Fort William, and that the ministers here had efused to christen her child, because she did not know who vas the father of it. Then she renewed her grief; and hanging down her head over the infant, she talked to it as if it must ertainly be damned if it should die without baptism. To be hort, several of us together prevailed to have the child christened; not that we thought the infant in danger, but to relieve the mother from her dreadful apprehensions.

I take this refusal to be partly political, and used as a means whereby to find out the male transgressor. But that knowledge would have been to little purpose in this case, it being a *regimental child:* and, indeed, this was our principal argument; for any dispute against the established rules of the kirk would be deemed impertinence, if not profaneness.

LETTER VII

|| Shall I venture at one only instance of cookery? I will, – and that a recent one, and therefore comes first to hand: but it does not come up to many others that I know, and are not fit to be told to any one that has not an immoveable stomach.

An officer, who arrived here a few days ago with his wife and son (a boy of about five or six years old), told me, that at a house not far distant from this place, as they were waiting for dinner, the child, who had been gaping about the kitchen came running into the room and fell a-crying; of which the mother asking the reason, he sobbed, and said, 'Mamma, don't eat any of the greens.' This occasioned a further inquiry; by which it appeared, the maid had been wringing the cale with her hands, as if she was wringing a dish-clout, and was setting it up in pyramids round the dish by way of ornament, and that her hands were very dirty, and her fingers in a lamentable condition with the itch.

Soon after, the coleworts were brought to table just as the child had described their figure and situation, and the wench's hands convinced them that his whole complaint was just and reasonable.

But I would not be thought by this to insinuate that there is nothing but cleanliness in England; for I have heard of foul practices there, especially by the men-cooks in the kitchens of persons of distinction: among whom I was told by one, that happening to go into his kitchen, where he had hardly ever been before, (probably by some information), he observed his cook had stuck upon the smoky chimneypiece a large lump of butter, and had raked part of it off with his fingers by handfuls, as he had occasion to throw them into the saucepan.

We have one great advantage, that makes amends for many inconveniences, that is, wholesome and agreeable drink, I mean French claret, which is to be met with almost every-where in public-houses of any note, except in the heart of the Highlands, and sometimes even there; but the concourse of my countrymen has raised the price of it considerably. At my first coming it was but sixteen-pence a bottle, and now it is raised to two shillings, although there be no more duty paid upon it now than there was before, which, indeed, was often none at all.

French brandy, very good, is about three shillings and sixpence or four shillings a gallon, but in quantities, from hovering ships on the coast, it has been bought for twenty-pence.

Lemons are seldom wanting here; so that punch, for those that like it, is very reasonable; but few care to drink it, as thinking the claret a much better liquor, in which I agree with them.

There lives in our neighbourhood, at a house (or castle) called Culloden, a gentleman whose hospitality is almost without bounds. It is the custom of that house, at the first visit or introduction, to take up your freedom by cracking his nut (as he terms it), that is, a cocoa-shell, which holds a pint filled with champagne, or such other sort of wine as you shall choose. You may guess by the introduction, at the contents of the volume. Few go away sober at any time; and for the greatest part of his guests, in the conclusion, they cannot go at all.

‖ In some parts, within less than ten miles of us near the coast, the hares are in such numbers there is but little diversion in hunting, for one being started soon turns out a fresh one; then the pack is divided, and must be called off, etc. insomuch that a whole day's hunting has been entirely fruitless. The country-people are very forward to tell us where the *maukin* is, as they call a hare, and are pleased to see them destroyed, because they do hurt to their caleyards.

Besides the hares, there are numbers of foxes; but they take to the mountains, which are rocky, and sometimes inaccessible to the dogs, of which several have been lost by falling from precipices in the pursuit; for the fox in his flight takes the most dangerous way. But when we happen to kill one of them, it is carried home through the blessings of the people, like a dangerous captive in a Roman triumph.

In this little town there are no less than four natural fools. There are hardly any crooked people (except by accidents), because there has been [   ] care taken to mend their shapes when they were young.[1]

The beggars are numerous, and exceedingly importunate, for there is no parish-allowance to any.

I have been told, that before the union they never presumed to ask for more than a *bodle* (or the sixth part of a penny), but now they beg for a *baubee* (or halfpenny). And some of them, that they may not appear to be ordinary beggars, tell you it is to buy snuff. Yet still it is common for the inhabitants, (as I have seen in Edinburgh), when they have none of the smallest money, to stop in the street, and giving a halfpenny, take from the beggar a *plack*, i.e. two bodles (or the third part of a penny) in change. Yet although the beggars frequently receive so small an alms from their benefactors, I don't know how it is, but they are generally shod, when the poor working women go barefoot. But here are no idle young fellows and wenches begging about the streets, as with you in London, to the disgrace of all order, and, as the French call it, *police*. By the way, this police is still a great office in Scotland; but, as they phrase it, is grown into *disuetude*, though the salaries remain.

LETTER VIII

As I have, in point of time, till the last post, been perfectly punctual in this my tattling correspondence, though not so exact in my letters upon other subjects, you may, possibly expect I should give you a reason for this failure, at least I am myself inclined to do so.

Several of us (the English) have been, by invitation, to dine

[1] The text reads 'because there has been no care taken', which does not make sense. But the emendation seems unlikely. A.J.Y.

with an eminent chief, not many miles from hence, in the Highlands; but I do assure you it was his importunity (the effect of his interest), and our own curiosity, more than any particular inclination, that induced us to a compliance.

We set out early in the morning without guide or interpreter, and passed a pretty wide river into the county of Ross, by a boat that we feared would fall to pieces in the passage. This excursion was made in order to a short visit on that side the Murray Frith, and to lengthen out the way, that we might not be too early with our noble host.

Our first visit being dispatched, we changed our course, and, as the sailor says, *stood* directly, as we thought, for the castle of our inviter; but we soon strayed out of our way among the hills, where there was nothing but heath, bogs, and stones, and no visible tract to direct us, it being across the country.

In our way we inquired of three several Highlanders, but could get nothing from them but *Haniel Sasson Ugget.*[1] We named the title of our chief, and pointed with the finger; but he was known to none of them, otherwise than by his *patronymick*, which none of us knew at that time. (I shall have something to say of this word, when I come to speak of the Highlands in general). But if we had been never so well acquainted with his ancestry name, it would have stood us in little stead, unless we had known likewise how to persuade some one of those men to show us the way. At length we happened to meet with a gentleman, as I supposed, because he spoke English, and he told us we must go west *a piece* (though there was no appearance of the sun), and then incline to the north; that then we were to go along the side of a hill, and ascend another (which to us was then unseen), and from the top of it we should see the castle.

I should have told you, that in this part of our peregrination we were upon the borders of the mountains only; and the hills, for the most part, not much higher than Hampstead or High-gate.

No sooner had he given us this confused direction, but he skipped over a little bog, that was very near us, and left us to

---

[1] A very inexpert rendering of 'Chan eil Sasunnach agam', literally, there is no English to me; or, I do not speak English. A.J.Y.

our perplexed consultations. However, at last we gained the height: but when we were there, one of our company began to curse the Highlander for deceiving us, being prepossessed with the notion of a *castle*, and seeing only a house hardly fit for one of our farmers of fifty pounds a year; and in the court-yard a parcel of low outhouses, all built with turf, like other Highland-huts.

When we approached this *castle*, our chief, with several attendants; (for he had seen us on the hill), came a little way to meet us; gave us a welcome, and conducted us into a parlour pretty well furnished.

After some time, we had notice given us that dinner was ready in another room; where we were no sooner sat down to table, but a band of music struck up in a little place out of sight, and continued playing all the time of dinner.

These concealed musicians he would have had us think were his constant domestics; but I saw one of them some time after dinner, by mere chance, whereby I knew they were brought from this town to regale us with more magnificence.

Our entertainment consisted of a great number of dishes, at a long table, all brought in under covers, but almost cold. What the greatest part of them were I could not tell, nor did I inquire, for they were disguised after the French manner; but there was placed next to me a dish, which I guessed to be boiled beef; I say that was my conjecture, for it was covered all over with stewed cabbage, like a smothered rabbit, and over all a deluge of bad butter.

When I had removed some of the incumbrance, helped myself, and tasted, I found the pot it was boiled in had given it too high a *goût* for my palate, which is always inclined to plain eating.

I then desired one of the company to help me to some roasted mutton, which was indeed delicious, and therefore served very well for my share of all this inelegant and ostentatious plenty.

We had very good wine, but did not drink much of it; but one thing I should have told you was intolerable, *viz.* The number of Highlanders that attended at table, whose feet and foul linen or woollen, I don't know which, were more than a match for the odour of the dishes.

The conversation was greatly engrossed by the chief, before, at, and after dinner; but I do not recollect any thing was said that is worth repeating.

There were, as we went home, several descants upon our feast; but I remember one of our company said he had tasted a pie, and that many a *peruke* had been baked in a better crust.

When we returned hither in the evening, we supped upon beef-steaks; which some, who complained they had not made a dinner, rejoiced over, and called them a luxury.

I make little doubt, but, after our noble host had gratified his ostentation and vanity, he cursed us in his heart for the expense, and that his family must starve for a month to retrieve the profusion; for this is according to his known character.

‖ There is another thing very inconvenient to the traveller which I had omitted. He is made to wait a most unreasonable while for everything for which he has occasion. I shall give you only one instance among a hundred.

At the Blair of *Athol*, benighted, tired, and hungry, I came to the inn, and was put into a room without any light; where, knowing the dilatory way of those people, I sat patiently waiting for a candle near half an hour; at last, quite tired with expectation, I called pretty hastily, and I must confess not without anger, for a light and some wine: this brought in a servant maid, who, as usual, cried out, 'What's your wull?' I then again told her my wants; but had no other answer than that her mistress had the keys, and was at supper, and she could not be disturbed. Her mistress, it is true, is a *gentlewoman;* but before she was married to the stately beggar who keeps that house, she lived in this town, and was humble enough to draw *two-penny*.

The two-penny, as they call it, is their common ale, the price of it is two-pence for a Scots pint, which is two quarts.

In sliding thus from the word two-penny, to a description of that liquor, there came to my memory a ridiculing dissertation upon such kind of transitions in one of the Tatlers; for those books I have with me, which, indeed, are here good part of my library.

This liquor is disagreeable to those who are not used to it;

but time and custom will make almost any thing familiar. The malt, which is dried with peat, turf, or furzes, gives to the drink a taste of that kind of fuel: it is often drank before it is cold, out of a *cap* or *coif* as they call it: this is a wooden dish, with two ears or handles, about the size of a tea-saucer, and as shallow, so that a steady hand is necessary to carry it to the mouth, and, in windy weather, at the door of a change, I have seen the liquor blown into the drinker's face. This drink is of itself apt to give a diarrhoea; and therefore when the natives drink plentifully of it, they interlace it with brandy or usky.

I have been speaking only of the common ale; for in some few gentlemen's houses I have drank as good as I think I ever met with in any part of England, but not brewed with the malt of this country.

‖ The principal importation of these parts consists in wines, brandy, tea, silks, etc. which is no great advantage to those who deal that way, when their losses by bad debts, seizures, and other casualties, are taken into the account: and it is injurious to the community, by exchanging their money for those commodities which are consumed among themselves, excepting the soldiery and a few strangers who bring their money with them.

Every now and then, by starts, there have been agreements made among the landed men, to banish, as much as in them lay, the use of brandy in particular. By these contracts they have promised to confine themselves to their own growth, and to enjoin the same to their families, tenants, and other dependants; but, like some salutary laws made for the public, these resolutions have not been long regarded.

I wish the reformation could be made for the good of the country (for the evil is universal); but I cannot say I should even be contented it should extend to the claret, till my time comes to return to England and humble port, of which, if I were but only inclined to taste, there is not one glass to be obtained for love or money, either here or in any other part of Scotland that has fallen within my knowledge: but this does not at all excite my regret.

‖ What I shall say of the ministers of this town is, that they are men of good lives and sober conversation, and less stiff in many indifferent matters than most of their brethren in other parts of Scotland; and to say the truth, the Scottish clergy (except some rare examples to the contrary) lead regular and unblamable lives.

What I have further to say on this head shall be more general, but nothing of this kind can be applied to all.

The subjects of their sermons are, for the most part, grace, free-will, predestination, and other topics hardly ever to be determined: they might as well talk Hebrew to the common people, and I think to any body else. But *thou shalt do no manner of work* they urge with very great success. The text relating to Caesar's tribute is seldom explained, even in places where great part of the inhabitants live by the contrary of that example. In England you know, the minister, if the people were found to be negligent of their clothes when they came to church, would recommend decency and cleanliness, as a mark of respect due to the place of worship; and indeed, humanly speaking, it is so to one another. But on the contrary, if a woman, in some parts of Scotland, should appear at kirk dressed, though not better than at an ordinary visit, she would be in danger of a rebuke from the pulpit, and of being told she ought to purify her soul, and not employ part of the sabbath in decking out her body; and I must needs say, that most of the females in both parts of the kingdom follow, in that particular, the instructions of their spiritual guides, religiously.

The minister here in Scotland would have the ladies come to kirk in their plaids, which hide any loose dress, and their faces too, if they will be persuaded, in order to prevent the wandering thoughts of young fellows, and perhaps some young old ones too: for the minister looks upon a well-dressed young woman to be an object unfit to be seen in the time of divine service, especially if she be handsome.

LETTER IX

I wish these ministers would speak oftener, and sometimes more civilly than they do, of morality.

To tell the people they may go to hell with all their morality at their back, – this surely may insinuate to weak minds, that it is to be avoided as a kind of sin; at best that it will be of no use to them. And then no wonder they neglect it, and set their enthusiastic notions of grace in the place of righteousness. This is in general; but I must own in particular, that one of the ministers of this town has been so careful of the morals of his congregation, that he earnestly exhorted them from the pulpit, to fly from the example of a wicked *neighbouring nation*.

Their prayers are often more like narrations to the Almighty, than petitions for what they want; and the *sough*, as it is called, (the whine), is unmanly, and much beneath the dignity of their subject.

‖ Their preaching extempore exposes them to the danger of exhibiting undigested thoughts and mistakes; as indeed it might do to any others who make long harangues without some previous study and reflection. But that some of them make little preparation, I am apt to conclude from their immethodical ramblings.

I shall mention one mistake, – I may call it an absurdity.

The minister was explaining to his congregation the great benefits arising from the sabbath. He told them it was a means of frequently renewing their covenant, etc., and likewise, it was a worldly good; as a day of rest for themselves, their servants, and cattle. Then he recounted to them the different days observed in other religions; as the seventh day by the Jews, etc. 'But,' says he, 'behold the particular wisdom of our institution, in ordaining it to be kept on the first: for if it were any other day, it would make a *broken week*.'

The cant is only approved of by the ignorant (poor or rich) into whom it instils a kind of enthusiasm, in moving their passions by sudden starts of various sounds. They have made of it a kind of art not easy to attain. But people of better understanding make a jest of this drollery, and seem to be highly pleased when they meet with its contrary.

‖ One of the ministers of this town (an old man who died some time ago) undertook one day to entertain us with a dialogue from the pulpit relating to the fall of man, in the following manner, which cannot so well be conveyed in writing as by word of mouth :—

First he spoke in a low voice – 'And the L.G. came into the garden and said –'

Then loud and angrily – 'Adam, where art ?'

Low and humbly – 'Lo, here am I, Lord !'

Violently – 'And what are ye deeing there ?'

With a fearful trembling accent – 'Lord, I was nacked, and I hid mysel.'

Outrageously – 'Nacked ! And what then ? Hast thou eaten, etc. ?'

Thus he profanely (without thinking it so) described the omniscient and merciful God in the character of an angry master, who had not patience to hear what his poor offending servant had to say in excuse of his fault. And this they call speaking in a familiar way to the understandings of the ordinary people.

But perhaps they think what the famous astrologer Lilly declared to a gentleman who asked him how he thought any man of good sense would buy his predictions. This question started another, which was – What proportion the men of sense bore to those who could not be called so ? And at last they were reduced to one in twenty. 'Now,' says the conjurer, 'let the nineteen buy my prophecies, and then' (snapping his fingers) 'that ! for your one man of good sense.'

Not to trouble you with any more particulars of their oddities from the pulpit, I shall only say, that since I have been in this country, I have heard so many (and of so many), that I really think there is nothing set down in the book called 'Scots Presbyterian Eloquence,' but what, at least, is probable. But the young ministers are introducing a manner more decent and reasonable, which irritates the old stagers against them; and therefore they begin to preach at one another.

If you happen to be in company with one or more of them, and wine, ale, or even a dram is called for, you must not drink till a long grace be said over it, unless you could be contented to be thought irreligious and unmannerly.

Some time after my coming to this country, I had occasion

to ride a little way with two ministers of the Kirk; and as we were passing by the door of a *change*, one of them (the weather being cold) proposed a dram.

As the alehouse-keeper held it in his hand, I could not conceive the reason of their bowing to each other, as pleading by signs to be excused, without speaking one word.

I could not but think they were contending who should drink last, and myself, a stranger, out of the question; but in the end the glass was forced upon me, and I found the compliment was, which of them should give the preference to the other of saying grace over the brandy. For my part I thought they did not well consider to whom they were about to make their address, when they were using all this ceremony one to another in his presence. And (to use their own way of argument) concluded they would not have done it in the presence at St James's.

They seem to me to have but little knowledge of men, being restrained from all free conversation, even in coffee houses, by the fear of scandal, which may be attended with the loss of their livelihood; and they are exceedingly strict and severe upon one another in every thing which, according to their way of judging, might give offence.

Not long ago, one of them, as I am told, was suspended for having a shoulder of mutton roasted on a Sunday morning; another for powdering his peruke on that day. Six or seven years ago, a minister (if my information be right) was suspended by one of the presbyteries – The occasion this:

He was to preach at a kirk some little way within the Highlands, and set out on the Saturday; but, in his journey, the rains had swelled the rivers to such a degree, that a ford which lay in his way was become impassable.

This obliged him to take up his lodging for that night at a little hut near the river; and getting up early the next morning, he found the waters just enough abated for him to venture a passage, which he did with a good deal of hazard, and came to the kirk in good time, where he found the people assembled and waiting his arrival.

This riding on horseback of a Sunday was deemed a great scandal. It is true, that when this affair was brought by appeal before the general assembly in Edinburgh, his suspension was removed, but not without a good many debates on the subject.

Though some things of this kind are carried too far, yet I cannot but be of opinion, that these restraints on the conduct of the ministers, which produce so great regularity among them, contribute much to the respect they meet with from the people; for although they have not the advantage of any outward appearance, by dress, to strike the imagination, or to distinguish them from other men who happen to wear black or dark gray, yet they are, I think I may say, ten times more reverenced than our ministers in England.

LETTER X

‖ The day before yesterday, an occasion called me to make a progress of about six or seven miles among the mountains; but before I set out, I was told the way was dangerous to strangers, who might lose themselves in the hills if they had not a conductor. For this reason, about two miles from hence I hired a guide, and agreed with him for sixpence to attend me the whole day. This poor man went barefoot, sometimes by my horse's side, and in dangerous places leading him by the bridle, winding about from side to side among the rocks, to such gaps where the horses could raise their feet high enough to mount the stones, or stride over them.

In this tedious passage, in order to divert myself (having an interpreter with me), I asked my guide a great many questions relating to the Highlands, all which he answered very properly.

In his turn, he told me, by way of question, to hear what I would say, that he believed there would be no war; but I did not understand his meaning till I was told. By *war* he meant *rebellion*; and then, with a dismal countenance, he said he was by trade a weaver, and that in the year 1715 the *sidier roy*, or red soldiers, as they call them (to distinguish them from the Highland companies, whom they call *sidier dou*, or the black soldiers) – I say he told me, that they burnt his house and his loom, and he had never been in condition since that time to purchase materials for his work, otherwise he had not needed to be a guide; and he thought his case very hard, because he had not been in the *affair*, or the *scrape* as they call it all over Scotland, being cautious of using the word Rebellion. But this last declaration of his I did not so much depend on.

When he had finished his story, which, by interpreting, took up a good deal of time, I recounted to him the fable of the pigeon's fate that happened to be among the jackdaws, at which he laughed heartily, notwithstanding his late grief for his loss; and doubtless the fable was to him entirely new.

I then asked his reason why he thought there would not be another war (as he called it); and his answer was, he believed the English did not expect one, because they were *fooling* away their money, in removing great stones and blowing up of rocks.

Wade

Here he spoke his grievance as a guide; and indeed, when the roads are finished according to the plan proposed, there will be but little occasion for those people, except such as can speak English, and may by some be thought necessary for interpreters in their journeys: I say they will be useless as guides alone, reckoning from the south of Scotland to this town the mountain way (for along the coast hither, the road can hardly be mistaken), and counting again from the Lowlands to the west end of the opening among the mountains that run from hence quite across the island.

But all the Highlands be-north this town and the said opening will remain as rugged and dangerous as ever.

At length I arrived at the spot, of which I was able to take a view, and found it most horrible; but in the way that I went, being the shortest cut going southward, it is not to be avoided.

This is a deep narrow hollow, between very steep mountains, where into huge parts of rocks have fallen. It is a terrifying sight to those who are not accustomed to such views; and at bottom is a small but dangerous burne, running wildly among the rocks, especially in times of rain. You descend by a declivity in the face of the mountain, from whence the rocks have parted (for they have visibly their decay), and the rivulet is particularly dangerous, when the passenger is going along with the stream, and pursued by the torrent. But you have not far to go in this bottom, before you leave the current, which pursues its way, in continued windings, among the feet of the mountains; and soon after you descend by a steep and rocky hill, and when the height is attained, you would think the most rugged ways you could possibly conceive of to be a happy variety.

When I was returned to the hut where I took my guide, being pleased with the fellow's good humour, and frankness in answering my questions, instead of six-pence I gave him a shilling. At first he could not trust his own eyes, or thought I was mistaken; but being told what it was, and that it was all his own, he fell on his knees and cried out, he never, in all his life before, knew any body give more than they bargained for. This done, he ran into his hut, and brought out four children almost naked, to show them to me, with a prayer for the English. Thus I had, for so small a price as one sixpence, the exquisite pleasure of making a poor creature happy for a time.

LETTER XI

|| I shall now, for a while, confine myself to some customs in this town; and shall not wander, except something material starts in my way.

The evening before a wedding, there is a ceremony called the *feet-washing*, when the bride-maids attend the future bride, and wash her feet.

They have a penny-wedding, that is, when a servant-maid has served faithfully, and gained the good will of her master and mistress, they invite their relations and friends, and there is a dinner or supper on the day the servant is married, and music and dancing follow to complete the evening.

The bride must go about the room, and kiss every man in the company, and in the end every body puts money into a dish, according to their inclination and ability. By this means, a family in good circumstances, and respected by those they invite, have procured for the new couple wherewithall to begin the world pretty comfortably for people of their low condition. But I should have told you, that the whole expense of the feast and fiddlers is paid out of the contribution. This and the former are likewise customs all over the Lowlands of Scotland.

I never was present at one of their weddings, nor have I heard of any thing extraordinary in that ceremony, only they do not use the ring in marriage as in England. But it is a most comical farce to see an ordinary bride conducted to church by two men, who take her under the arm and hurry the poor unwilling creature along the streets, as you may have seen a pickpocket dragged to a horse-pond in London. I have somewhere read of a kind of force, of old, put upon virgins in the article of marriage, in some eastern country, where the practice was introduced to conquer their modesty: but I think in this age and nation there is little occasion for any such violence. And perhaps (with reverence to antiquity, though it often reproaches our time) it was then only used to save appearances.

The moment a child is born, in these northern parts, it is immersed in cold water, be the season of the year never so rigorous.

When I seemed, at first, a little shocked at the mention of this strange extreme, the good women told me, the midwives would not forego that practice, if my wife, though a stranger, had a child born in this country.

At the christening, the husband holds up the child before the pulpit, from whence the minister gives him a long extemporary admonition concerning its education. In most places, the infant's being brought to the church is not to be dispensed with, though it be in never so weak a condition; but here, as I said before, they are not so scrupulous in that and some other particulars.

For inviting people to ordinary buryings in all parts of the low-country, as well as here, a man goes about with a bell; and when he comes to one of his stations, suppose the deceased was a man, he cries, 'All brethren and sisters, I let you to wot, that there is a brother departed this life, at the pleasure of Almighty God; they called him, &c. – he lived at, &c.' And so for a woman, with the necessary alterations. The corpse is carried, not upon men's shoulders, as in England, but, under hand, upon a bier; and the nearest relation to the deceased carries the head, the next of kin on his right-hand, &c. and if the church-yard be anything distant, they are relieved by others as occasion may require. The men go two-and-two before the bier, and the women, in the same order, follow after it; and all the way the bellman goes tinkling before the procession, as is done before the host in popish countries.

Not long ago a Highland-man was buried here. There were few in the procession besides Highlanders in their usual garb; and all the way before them a piper played on his bagpipe, which was hung with narrow streamers of black crape.

When people of some circumstance are to be buried, the nearest relation sends printed letters, signed by himself; and sometimes, but rarely, the invitation has been general, and made by beat of drum.

The friends of the deceased usually meet at the house of mourning the day before the funeral, where they sit a good while like Quakers at a silent meeting, in dumb show of sorrow; but in time the bottle is introduced, and the ceremony quite reversed.

It is esteemed very slighting, and scarcely ever to be forgiven, not to attend after invitation, if you are in health; the only means to escape resentment, is to send a letter, in answer, with some reasonable excuse.

The company, which is always numerous, meets in the street at the door of the deceased; and when a proper number of them are assembled, some of those among them, who are of highest rank, or most esteemed, and strangers, are the first invited to walk into a room, where there usually are several pyramids of plum-cake, sweetmeats, and several dishes, with pipes and tobacco; the last is according to an old custom, for it is very rare to see any body smoke in Scotland.

The nearest relations and friends of the person to be interred, attend, and, like waiters, serve you with wine for about a quarter of an hour; and no sooner have you accepted of one glass, but another is at your elbow, and so a third, &c. There is no excuse to be made for not drinking, for then it will be said; 'You have obliged my brother, or my cousin such-a-one; pray, sir, what have I done to be refused?' When the usual time is expired, this detachment goes out, and another succeeds; and

when all have had their *tour*, they accompany the corpse to th
grave, which they generally do about noon.

The minister, who is always invited, performs no kind c
funeral service for those of any rank whatever, but mos
commonly is one of the last that leaves the place of burial.

When the company are about to return, a part of them ar
selected to go back to the house, where all sorrow seems to b
immediately banished, and wine is filled about as fast as it ca
go round, till there is hardly a sober person among them. And
by the way, I have been often told, that some have kept thei
friends drinking upon this occasion for more days together tha
I can venture to mention.

In the conclusion, some of the sweetmeats are put into you
hat, or thrust into your pocket, which enable you to make
great compliment to the women of your acquaintance.

LETTER XIII

I shall now return to the neighbouring country. Here are bu
two houses of any note within many miles of us, on this side th
Murray Frith; one is the house of Culloden, which I hav
mentioned in a former letter.

This is about two miles off, and is a pretty large fabric, buil
with stone, and divided into many rooms, among which th
hall is very spacious.

There are good gardens belonging to it, and a noble plante
avenue, of great length, that leads to the house, and a plantatio
of trees about it.

This house (or castle) was besieged in the year 1715 by a bod
of the rebels; and the laird being absent, in parliament, his lad
baffled all their attempts, with extraordinary courage an
presence of mind.

Nearly adjoining are the parks, that is, one large tract c
ground, surrounded with a low wall of loose stones, an
divided into several parts by partitions of the same. The surfac
of the ground is all over heath, or, as they call it, *heather*, withou
any trees; but some of it has been lately sown with the seed c

rs, which are now grown about a foot and a half high, but are
ardly to be seen for the heath.

An English captain, the afternoon of the day following his
rrival here from London, desired me to ride out with him, and
1ow him the parks of Culloden, without telling me the reason
f his curiosity. Accordingly we set out; and when we were
retty near the place, he asked me, 'Where are these parks?
or,' says he, 'there is nothing near in view but heath, and, at
distance, rocks and mountains.' I pointed to the inclosure;
nd, being a little way before him, heard him cursing in
oliloquy, which occasioned my making a halt, and asking if
nything had displeased him. Then he told me, that at a coffee-
ouse in London, he was one day commending the park of
tudley in Yorkshire, and those of several other gentlemen in
ther parts of England, when a Scots captain, who was by,
ried out, 'Ah! sir, but if you were to see the parks of Culloden
1 Scotland!'

This my companion repeated several times with different
1odulations of voice; and then, in an angry manner, swore, if
e had known how grossly he had been imposed on, he could
ot have put up so great an affront. But I should have told you,
1at every one of the small divisions above mentioned is called
separate park, and that the reason for making some of the
1ner walls has been to prevent the hares (with which as I said
efore the country abounds) from cropping the tender tops of
1ose young firs, which, indeed, effectually spoils their regular
rowth.

The other house I spoke of is not much further distant from
1e contrary side of the town, and belongs to the younger
rother of the gentleman above-mentioned. He is lord-
dvocate, or attorney-general, for Scotland: it is a good old
uilding, but not so large as the other; and near it there is a
1ost romantic wood, whereof one part consists of great heights
nd hollows; and the brush-wood at the foot of the trees, with
1e springs that issue out of the sides of the hills invite the
oodcocks, which, in the season, are generally there in great
umbers, and render it the best spot for cock-shooting that ever
knew.

Neither of these houses are to be seen from any part near the town.

The gentleman, of whose house I have last been speaking, were it not for a valetudinary state of health, and the avocation of his office, would be as highly pleased to see his friends about him at table, and over a bottle, as his hospitable brother.

In the spots of arable land near the town, the people sometimes plough with eight small beasts, part oxen and part cows. They do not drive them with a goad, as in England, but beat them with a long stick, making a hideous Irish noise in calling to them as they move along.

The poverty of the field-labourers hereabouts is deplorable. was one day riding out for air and exercise; and in my way saw a woman cutting green barley in a little plot before her hut.

This induced me to turn aside, and ask her what use she intended it for; and she told me it was to make bread for her family.

The grain was so green and soft, that I easily pressed some of it between my fingers; so that when she had prepared it, certainly it must have been more like a poultice than what she called it, bread. There was a gentleman with me, who was my interpreter; and though he told me what the woman said, yet he did not seem greatly to approve of my curiosity.

Their harvest-labourers are often paid in kind, *viz.* oats or barley; and the person thus paid, goes afterwards about with the sheaves, to sell them to such as will purchase them.

If they are paid in money, their wages is two-pence halfpenny or three-pence a day, and their dinner, which I suppose is oatmeal.

There is no other sort of grain hereabouts, besides oats, barley, and beer, which last is an inferior species of barley, but of greater increase. A field of wheat would be as great a rarity as a nightingale in any part of Scotland, or a cat-a-mountain in Middlesex. And yet I have seen good wheat in some of the lowland part of the shire of Murray; which is, indeed, but a narrow space between the sea and the mountains not very far south of us. It is true, a certain gentleman, not far from the coast in the county of Ross, which is further north than we are, by favour of an extraordinary year, and a piece of new ground, raised some wheat; but he made so much parade of it, that the stack stood in his court-yard till the rats had almost devoured it. This, and a good melon he treated me with, which was raised under a rock facing the south, and strongly reflecting the heat of the sun, so equally flattered him, that he afterwards made use of me as a witness of both upon several occasions. But melons may be produced in Lapland.

‖ About the time of one great scarcity here, the garrison of Fort-William, opposite to us on the west coast, was very low in oatmeal, and the little hovel town of Maryburgh, nearly adjoining to it, was almost destitute.

Some affairs at that time called me to the fort; and being at the governor's house, one of the townswomen came to his lady, and besought her to use her interest that she might be spared out of the stores, for her money, or to repay it in kind, only one peck of oatmeal, to keep her children from starving; for that there was none to be sold in the town, or other food to be had whatever. The lady, who is one of the best and most agreeable of women, told her she feared her husband could not be prevailed on to part with any at that time. This she said, as knowing that kind of provision was almost exhausted, and a great number of mouths to be fed; that there was but a very precarious dependance upon the winds for a supply, and that other sea accidents might happen: – but to show her good will, she gave her a shilling. The poor woman, holding up the money, first looked at that, in a musing manner, then at the lady, and bursting out into tears, cried – 'Madam, what must I do with this? My children cannot eat it!' And laid the shilling down upon the table in the greatest sorrow and despair. It would be too trite to remark upon the uselessness of money, when it cannot be bartered for something absolutely necessary to life. But I do assure you I was hardly ever more affected with distress than upon this occasion, for I never saw such an example of it before.

I must not leave you in suspense. The governor commiserating the poor woman's circumstance, spared her that small quantity; and then the passion of joy seemed more unruly in the poor creature's breast, than all her grief and fear had been before.

Some few days afterwards, a ship that had laid wind-bound in the Orkneys, arrived; and upon my return hither, I found there had been a supply likewise, by sea, from the low-country.

I shall make no apology for going a little out of my way to give you a short account of the fortress Fort-William, and the town of Maryburgh that belongs to it; because, upon a like occasion, you gave me a hint in one of your letters, that such sudden starts of variety were agreeable to you.

The fort is situate in Lochaber, a country which, though bordering upon the western ocean, yet is within the shire of Inverness. Oliver Cromwell made there a settlement, as I have said before; but the present citadel was built in the reign of king William and queen Mary, and called after the name of the king. It was in great measure originally designed as a check upon the chief of the Camerons, a clan which in those days was greatly addicted to plunder, and strongly inclined to rebellion.

It stands in a most barren rocky country, and is washed on one of the faces of the fortification by a navigable arm of the sea. It is almost surrounded on the land sides with rivers not far distant from it, which, though but small, are often impassable from their depth and rapidity. And lastly, it is near the foot of an exceedingly high mountain, called Ben-Nevis, of which I may have occasion to say something in some future letter relating particularly to the high-country. The town was erected into a barony in favour of the governor of the fort for the time being, and into a borough bearing the name of queen Mary. It was originally designed as a sutlery to the garrison in so barren a country, where little can be had for the support of the troops.

The houses were neither to be built with stone nor brick, and are to this day composed of timber, boards, and turf. This was ordained, to the end they might the more suddenly be burnt, or otherwise destroyed, by order of the governor, to prevent any lodgment of an enemy that might annoy the fort, in case of rebellion or invasion.

LETTER XV

The 2d of October, 172–

‖ Set out with one servant, and a guide; the latter, because no stranger (or even a native, unacquainted with the way) can venture among the hills without a conductor; for if he once goes aside, and most especially if snow should fall (which may happen on the very high hills at any season of the year), in that, or any other case, he may wander into a bog, to impassable bourns or rocks, and every *ne plus ultra* oblige him to change his course, till he wanders from all hopes of ever again seeing the face of a human creature.

Or if he should accidentally hit upon the way from whence he strayed, he would not distinguish it from another, there is such a seeming sameness in all the rocky places.

Or again, if he should happen to meet with some Highlander, and one that was not unwilling to give him directions, he could not declare his wants, as being a stranger to the language of the country. In short, one might as well think of making a sea voyage without sun, moon, stars, or compass, as pretend to know which way to take, when lost among the hills and mountains.

But to return to my journal, from which I have strayed, though not with much danger, it being at first setting out, and my guide with me.

After riding about four miles of pretty good road, over heathy moors, hilly, but none high or of steep ascent, I came to a small river, where there was a ferry; for the water was too deep and rapid to pass the ford above. The boat was patched almost everywhere with rough pieces of boards, and the oars were kept in their places by small bands of twisted sticks.

I could not but inquire its age, seeing it had so many marks of antiquity; and was told by the ferryman, it had belonged to his father, and was above sixty years old. This put me in mind of the knife, which was of an extraordinary age, but had, at times, been repaired with many new blades and handles. But in most places of the Highlands, where there is a boat (which is very rare), it is much worse than this, and not large enough to receive a horse; and therefore he is swum at the stern, while somebody holds up his head by a halter or bridle.

The horses swim very well at first setting out; but if the water be wide, in time they generally turn themselves on one of their sides, and patiently suffer themselves to be dragged along.

I remember one of these boats was so very much out of repair, we were forced to stand upon clods of turf, to stop the leaks in her bottom, while we passed across the river.

I shall here conclude, in the style of the news-writers – This to be continued in my next.

LETTER XVI

From the river's side I ascended a steep hill, so full of large stones, it was impossible to make a trot. This continued up and down about a mile and half.

At foot of the hill, tolerable way for a mile, there being no great quantity of stones among the heath, but very uneven; and at the end of it a small bourn descending from between two hills, worn deep among the rocks, rough, rapid and steep, and dangerous to pass. I concluded some rain had fallen behind the hills that were near me; which I could not see, because it had a much greater fall of water than any of the like kind I had passed before.

From hence a hill five miles over, chiefly composed of lesser hills; so stony, it was impossible to crawl above a mile in an hour. But I must except a small part of it from this general description; for there ran across this way (*or road*, as they call it) the end of a wood of fir-trees, the only one I had ever passed.

This, for the most part, was an easy rising slope of about half a mile. In most places of the surface it was bog about two feet deep, and beneath was uneven rock; in other parts the rock and roots of the trees appeared to view.

The roots sometimes crossed one another, as they ran along a good way upon the face of the rock, and often above the boggy part, by both which my horses' legs were so much entangled, that I thought it impossible to keep them upon their feet. But you would not have been displeased to observe how the roots had run along, and felt, as it were, for the crannies of the rock; and there shot into them, as a hold against the pressure of winds above.

At the end of this hill was a river, or rather rivulet, and near the edge of it a small grassy spot, such as I had not seen in all my way, but the place not inhabited. Here I stopped to bait. My own provisions were laid upon the foot of a rock, and the oats upon a kind of mossy grass, as the cleanest place for the horses' feeding.

While I was taking some refreshment, chance provided me with a more agreeable repast – the pleasure of the mind. I happened to espy a poor Highlander at a great height, upon the declivity of a high hill, and ordered my guide to call him down. The *traucho* (or come hither) seemed agreeable to him, and he came down with wonderful celerity, considering the roughness of the hill; and asking what was *my will* (in his language), he was given to understand I wanted him only to eat and drink. This unexpected answer raised such joy in the poor creature, as he could not help showing it by skipping about, and expressing sounds of satisfaction. And when I was retired a little way down the river, to give the men an opportunity of enjoying themselves with less restraint, there was such mirth among the three, as I thought a sufficient recompense for my former fatigue.

But perhaps you may question how there could be such merriment, with nothing but water?

I carried with me a quart-bottle of brandy, for my man and the guide; and for myself, I had always in my journeys a *pocket-pistol*, loaded with brandy, mixed with juice of lemons (when they were to be had), which again mingled with water, in a wooden cup, was upon such occasions my table drink.

When we had trussed up our baggage, I entered the ford, and passed it not without danger, the bottom being filled with large stones, the current rapid, a steep rocky descent to the water, and a rising on the farther side, much worse; for having mounted a little way up the declivity, in turning the corner of a rock I came to an exceeding steep part before I was aware of it, where I thought my horse would have gone down backwards, much faster than he went up: but I recovered a small flat of the rock, and dismounted.

There was nothing remarkable afterwards, till I came near the top of the hill; where there was a seeming plain of about a hundred and fifty yards, between me and the summit.

No sooner was I upon the edge of it, but my guide desired me to alight; and then I perceived it was a bog, or peat-moss, as they call it.

I had experience enough of these deceitful surfaces to order that the horses should be led in separate parts; lest, if one broke the turf, the other, treading in his steps, might sink.

The horse I used to ride, having little weight but his own, went on pretty successfully; only now and then breaking the surface a little; but the other, that carried my portmanteau, and being not quite so nimble, was much in danger, till near the further end, and here he sank. But it luckily happened to be in a part where his long legs went to the bottom, which is generally hard gravel, or rock; but he was in almost up to the back.

By this time my own (for distinction) was quite free of the bog, and being frightened, stood very tamely by himself; which he would not have done at another time. In the mean while we were forced to wait at a distance, while the other was flouncing and throwing the dirt about him; for there was no means of coming near him to ease him of the heavy burthen he had upon his loins, by which he was sometimes in danger to be turned upon his back, when he rose to break the bog before him. But in about a quarter of an hour he got out, bedaubed with the slough, shaking with fear, and his head and neck all over in a foam.

This bog was stiff enough at that time to bear the country *garrons* in any part of it. But it is observed of the English horses, that when they find themselves hampered, they stand still, and tremble till they sink, and then they struggle violently, and work themselves further in; and if the bog be deep, as most of them are, it is next to impossible to get them out, otherwise than by digging them a passage. But the little Highland hobbies, when they find themselves bogged, will lie still till they are relieved. And besides, being bred in the mountains, they have learnt to avoid the weaker parts of the mire; and sometimes our own horses, having put down their heads and smelt to the bog, will refuse to enter upon it.

|| I had now five computed miles to go, before I came to my first asylum; that is, five Scots miles, which, as in the north of England, are longer than yours, as three is to two. And if the difficulty of the way were to be taken into the account it might well be called fifteen.

This (except about three quarters of a mile of heathy ground, pretty free from stones and rocks) consisted of stony moors, almost impracticable for a horse with his rider; and likewise of rocky way, where we were obliged to dismount, and sometimes climb, and otherwhile slide down. But what vexed me most of all, they called it a road: yet, after all, I must confess it was preferable to a boggy way. The great difficulty was to wind about with the horses, and find such places as they could possibly be got over.

When we came near the foot of the lowermost hill, I discovered a pretty large glen, which before was not to be seen. I believe it might be about a quarter of a mile wide, enclosed by exceeding high mountains, with nine dwelling-huts, besides a few others of a lesser size, for barns and stables. This they call a town, with a pompous name belonging to it; but the comfort of being near the end of my day's journey (heartily tired) was mixed with the allay of a pretty wide river, that ran between me and my lodging.

Having passed the hill, I entered the river; my horse being almost at once up to his midsides. The guide led him by the bridle, as he was sometimes climbing over the loose stones, which lay in all positions, and many of them two or three feet diameter; at other times, with his nose in the water, and mounted up behind. Thus he proceeded with the utmost caution, never removing one foot, till he found the others firm; and all the while seeming impatient of the pressure of the torrent, as if he was sensible, that once losing his footing, he should be driven away, and dashed against the rocks below.

|| The instant I had recovered the farther side of the river,

there appeared near the water six Highland men and a woman. These I suppose had coasted the stream over rocks, and along the sides of steep hills; for I had not seen them before.

Seeing they were preparing to wade, I stayed to observe them. First, the men and the woman tucked up their petticoats, then they cast themselves into a rank, with the female in the middle, and laid their arms over one another's shoulders; and I saw they had placed the strongest toward the stream, as best able to resist the force of the torrent.

In their passage the large slippery stones made some of them now and then to lose their footing; and on those occasions the whole rank changed colour and countenance.

I believe no painter ever remarked so strong impressions of fear and hope on a human face, with so many and sudden successions of those two opposite passions, as I observed among those poor people; but in the Highlands this is no uncommon thing.

Perhaps you will ask – How does a single Highlander support himself against so great a force? He bears himself up against the stream with a stick, which he always carries with him for that purpose.

|| When I came to my *inn*, I found the stable-door too low to receive my large horses, though high enough for the country garrons; so the frame was taken out, and a small part of the roof pulled down for their admittance; for which damage I had a shilling to pay the next morning. My fear was, the hut being weak and small, they would pull it about their ears; for that mischance had happened to a gentleman who bore me company in a former journey, but his horses were not much hurt by the ruins.

When oats were brought, I found them so light and so much sprouted, that, taking up a handful, others hung to them, in succession, like a cluster of bees; but of such corn it is the custom to give double measure.

My next care was to provide for myself; and to that end I entered the dwelling-house. There my landlady sat with a parcel of children about her, some quite and others almost naked, by a little peat fire, in the middle of the hut; and over the fire-place was a small hole in the roof for a chimney. The floor was common earth, very uneven, and no where dry, but near the fire, and in the corners, where no foot had carried the muddy dirt from without-doors.

The skeleton of the hut was formed of small crooked timber; but the beam for the roof was large out of all proportion. This is to render the weight of the whole more fit to resist the violent flurries of wind, that frequently rush into the plains from the openings of the mountains; for the whole fabric was set upon the surface of the ground, like a table, stool, or other moveable.

Hence comes the Highlander's compliment, or health, in drinking to his friend – For as we say, among familiar acquaintance – To your *fire-side;* he says, much to the same purpose – To your *roof tree*, alluding to the family's safety from tempests.

The walls were about four feet high, lined with sticks wattled like a hurdle, built on the out-side with turf; and thinner slices of the same served for tiling. This last they call *divet*.

When the hut has been built some time, it is covered with weeds and grass; and I do assure you I have seen sheep, that had got up from the foot of an adjoining hill, feeding upon the top of the house.

If there happens to be any continuance of dry weather, which is pretty rare, the worms drop out of the *divet,* for want of moisture; insomuch that I have shuddered at the apprehension of their falling into the dish when I have been eating.

LETTER XVII

At a little distance was another hut, where preparations were making for my reception. It was something less, but contained two beds, or boxes to lie in, and was kept as an apartment for people of distinction; or, which is all one, for such as seem by their appearance to promise expense. And indeed, I have often found but little difference in that article, between one of those huts and the best inn in England. Nay, if I were to reckon the value of what I had for my own use, by the country price, it would appear to be ten times dearer: but it is not the maxim of the Highlands alone (as we know), that those who travel must pay for such as stay at home; and really the Highland gentlemen themselves are less scrupulous of expense in these public huts than anywhere else. And their example in great measure authorises impositions upon strangers, who may complain, but can have no redress.

The landlord not only sits down with you, as in the northern Lowlands, but in some little time asks leave (and sometimes not) to introduce his brother, cousin, or more, who are all to drink your honour's health in usky; which, though a strong spirit, is to them like water. And this I have often seen them drink out of a scallop-shell. And in other journeys, notwithstanding their great familiarity with me, I have several times seen my servant at a loss how to behave, when the Highlander has turned about and very formally drank to him: and when I have baited, and eaten two or three eggs, and nothing else to be had, when I asked the question, 'What is there for eating?' The answer has been, 'Nothing for you, sir; but sixpence for your man.'

The host, who is rarely other than a gentleman, is interpreter between you and those who do not speak English; so that you lose nothing of what any one has to say relating to the antiquity of their family, or the heroic actions of their ancestors in war with some other clan.

If the guest be a stranger, not seen before by the man of the house, he takes the first opportunity to inquire of the servant, from whence his master came, who he is, whither he is going, and what his business in that country? And if the fellow happens to be surly, as thinking the enquiry impertinent, perhaps chiefly from the Highlander's poor appearance, then the master is sure to be subtly sifted (if not asked) for the secret; and if obtained, it is a help to conversation with his future guests.

Notice at last was brought me that my apartment was ready; but at going out from the first hovel, the other seemed to be all on fire within: for the smoke came pouring out through the ribs and roof all over; but chiefly out at the door, which was not four feet high, so that the whole made the appearance (I have seen) of a fuming dunghill removed and fresh piled up again, and pretty near the same in colour, shape, and size.

By the way, the Highlanders say they love the smoke; it keeps them warm. But I retired to my first shelter till the peats were grown red, and the smoke thereby abated.

This fuel is seldom kept dry, for want of convenience; and that is one reason why, in lighting or replenishing the fire, the smokiness continues so long a time. And Moggy's puffing of it with her petticoat instead of a pair of bellows is a dilatory way.

I believe you would willingly know (being an Englishman) what I had to eat. My fare was a couple of roasted hens (as they call them), very poor, new killed, the skins much broken with plucking; black with smoke, and greased with bad butter.

As I had no great appetite to that dish, I spoke for some hard eggs; made my supper of the yolks, and washed them down with a bottle of good small claret.

My bed had clean sheets and blankets; but which was best of all (though negative), I found no inconvenience from those troublesome companions with which most other huts abound. But the bare mention of them brings to my remembrance a passage between two officers of the army, the morning after a Highland night's lodging.

One was taking off the slowest kind of the two, when the other cried out, 'Z – ds, what are you doing? – Let us first secure the dragoons; we can take the foot at leisure.'

But I had like to have forgot a mischance that happened to me the next morning; for rising early, and getting out of my box pretty hastily, I unluckily set my foot in the chamber-pot— a hole in the ground by the bed-side, which was made to serve for that use in case of occasion.

I shall not trouble you with any thing that passed till I mounted on horseback; only, for want of something more proper for breakfast, I took up with a little brandy, water, sugar, and yolks of eggs, beat up together; which I think they call Old man's milk.

I was now provided with a new guide, for the skill of my first extended no further than this place: but this could speak no English, which I found afterwards to be an inconvenience.

Second day. At mounting I received many compliments from my host; but the most earnest was, that common one of wishing me good weather. For, like the seafaring man, my safety depended upon it; especially at that season of the year.

As the plain lay before me, I thought it all fit for culture; but in riding along I observed a good deal of it was bog, and here and there rock even with the surface: however, my road was smooth; and if I had had company with me, I might have said jestingly, as was usual among us after a rough way; – 'Come let us ride this over again.'

At the end of about a mile, there was a steep ascent, which they call a *carne;* that is, an exceeding stony hill, which at some distance seems to have no space at all between stone and stone. I thought I could compare it with no ruggedness so aptly as to suppose it like all the different stones in a mason's yard thrown promiscuously upon one another. This I passed on foot, at the rate of about half a mile in the hour. I do not reckon the time that was lost in backing my horses out of a narrow place without the side of a rock, where the way ended with a precipice of about twenty feet deep. Into this gap they were led by the mistake or carelessness of my guide. The descent from the top of this carne was short, and thence I ascended another hill not so stony; and at last, by several others (which, though very rough, are not reckoned extraordinary in the Highlands), I came to a precipice of about a hundred yards in length.

The side of the mountain below me was almost perpendicular, and the rest above, which seemed to reach the clouds, was exceedingly steep. The path which the Highlanders and their little horses had worn was scarcely two feet wide, but pretty smooth and below was a lake, whereinto vast pieces of rock had fallen, which I suppose had made in some measure the steepness of the precipice; and the water that appeared between some of them seemed to be under my stirrup. I really believe the path where I was is twice as high from the lake, as the cross of St Paul's is from Ludgate-Hill: and I thought I had good reason to think so; because a few huts beneath, on the further side of the water, which is not very wide, appeared to me, each of them, like a black spot not much bigger than the standish[1] before me.

---

[1] Standish: a stand containing ink, pens, etc. A. J. Y.

‖ I shall not trouble you with any more at present, than that I safely arrived at my baiting-place; for, as I hinted before, there is such a sameness in the parts of the hills, that the description of one rugged way, bog, ford, &c. will serve pretty well to give you a notion of the rest.

Here I desired to know what I could have for dinner; and was told there was some undressed mutton. This I esteemed as a rarity; but as I did not approve the fingers of either maid or mistress, I ordered my man (who is an excellent cook so far as a beef-stake or a mutton-chop) to broil me a chop or two, while I took a little turn to ease my legs, weary with sitting so long on horseback.

‖ Here was no wine to be had; but as I carried with me a few lemons in a net, I drank some small punch for refreshment. When my servant was preparing the liquor, my landlord came to me, and asked me seriously, If those were apples he was squeezing? And indeed there are as many lemon-trees as apple-trees in that country; nor have they any kind of fruit in their glens that I know of.

Their huts are mostly built on some rising rocky spot, at the foot of a hill, secure from any bourne or springs that might descend upon them from the mountains; and, thus situated, they are pretty safe from inundations from above or below, and other ground they cannot spare from their corn. And even upon the skirts of the Highlands, where the laird has indulged two or three trees not far from his house, I have heard the tenant lament the damage done by the droppings and shade of them, as well as the space taken up by the trunks and roots.

The only fruit the natives have, that I have seen, is the bilberry, which is mostly found near springs, in hollows of the heaths. The taste of them, to me, is not very agreeable; but they are much esteemed by the inhabitants, who eat them with their milk. Yet in the mountain-woods, which for the most part are distant, and difficult of access, there are nuts, raspberries, and strawberries; the two last, though but small, are very grateful to the taste: but those woods are so rare, (at least it has always appeared so to me), that few of the Highlanders are near enough to partake of the benefit.

I now set out on my last stage; of which I had gone about five miles, in much the same manner as before, when it began to rain below; but it was snow above, to a certain depth from the summits of the mountains.

In about half an hour afterwards, at the end of near a mile there arose a most violent tempest. This in a little time began to scoop the snow from the mountains, and made such a furious drift, which did not melt as it drove, that I could hardly see my horse's head.

The horses were blown aside from place to place, as often as the sudden gusts came on, being unable to resist those violent eddy-winds; and at the same time they were very near blinded with the snow.

Now I expected no less than to perish, was hardly able to keep my saddle, and for increase of misery, my guide led me out of the way, having entirely lost his land-marks.

When he perceived his error, he fell down on his knees by my horse's side; and in a beseeching posture, with his arms extended, and in a howling tone, he seemed to ask forgiveness.

I imagined what the matter was, for I could but just see him and that too by fits; and spoke to him with a soft voice, to signify I was not in anger. And it appeared afterwards that he expected to be shot, as they have a dreadful notion of the English.

Thus finding himself in no danger of my resentment, he addressed himself to the searching about for the way from which he had deviated; and in some little time I heard a cry of joy and he came and took my horse by the bridle, and never afterwards quitted it till we came to my new lodging, which was about a mile; for it was almost as dark as night. In the mean time I had given direction to my man for keeping close to my horse's heels; and if any thing should prevent it, to call to me immediately, that I might not lose him.

As good luck would have it, there was but one small river in the way; and the ford, though deep and winding, had a smooth sandy bottom, which is very rare in the Highlands.

There was another circumstance favourable to us, (I shall

not name a third as one, which is our being not far from the village; for we might have perished with cold in the night, as well near it as further off), there had not a very great quantity of snow fallen upon the mountains, because the air began a little to clear, though very little, within about a quarter of a mile of the glen, otherwise we might have been buried in some cavity hid from us by the darkness and the snow.

But if this drift which happened to us upon some one of the wild moors had continued, and we had had far to go, we might have perished, notwithstanding the knowledge of any guide whatever.

These drifts are, above all other dangers, dreaded by the Highlanders; for my own part, I could not but think of Mr Addison's short description of a whirlwind, in the wild sandy deserts of Numidia.

LETTER XVIII

Every high wind, in many places of the Highlands, is a whirlwind. The agitated air pouring into the narrow and high spaces between the mountains, being confined in its course, and, if I may use the expression, pushed on by a crowding rear, till it comes to a bounded hollow, or kind of amphitheatre; I say, the air, in that violent motion, is there continually repelled by the opposite hill, and rebounded from others, till it finds a passage; insomuch that I have seen in the western highlands, in such a hollow, some scattering oaks, with their bark twisted almost as if it had been done with a lever.

This I suppose was effected when they were young, and consequently the rest of their growth was in that figure. And I myself have met with such rebuffs on every side, from the whirling of such winds, as are not easy to be described.

When I came to my inn, (you will think the word a burlesque), I found it a most wretched hovel, with several pretty large holes in the sides; and, as usual, exceeding smoky.

My apartment had a partition about four feet high, which separated it from the lodging of the family. And being entered, I called for straw or heather, to stop the gaps. Some straw was brought; but no sooner was it applied, but it was pulled away on the outside.

This put me in very ill humour, thinking some malicious Highlander did it to plague or affront me; and therefore I sent my man (who had just housed his horses, and was helping me) to see who it could be; and immediately he returned laughing, and told me it was a poor hungry cow, that was got to the backside of the hut for shelter, and was pulling out the straw for provender.

The smoke being something abated, and the edifice repaired, I began to reflect on the miserable state I had lately been in; and esteemed that very hut, which at another time I should have greatly despised, to be to me as good as a palace; and, like a keen appetite with ordinary fare, I enjoyed it accordingly, not envying even the inhabitants of Buckingham-House.

Here I conclude my journal, which I fear you will think as barren and tedious as the ground I went over; but I must ask your patience a little while longer concerning it, as no great reason yet appears to you why I should come to this wretched place, and go no further.

By a change of the wind, there happened to fall a good deal of rain in the night; and I was told by my landlord, the hill presaged more of it; that a wide river before me was become impassable, and if I remained longer in the hills at that season of the year, I might be shut in for most part of the winter; for if fresh snow should fall, and lie lower down on the mountain than it did the day before, I could not repass the precipice, and must wait till the lake was frozen so hard as to bear my horses; and even then it was dangerous in those places where the springs bubble up from the bottom, and render the ice thin, and incapable to bear any great weight: – but that, indeed, those weak spots might be avoided by means of a skilful guide.

As to the narrow path, he said he was certain that any snow which might have lodged on it from the drift, was melted by the rain, which was then ceased. To all this he added a piece of news (not very prudently, as I thought), which was, that some time before I passed the precipice, a poor Highlander leading over it his horse laden with *creels*, or small paniers, one of the struck against the upper part of the hill, as he supposed; and whether the man was endeavouring to save his horse, or how it was he could not tell, but that they both fell down, and were dashed to pieces among the rocks. This to me was very affecting, especially as I was to pass the same way in my return.

Thus I was prevented from meeting a number of gentlemen of a clan, who were to have assembled in a place assigned for our interview, about a day-and-half's journey further in the Hills; and on the other side of the river were numbers of Highlanders waiting to conduct me to them. But I was told, before I entered upon this peregrination, that no Highlander would venture upon it at that time of the year; yet I piqued myself upon following the unreasonable directions of such as knew nothing of the matter.

Now I returned with as hasty steps as the way you have seen would permit, having met with no more snow or rain till I got into the lower country; and then there fell a very great *storm* (as they call it), for by the word *storm* they only mean snow. And you may believe I then hugged myself, as being got clear of the mountains.

|| The Highlanders are exceeding proud to be thought an unmixed people, and are apt to upbraid the English with being a composition of all nations; but for my own part, I think a little mixture in that sense would do themselves no manner of harm.

The stature of the better sort, so far as I can make the comparison, is much the same with the English, or Low-Country Scots, but the common people are generally small; nor is it likely that, by being half starved in the womb, and never afterwards well fed, they should by that means be rendered larger than other people. *Nor do it.*

How often have I heard them described in London as almost giants in size; and certainly there are a great many tall men of them in and about that city: but the truth is, when a young fellow of any spirit happens (as Kite says) to be born to be a *great man*, he leaves the country, to put himself into some foreign service (chiefly in the army), but the short ones are not commonly seen in other countries than their own. I have seen a hundred of them together come down to the Lowlands for harvest-work, as the Welsh come to England for the same purpose; and but few sizeable men among them, and their women are generally very small.

|| In one expedition where I was well attended, as I have said before, there was a river in my way so dangerous, that I was set upon the shoulders of four Highlanders; my horse not being to be trusted to in such roughness, depth, and rapidity. And I really thought sometimes, we whould all have gone together.

In the same journey the shoulders of some of them were employed to ease the horses down from rock to rock; and all that long day I could make out but nine miles. This also was called a road.

Toward the end of another progress in my return to this town, after several hazards from increasing waters, I was at length stopped by a small river that was become impassable. There happened, luckily for me, to be a public hut in this place, for there was no going back again; but there was nothing to drink, except the water of the river.

This I regretted the more, as I had refused at one of the barracks to accept of a bottle of old hock, on account of the carriage, and believing I should reach hither before night. In about three hours after my arrival at this hut, there appeared on the other side of the water a parcel of merchants, with little horses loaded with roundlets of usky.

Within sight of the ford was a bridge (as they called it) made for the convenience of this place. It was composed of two small fir-trees not squared at all, laid one beside the other, across a narrow part of the river, from rock to rock. There were gaps and intervals between those trees, and beneath a most tumultuous fall of water.

Some of my merchants bestriding the bridge, edged forwards, and moved the usky vessels before them; but the others afterwards, to my surprise, walked over this dangerous passage, and dragged their *garrons* through the torrent, while the poor little horses were almost drowned with the surge.

I happened to have a few lemons left, and with them I so far qualified the ill taste of the spirit, as to make it tolerable; but eatables there were none except eggs, and poor starved fowls as usual.

The usky men were my companions, whom it was expected I should treat according to custom; there being no partition to separate them from me. And thus I passed a part of the day, and great part of the night in the smoke, and dreading the bed.

LETTER XX

The gentry may be said to be a handsome people, but the commonalty much otherwise; one would hardly think, by their faces, they were of the same species, at least of the same country, which plainly proceeds from their bad food, smoke at home, and sun, wind, and rain abroad; because the young children have as good features as any I have seen in other parts of the island.

I have mentioned the sun in this northern climate as partly the cause of their disguise, for that (as I said before) in summer the heat, by reflection from the rocks, is excessive; at the same time the cold on the tops of the hills is so vast an extreme as cannot be conceived by any but those who have felt the difference, and know the danger of so sudden a transition from one to the other; and this likewise has its effect upon them.

The ordinary natives are, for the most part, civil when they are kindly used, but most mischievous when much offended, and will hardly ever forgive a provocation, but seek some open or secret revenge, and generally speaking, the latter of the two.

A Highland town, as before-mentioned, is composed of a few huts for dwellings, with barns and stables, and both the latter are of a more diminuitive size than the former, all irregularly placed, some one way, some another, and at any distance look like so many heaps of dirt; these are built in glens and straths, which are the corn-countries, near rivers and rivulets, and also on the sides of lakes where there is some arable land for the support of the inhabitants.

But I am now to speak of the manner in which the lower order of Highlanders live; and shall begin with the spring of the year.

This is a bad season with them; for then their provision of

oatmeal begins to fail, and for a supply they bleed their cattle, and boil the blood into cakes, which, together with a little milk and a short allowance of oatmeal, is their food.

It is true, there are small trouts, or something like them, in some of the little rivers, which continue in holes among the rocks, which are always full of water when the stream is quite ceased for want of rain; these might be a help to them in this starving season; but I have had so little notion in all my journeys that they made those fish a part of their diet, that I never once thought of them, as such, till this very moment. It is likely they cannot catch them for want of proper tackle, but I am sure they cannot be without them for want of leisure. What may seem strange is, that they do not introduce roots among them (as potatoes, for the purpose); but the land they occupy is so very little, they think they cannot spare any part of it from their corn, and the landlord's demand of rent in kind is another objection. You will perceive I am speaking only of the poor people in the interior parts of the mountains; for near the coast, all round them, there are few confined to such diminutive farms, and the most necessitous of all may share, upon occasion, the benefit of various kinds of shell-fish, only for seeking and fetching.

Their cattle are much weakened by want of sufficient food in the preceding winter, and this immoderate bleeding reduces them to so low a plight, that in a morning they cannot rise from the ground, and several of the inhabitants join together to help up each other's cows, &c.

In summer the people remove to the hills, and dwell in much worse huts than those they leave below: these are near the spots of grazing, and are called *shealings*, scattered from one another as occasion requires. Every one has his particular space of pasture, for which, if it be not a part of his farm, he pays, as I shall mention hereafter.

Here they make their butter and cheese. By the way, I have seen some of the former with blueish veins, made, as I thought, by the mixture of smoke, not much unlike to Castile soap; but some have said it was a mixture of sheep's milk which gave a part of it that tincture of blue.

When the grazing fails, the Highlanders return to their former habitations, and the cattle to pick up their sustenance among the heath, as before.

At other times the children share the milk with the calves, lambs, and kids; for they milk the dams of them all, which keeps their young so lean, that when sold in the low-country they are chiefly used, as they tell me, to make soups withal; and when a side of any one of these kinds hangs up in our market, the least disagreeable part of the sight is the transparency of the ribs.

About the latter end of August or the beginning of September the cattle are brought into good order by their summer feed, and the beef is extremely sweet and succulent; which I suppose is owing, in good part, to their being reduced to such poverty in the spring, and made up again with new flesh.

Now the drovers collect their herds, and drive them to fairs and markets on the borders of the Lowlands, and sometimes to the North of England; and in their passage they pay a certain tribute, proportionable to the number of cattle, to the owner of the territory they pass through, which is in lieu of all reckonings for grazing.

I have several times seen them driving great numbers of cattle along the sides of the mountains at a great distance, but never, except once, was near them. This was in a time of rain, by a wide river where there was a boat to ferry over the drovers. The cows were about fifty in number, and took the water like spaniels; and when they were in, their drivers made a hideous cry to urge them forwards: this, they told me, they did to keep the foremost of them from turning about; for in that case the rest would do the like, and then they would be in danger, especially the weakest of them, to be driven away and drowned by the torrent.

I thought it a very odd sight to see so many noses and eyes just above the water, and nothing of them more to be seen; for they had no horns; and upon the land they appeared in size and shape like so many large Lincolnshire calves.

I shall speak of the Highland harvest, that is, the autumn, when I come to the article of their husbandry. But nothing is more deplorable than the state of these people in time of winter.

They are in that season often confined to their glens by swoln rivers, snow, or ice on the paths in the sides of the hills, which is accumulated by drippings from the springs above, and so by little and little formed into knobs like a stick of sugar-candy; only the parts are not angular like those, but so uneven and slippery no foot can pass.

They have no diversions to amuse them, but sit brooding in the smoke over the fire till their legs and thighs are scorched to an extraordinary degree; and many have sore eyes, and some are quite blind.

This long continuance in the smoke makes them almost as black as chimney-sweepers; and when the huts are not water-tight, which is often the case, the rain that comes through the roof and mixes with the sootiness of the inside, where all the sticks look like charcoal, falls in drops like ink. But in this circumstance the Highlanders are not very solicitous about their outward appearance.

To supply the want of candles, when they have occasion for more light than is given by the fire, they provide themselves with a quantity of sticks of fir, the most resinous that can be procured: some of these are lighted and laid upon a stone; and as the light decays, they revive it with fresh fuel. But when they happen to be destitute of fire, and none is to be got in the neighbourhood, they produce it by rubbing sticks together; but I do not recollect what kind of wood is fittest for that purpose.

If a drift of snow from the mountains happens, and the same should be of any continuance, they are thereby rendered completely prisoners. In this case the snow, being whirled from the mountains and hills, lodges in the plains below, till some-times it increases to a height almost equal with the tops of their huts; but then it is soon dissolved for a little space round them, which is caused by the warmth of the fire, smoke, family and cattle within.

Thus are they confined to a very narrow compass; and in the mean time, if they have any out-lying cattle in the hills, they are leaving the heights and returning home; for by the same means that the snow is accumulated in the glen, the hills are cleared of the incumbrance: but the cattle are sometimes intercepted by the depth of snow in the plain or deep hollows in their way. In such case, when the wind's drift begins to cease, from the wind having a little spent its fury, the people take the following method to open a communication.

If the huts are at any distance asunder, one of them begins at the edge of the snow next to his dwelling; and waving his body from side to side, presses forward and squeezes it from him on either hand; and if it be higher than his head he breaks down that part with his hands. Thus he proceeds till he comes to another hut, and when some of them are got together, they go on in the same manner to open a way for the cattle; and in thus doing they relieve one another, when too wet and weary to proceed further, till the whole is completed. Yet, notwithstanding all their endeavour, their cattle are sometimes lost.

As this may seem to you a little too extraordinary, and you will believe I never saw it, I shall assure you I had it from a gentleman, who being nearly related to a chief, has therefore a considerable farm in the inner Highlands, and would not deceive me in a fact that does not recommend his country; of which he is as jealous as any one I have known on this side of the Tweed.

A drift of snow, like that above described, was said to have been the ruin of the Swedish army, in the last expedition of Charles XII.

Before I proceed to their husbandry I shall give you some account of an animal necessary to it; that is, their horses, or rather (as they are called) garrons.

These horses in miniature run wild among the mountains; some of them till they are eight or ten years old, which renders them exceedingly restive and stubborn.

There be various ways of catching them, according to the nature of the spot of country where they chiefly keep their haunts. Sometimes they are hunted by numbers of Highland-men into a bog, in other places they are driven up a steep hill, where the nearest of the pursuers endeavours to catch them by the hind leg; and I have been told, that sometimes both horse and man have come tumbling down together.

In another place they have been hunted from one to another among the heath and rocks, till they have laid themselves down through weariness and want of breath.

They are so small that a middle-sized man must keep his legs almost in lines parallel to their sides when carried over the stony ways; and it is almost incredible to those who have not seen it, how nimbly they skip with a heavy rider among the rocks and large moor-stones, turning zig-zag to such places as are passable.

I think verily they all follow one another in the same irregular steps, because in those ways there appears some little smoothness, worn by their naked hoofs, which is not any-where else to be seen.

When I have been riding (or rather creeping) along at the foot of a mountain, I have discovered them by their colour, which is mostly white, and by their motion, which readily catches the eye; when at the same time they were so high above me they seemed to be no bigger than a lap-dog, and almost hanging over my head. But what has appeared to me very extraordinary, is, that when, at other times, I have passed near to them, I have perceived them to be (like some of our common beggars in London) in ragged and tattered coats, but full in flesh; and that, even toward the latter end of winter, when I think they could have nothing to feed upon but heath and rotten leaves of trees, if any of the latter were to be found.

The Highlanders have a tradition they came originally from Spain, by breeders left there by the Spaniards in former times; and they say, they have been a great number of years in dwindling to their present diminutive size.

I was one day greatly diverted with the method of taming these wild hobbies.

In passing along a narrow path on the side of a high hill among the mountains, at length it brought me to a part looking down into a little plain; there I was at once presented with the scene of a Highlandman beating one of these garrons most unmercifully with a great stick; and upon a stricter view I perceived the man had tied a rope, or something like it, about one of his hind legs, as you may have seen a single hog driven in England; and indeed in my situation he did not seem so big. At the same time the horse was kicking and violently struggling, and sometimes the garron was down and sometimes the Highlander, and not seldom both of them together, but still the man kept his hold.

After waiting a considerable time to see the event, though not so well pleased with the precipice I stood upon, I found the garron gave it up; and being perfectly conquered for that time, patiently suffered himself to be driven to a hut not far from the field of battle.

I was desirous to ask the Highlander a question or two by the help of my guide, but there was no means for me to get down but by falling; and when I came to a part of the hill where I could descend to the glen, I had but little inclination to go back again, for I never by choice made one retrograde step when I was leaving the mountains. But what is pretty strange, though very true (by what charm I know not), I have been well enough pleased to see them again, at my first entrance to them in my returns from England. And this has made my wonder cease that a native should be so fond of such a country.

The soil of the corn-lands is in some places so shallow, with rocky ground beneath it, that a plough is of no manner of use. This they dig up with a wooden spade; for almost all their implements for husbandry, which in other countries are made of iron, or partly of that metal, are in some parts of the Highlands entirely made of wood; such as the spade, plough-share, harrow, harness, and bolts; and even locks for doors are made of wood. By the way, these locks are contrived so artfully, by notches made at unequal distances within-side, that it is impossible to open them with any thing but the wooden keys that belong to them. But there would be no great difficulty in opening the wall of the hut; as the Highlander did by the portmanteau that he saw lying upon a table, and nobody near it but his companion.

'Out!' says he; 'what fool was this that put a lock upon leather?' and immediately ripped it open with his dirk.

Where the soil is deeper, they plough with four of their little horses abreast: The manner this: –

Being thus ranked, they are divided by a small space into pairs, and the driver, or rather leader of the plough, having placed himself before them, holding the two innermost by their heads, to keep the couples asunder; he with his face toward the plough goes backward, observing, through the space between the horses, the way of the plough-share.

When I first saw this awkward method, as I then thought it, I rid up to the person who guided the machine, to ask him some questions concerning it: he spoke pretty good English, which made me conclude he was a gentleman; and yet in quality of a proprietor and conductor might without dishonour employ himself in such a work.

My first question was, whether that method was common to the Highlands, or peculiar to that part of the country; and by way of answer, he asked me, If they ploughed otherwise any where else. Upon my further inquiry, why the man went backwards, he stopped and very civilly informed me, that there were several small rocks which I did not see, that had a little part of them just peeping on the surface, and therefore it was necessary his servant should see and avoid them, by guiding the horses accordingly; or otherwise his plough might be spoiled by the shock.

The answer was satisfactory and convincing; and I must here take notice that many other of their methods are too well suited to their own circumstances and those of the country, to be easily amended by such as undertake to deride them.

In the western Highlands they still retain that barbarous custom (which I have not seen any where else) of drawing the harrow by the horse's dock, without any manner of harness whatever. And when the tail becomes too short for the purpose they lengthen it out with twisted sticks. This unnatural practice was formerly forbidden in Ireland by act of parliament, as my memory informs me, from accounts I have formerly read of that country; for being almost without books, I can have little other help wherefrom to make quotations.

When a burthen is to be carried on horseback, they use two baskets, called _creels,_ one on each side of the horse; and if the load be such as cannot be divided, they put it into one of them, and counterbalance it with stones in the other; so that one half of the horse's burthen is – I cannot say unnecessary, because I do not see how they could well do otherwise in the mountains.

Their harvest is late in the year, and therefore seldom got in dry, as the great rains usually come on about the latter end of August: nor is the corn well preserved afterwards in those miserable hovels they call barns, which are mostly not fit to keep out the bad weather from above; and were it not for the high winds that pass through the openings of the sides in dry weather, it would of necessity be quite spoiled. But as it is, the grain is often grown in the sheaves, as I have observed in a former letter.

To the lightness of the oats, one might think they contributed themselves; for if there be one part of their ground that produces worse grain than another, they reserve that, or part of it, for seed; believing it will produce again as well in quantity and quality as the best; but whether in this they are right or wrong, I cannot determine.

Another thing, besides the bad weather, that retards their harvest, is, they make it chiefly the work of the women of the family. Near the Lowlands I have known a field of corn to employ a woman and a girl for a fortnight; which, with proper help, might have been done in two days. And although the owner might not well afford to employ many hands, yet his own labour would have prevented half the risk of bad weather at that uncertain season.

An English lady, who found herself something decaying in her health, and was advised to go among the Hills, and drink goat's milk or whey, told me lately, that seeing a Highlander basking at the foot of a hill in his full dress, while his wife and her mother were hard at work in reaping the oats, she asked the old woman how she could be contented to see her daughter labour in that manner, while her husband was only an idle spectator? And to this the woman answered, that her son-in-law was a _gentleman,_ and it would be a disparagement to him to do any such work; and that both she and her daughter too were sufficiently honoured by the alliance.

This instance I own has something particular in it, as such, but the thing is very common, *à la Palatine*, among the middling sort of people.

Not long ago, a French officer, who was coming hither the Hill way, to raise some recruits for the Dutch service, met a Highland-man with a good pair of brogues on his feet, and his wife marching bare-foot after him.

This indignity to the sex raised the Frenchman's anger to such a degree, that he leaped from his horse, and obliged the fellow to take off the shoes, and the woman to put them on.

By this last instance (not to trouble you with others) you may see it is not in their harvest-work alone they are something in the *Palatine* way with respect to their women.

The Highlanders have a notion that the moon, in a clear night, ripens their corn much more than a sunshiny day; for this they plead experience; yet they cannot say by what rule they make the comparison. But by this opinion of theirs I think they have little knowledge of the nature of those two planets.

In larger farms, belonging to gentlemen of the clan, where there are any number of women employed in harvest-work, they all keep time together, by several barbarous tones of the voice; and stoop and rise together, as regularly as a rank of soldiers, when they ground their arms. Sometimes they are incited to their work by the sound of a bagpipe; and by either of these, they proceed with great alacrity, it being disgraceful for any one to be out of time with the sickle. They use the same tone, or a piper, when they thicken the new-woven plaiding, instead of a fulling-mill.

This is done by six or eight women sitting upon the ground near some river or rivulet, in two opposite ranks, with the wet cloth between them; their coats are tucked up, and with their naked feet they strike one against another's, keeping exact time as above-mentioned. And among numbers of men, employed in any work that requires strength and joint labour, as the launching a large boat, or the like, they must have the piper to

gulate their time, as well as usky, to keep up their spirits in
e performance; for pay they often have little, or none at all.

Nothing is more common than to hear the Highlanders boast
w much their country might be improved, and that it would
oduce double what it does at present, if better husbandry
re introduced among them. For my own part, it was always
e only amusement I had among the Hills, to observe every
inute thing in my way; and I do assure you, I do not remem-
r to have seen the least spot that would bear corn unculti-
ted, not even upon the sides of the hills, where it could be no
herwise broke up than with a spade. And as for manure to
pply the salts, and enrich the ground, they have hardly any.
summer their cattle are dispersed about the *sheelings*, and
most all the rest of the year in other parts of the hills; and
erefore all the dung they can have, must be from the trifling
antity made by the cattle while they are in the house. I never
ew or heard of any limestone, chalk, or marl, they have in
e country; and if some of their rocks might serve for limestone,
that case their kilns, carriage, and fuel would render it so
pensive, it would be the same thing to them as if there was
ne. Their great dependance is upon the nitre of the snow;
d they lament the disappointment if it does not fall early in
e season. Yet I have known, in some, a great inclination to
provement; and shall only instance in a very small matter,
ich perhaps may be thought too inconsiderable to mention.

Not far from Fort William, I have seen women with a little
rse-dung brought upon their backs, in *creels*, or baskets, from
at garrison; and on their knees, spreading it with their hands
on the land, and even breaking the balls, that every part of
e little spot might have its due proportion.

These women have several times brought me hay to the fort,
ich was made from grass cut with a knife, by the way-side;
d from one I have bought two or three pennyworth; from
other, the purchase has been a groat; but six pennyworth
s a most considerable bargain.

At their return from the hay-market they carried away the
ng of my stable (which was one end of a dwelling-hut) in
anner above-mentioned.

Speaking of grass and hay, it comes to my remembrance, that in passing through a space between the mountains, not far from Keppoch in Lochaber, I observed, in the hollow (though too narrow to admit much of the sun) a greater quantity of grass than I remembered to have seen in any such spot in the inner parts of the Highlands. It was in the month of August, when it was grown rank and flagged pretty much, and therefore I was induced to ask why the owner did not cut it? To this I was answered, it never had been mowed, but was left every year as natural hay for the cattle in winter, that is, to lie upon the ground like litter, and (according to their description) the cows routed for it in the snow, like hogs in a dunghill; but the people have no barns fit to contain a quantity of hay, and it would be impossible to secure it in mows from the tempestuous eddy winds, which would soon carry it over the mountains: besides, it could not well be made, by reason of rains and want of sun, and therefore they think it best to let it lie, as it does, with the roots in the ground.

The advantage of enclosures is a mighty topic with the Highlanders, though they cannot spare for grass one inch o land that will bear corn; or if they could, it would be a much more expensive way of grazing their cattle than letting them run, as they do, in the hills; but enclosures, simply as such, do not better the soil, or, if they might be supposed to be an advantage to it, where is the Highland tenant that can lay ou ten shillings for that purpose? and what would he be gainer by it in the end, but to have his rent raised, or his farm divided with some other? Or, lastly, where are the number of High landers that would patiently suffer such an inconvenien innovation? For my part, I think nature has sufficientl enclosed their lands by the feet of the surrounding mountain. Now, after what has been said, where can this improvement be

But it seems, they had rather you should think them ignorant lazy, or any thing else, than entertain a bad opinion of thei country. – But I have dwelt too long upon this head.

Their rent is chiefly paid in kind, that is to say, great part of it in several species arising from the product of the farm; such as barley, oatmeal, and what they call *customs*, as sheep, lamb

oultry, butter, &c. and the remainder, if any, is paid in
money, or an addition of some one of the afore-mentioned
pecies, if money be wanting.

The gentlemen, who are near relations of the chief, hold
retty large farms, if the estate will allow it, perhaps twenty or
hirty pounds a year, and they again, generally, parcel them
ut to under-tenants in small portions. Hence it comes, that by
uch a division of an old farm (part of an upper-tenant's
olding), suppose among eight persons, each of them pays an
ighth part of every thing, even to the fraction of a capon, which
annot in the nature of it be paid in kind, but the value of it is
ast in with the rest of the rent, and, notwithstanding the
bove-mentioned customs are placed in an upper-tenant's
ental, yet they properly belong to the chief, for the maintenance
f the family in provisions.

Every year, after the harvest, the sheriff of the county, or his
eputy, together with a jury of landed men, sets a rate upon
orn provisions, and the custom of the country regulates the
est.

The sheriff's regulation for the year is called the *feers-price*,
nd serves for a standard whereby to determine every thing
elating to rents and bargains; so that if the tenant is not
rovided with all the species he is to pay, then that which is
anting may be converted into money, or something else with
ertainty.

Before I conclude this letter, I shall take notice of one thing,
hich, at first, I thought pretty extraordinary, and that is, If
ny landed man refuses or fails to pay the king's tax; then, by a
arrant from the civil magistrate, a proportionable number of
oldiers are quartered upon him, with sometimes a commis-
oned-officer to command them; all whom he must maintain
ll the cess is fully discharged. This is a penalty for his default,
ven though he had not the means to raise money in all that
me; and let it be ever so long, the tax in the end is still the
ame. You will not doubt that the men, thus living upon free
uarters, use the best interest with their officers to be sent on
uch parties.

LETTER XXI

|| There are in the mountains both red-deer and roes, but neither of them in any great numbers, that ever I could find. The red-deer are large, and keep their haunts in the highest mountains; but the roe is less than our fallow-deer, and partakes, in some measure, of the nature of the hare; having no fat about the flesh, and hiding in the clefts of rocks, and other hollows, from the sight of pursuers. These keep chiefly in the woods.

A pack of hounds, like that of Actaeon, in the same metaphorical sense, would soon devour their master. But, supposing they could easily be maintained, they would be of no use, it being impossible for them to hunt over such rocks and rugged steep declivities; or if they could do this, their cry in those open hills would soon fright all the deer out of that part of the country. This was the effect of one single hound, whose voice I have often heard in the dead of the night (as I lay in bed) echoing among the mountains; he was kept by an English gentleman at one of the barracks, and it was loudly complained of by some of the lairds, as being prejudicial to their estates.

When a solemn hunting is resolved on, for the entertainment of relations and friends, the haunt of the deer being known, a number of the vassals are summoned, who readily obey by inclination; and are besides obliged by the tenure of their lands, of which one article is, that they shall attend the *master* at his huntings. This, I think, was part of the ancient vassalage in England.

The chief convenes what numbers he thinks fit, according to the strength of his clan: perhaps three or four hundred. With these he surrounds the hill; and as they advance upwards, the deer flies the sight of them, first of one side, then of another; and they still, as they mount, get into closer order, till in the end he is enclosed by them in a small circle, and there they hack him down with their broad-swords. And they generally do it so dexterously, as to preserve the hide entire.

If the chase be in a wood, which is mostly upon the declivity of a rocky hill, the tenants spread themselves as much as they can, in a rank extending upwards; and march, or rather crawl forward, with a hideous yell. Thus they drive every thing before them, while the laird and his friends are waiting at the farther end with their guns to shoot the deer. But it is difficult to force the roes out of their cover; insomuch that when they come into the open light, they sometimes turn back upon the huntsmen, and are taken alive.

What I have been saying on this head is only to give you some taste of the Highland hunting; for the hills, as they are various in their form, require different dispositions of the men that compose the pack. The first of the two paragraphs next above, relates only to such a hill as rises something in the figure of a cone; and the other you see, is the side of a hill which is clothed with a wood; and this last is more particularly the shelter of the roe. A further detail I think would become tedious.

When the chief would have a deer only for his household, the game-keeper and one or two more are sent into the hills with guns, and oatmeal for their provision; where they often lie night after night, to wait an opportunity of providing venison for the family. This has been done several times for me, but always without effect.

The foxes and wild cats (or cat-a-mountain) are both very large in their kind, and always appear to have fed plentifully. They do the Highlanders much more hurt in their poultry, &c. than they yield them profit by their furs: and the eagles do them more mischief than both the others together. It was one of their chief complaints, when they were disarmed in the year 1725,[1] that they were deprived of the means to destroy those noxious animals, and that a great increase of them must necessarily follow the want of their fire-arms.

Of the eatable part of the feathered kind peculiar to the mountains is, first, the *cobberkely*, which is sometimes called a wild turkey; but not like it, otherwise than in size. This is very seldom to be met with (being an inhabitant of very high and unfrequented hills), and is therefore esteemed a great rarity for the table.

[1] An Act forbidding the Highlanders to possess arms was passed in 1725. A.J.Y.

Next is the *black cock*, which resembles in size and shape a pheasant, but is black and shining like a raven; but the hen is not, in shape or colour, much unlike to a hen-pheasant.

And lastly, the *tormican* is near about the size of the moor-fowl (or grouse), but of a lighter colour, which turns almost white in winter. These I am told feed chiefly upon the tender tops of the fir branches, which I am apt to believe; because the taste of them has something tending to turpentine, though not disagreeable. It is said, If you throw a stone so as to fall beyond it, the bird is thereby so much amused or daunted, that it will not rise till you are very near; but I have suspected this to be a sort of conundrum, signifying they are too shy to suffer an approach near enough for that purpose, like what they tell the children about the salt and the bird.

The tribes will not suffer strangers to settle within their precinct, or even those of another clan to enjoy any possession among them; but will soon constrain them to quit their pretensions, by cruelty to their persons, or mischief to their cattle or other property.

LETTER XXII

‖ The Highland dress consists of a bonnet made of thrum without a brim, a short coat, a waistcoat longer by five or six inches, short stockings, and brogues or pumps without heels. By the way, they cut holes in their brogues, though new made, to let out the water when they have far to go and rivers to pass; this they do to preserve their feet from galling.

Few besides gentlemen wear the *trowze*, that is, the breeches and stockings all of one piece and drawn on together; over this habit they wear a plaid, which is usually three yards long and two breadths wide, and the whole garb is made of chequered tartan or plaiding: this, with the sword and pistol, is called a *full dress*, and to a well-proportioned man with any tolerable air, it makes an agreeable figure; but this you have seen in London, and it is chiefly their mode of dressing when they are in the Lowlands, or when they make a neighbouring visit, or go any-where on horseback; but when those among them who travel on foot, and have not attendants to carry them over the waters, they vary it into the *quelt*, which is a manner I am about to describe.

The common habit of the ordinary Highlanders is far from being acceptable to the eye: with them a small part of the plaid, which is not so large as the former, is set in folds and girt round the waist to make of it a short petticoat that reaches half way down the thigh, and the rest is brought over the shoulders, and then fastened before, below the neck, often with a fork, and sometimes with a bodkin, or sharpened piece of stick, so that they make pretty near the appearance of the poor women in London when they bring their gowns over their heads to shelter them from the rain. In this way of wearing the plaid, they have sometimes nothing else to cover them, and are often barefoot; but some I have seen shod with a kind of pumps made out of a raw cowhide with the hair turned outward, which being ill made, the wearer's feet looked something like those of a rough-footed hen or pigeon: these are called *quarrants*, and are not only offensive to the sight, but intolerable to the smell of those who are near them. The stocking rises no higher than the thick of the calf, and from the middle of the thigh to the middle of the leg is a naked space, which being exposed to all weathers, becomes tanned and freckled; and the joint being mostly infected with the country distemper, the whole is very disagreeable to the eye.

This dress is called the *quelt*; and for the most part they wear the petticoat so very short, that in a windy day, going up a hill, or stooping, the indecency of it is plainly discovered.

A Highland gentleman told me one day merrily, as we were speaking of a dangerous precipice we had passed over together, that a lady of a noble family had complained to him very seriously, That as she was going over the same place with a *gilly*, who was upon an upper path leading her horse with a long string, she was so terrified with the sight of the abyss, that, to avoid it, she was forced to look up towards the bare Highlander all the way long.

I have observed before, that the plaid serves the ordinary people for a cloak by day and bedding at night: by the latter it imbibes so much perspiration, that no one day can free it from the filthy smell; and even some of better than ordinary appearance, when the plaid falls from the shoulder, or otherwise requires to be re-adjusted, while you are talking with them, toss it over again, as some people do the knots of their wigs, which conveys the offence in whiffs that are intolerable: of this they seem not to be sensible, for it is often done only to give themselves airs.

Various reasons are given both for and against the Highland dress. It is urged against it, that it distinguishes the natives as a body of people distinct and separate from the rest of the subjects of Great Britain, and thereby is one cause of their narrow adherence among themselves to the exclusion of all the rest of the kingdom; but the part of the habit chiefly objected to is the plaid (or mantle), which, they say, is calculated for the encouragement of an idle life in lying about upon the heath in the daytime, instead of following some lawful employment; that it serves to cover them in the night when they lie in wait among the mountains to commit their robberies and depredations, and is composed of such colours as altogether in the mass so nearly resemble the heath on which they lie, that it is hardly to be distinguished from it until one is so near them as to be within their power, if they have any evil intention.

That it renders them ready at a moment's warning to join in any rebellion, as they carry continually their tents about them.

And, lastly, it was thought necessary in Ireland to suppress that habit by act of parliament, for the above reasons, and no complaint for the want of it now remains among the mountaineers of that country.

On the other hand it is alleged, the dress is most convenient to those who, with no ill design, are obliged to travel from one part to another upon their lawful occasions, viz.

That they would not be so free to skip over the rocks and bogs with breeches, as they are in the short petticoat.

That it would be greatly incommodious to those who are frequently to wade through waters, to wear breeches, which must be taken off upon every such occurrence, or would not only gall the wearer, but render it very unhealthful and dangerous to their limbs to be constantly wet in that part of the body, especially in winter-time, when they might be frozen.

And with respect to the plaid in particular, the distance between one place of shelter and another is often too great to be reached before night comes on; and being intercepted by sudden floods, or hindered by other impediments, they are frequently obliged to lie all night in the hills, in which case they must perish, were it not for the covering they carry with them.

That even if they should be so fortunate as to reach some hospitable hut, they must lie upon the ground uncovered, there being nothing to be spared from the family for that purpose.

And to conclude, A few shillings will buy this dress for an ordinary Highlander, who very probably might hardly ever be in condition to purchase a Lowland suit, though of the coarsest cloth or stuff, fit to keep him warm in that cold climate.

‖ The young children of the ordinary Highlanders are miserable objects indeed, and are mostly overrun with that distemper which some of the old men are hardly ever freed of from their infancy. I have often seen them come out from the huts early in a cold morning stark naked, and squat themselves down (if I might decently use the comparison) like dogs on a dunghill, upon a certain occasion after confinement. And at other times they have but little to defend them from the inclemencies of the weather in so cold a climate: nor are the children of some gentlemen in much better condition, being strangely neglected till they are six or seven years old: this one might know by a saying I have often heard, viz. 'That a gentleman's bearns are to be distinguished by their speaking English.'

I was invited one day to dine with a laird, not very far within the Hills; and observing about the house an English soldier, whom I had often seen before in this town, I took an opportunity to ask him several questions. This man was a bird-catcher, and employed by the laird to provide him with small birds for the exercise of his hawks.

Among other things he told me, that for three or four days after his first coming, he had observed in the kitchen (an outhouse hovel) a parcel of dirty children half naked, whom he took to belong to some poor tenant, till at last he found they were a part of the family; but although these were so little regarded, the young laird, about the age of fourteen, was going to the university; and the eldest daughter, about sixteen, sat with us at table, clean and genteely dressed.

LETTER XXIII

|| They have been used to impose a tax upon the inhabitants of the Low-country, near the borders of the Highlands, called *black mail* (or rent), and levy it upon them by force; and sometimes upon the weaker clans among themselves. But as it was made equally criminal, by several acts of parliament, to comply with this exaction and to extort it, the people, to avoid the penalty, came to agreement with the robbers, or some of their correspondents in the Lowlands, to protect their houses and cattle. And as long as this payment was punctually made, the depredations ceased, or otherwise the collector of this imposition was by contract obliged to make good the loss, which he seldom failed to do.

These collectors gave regular receipts, as for safeguard money; and those who refused to pay it, were sure to be plundered, except they kept a continual guard of their own well armed, which would have been a yet more expensive way of securing their property.

And notwithstanding the guard of the independent Highland companies, which were raised chiefly to prevent thefts and impositions of this nature; yet I have been certainly informed, that this *black mail*, or evasive safe-guard money, has been very lately paid in a disarmed part of the northern Highlands; and, I make no doubt, in other places besides, though it has not yet come to my knowledge.

The gathering-in of rents is called *uplifting* them, and the stealing of cows they call *lifting*, a softening word for theft; as if it were only collecting their dues. This I have often heard; but it has often occurred to me, that we have the word *shop-lifting* in the sense of stealing, which I take to be an old English compound word. But as to the etymology of it, I leave that to those who are fond of such unprofitable disquisitions, though I think this is pretty evident.

When a design is formed for this purpose, they go out in parties from ten to thirty men, and traverse large tracts of mountains, till they arrive at the place where they intend to commit their depredations; and that they choose to do as distant as they can from their own dwellings.

The principal time for this wicked practice is, the Michaelmas moon, when the cattle are in condition fit for markets held on the borders of the Lowlands. They drive the stolen cows in the night-time, and by day they lie concealed with them in bye-places among the mountains, where hardly any others come; or in woods, if any such are to be found in their way.

I must here ask leave to digress a little, and take notice, that I have several times used the word *cows* for a drove of cattle. This is according to the Highland style; for they say A drove of cows, when there are bulls and oxen among them, as we say A flock of geese, though there be in it many ganders. And having just now mentioned the time of *lifting*, it revived in my memory a malicious saying of the Lowlanders, *viz.* that the Highland lairds tell out their daughters' *tockers*[1] by the light of the Michaelmas moon. – But to return:

Sometimes one band of these robbers has agreed with another to exchange the stolen cattle; and in this case they used to commit their robberies nearer home; and by appointing a place of rendezvous, those that *lifted* in the north-east (for the purpose) have exchanged with others toward the west, and each have sold them not many miles from home, which was commonly at a very great distance from the place where they were stolen. Nay further, as I have been well informed, in making this contract of exchange, they have by correspondence, long before they went out, described to each other the colour and marks of the cows destined to be stolen and exchanged.

I remember a story concerning a Highland-woman, who, begging a charity of a Lowland laird's lady, was asked several questions; and among the rest, how many husbands she had

[1] Tocker: dowry. A.J.Y.

had? To which she answered, Three. And being further questioned, if her husbands had been kind to her, she said the two first were honest men, and very careful of their family, for they both *died for the law*, that is, were hanged for theft. 'Well, but as to the last?' 'Hout!' says she, 'a fulthy peast! he dy'd at hame, lik an auld dug, on a *puckle* o' strae.'

Those that have lost their cattle sometimes pursue them by the track, and recover them from the thieves. Or if in the pursuit they are *hounded* (as they phrase it) into the bounds of any other chief, whose followers were not concerned in the robbery, and track is there lost, he is obliged by law to trace them out of his territory, or make them good to the owner.

By the way, the heath or heather, being pressed by the foot, retains the impression, or at least some remains of it, for a long while, before it rises again effectually; and besides, you know, there are other visible marks left behind by the cattle. But even a single Highlander has been found by the track of his foot, when he took to hills out of the common ways, for his greater safety in his flight; as thinking he could not so well be discovered from hill to hill every now and then, as he often might be in the road (as they call it) between the mountains.

If the pursuers overtake the robbers, and find them inferior in number, and happen to seize any of them, they are seldom prosecuted, there being but few who are in circumstances fit to support the expense of a prosecution; or if they were, they would be liable to have their houses burnt, their cattle hocked, and their lives put in danger, from some of the clan to which the banditti belonged.

But with the richer sort, the chief or chieftain generally makes a composition, when it comes to be well known the thieves belonged to his tribe, which he willingly pays, to save the lives of some of his clan; and this is repaid him by a contribution among the robbers, who never refuse to do their utmost to save those of their fraternity. But it has been said this payment has been sometimes made in cows stolen from the opposite side of the country, or paid out of the produce of them when sold at the market.

It is certain some of the Highlanders think of this kind of
depredation, as our deer-stealers do of their park and forest
enterprises; that is, to be a small crime, or none at all. And as
the latter would think it a scandalous reproach to be charged
with robbing a hen-roost, so the Highlander thinks it less
shameful to steal a hundred cows than one single sheep; for a
sheep-stealer is infamous even among them.

LETTER XXIV

The heritable power of *pit and gallows*, as they call it, which
still is exercised by some within their proper districts, is, I think,
too much for any particular subject to be intrusted withal. But
it is said, that any partiality or revenge of the chief in his own
cause is obviated by the law; which does not allow him himself
to sit judicially, but obliges him to appoint a substitute as
judge in his court, who is called the *baily of regality*.

I fear this is but a shadow of safety to the accused, if it may
not appear to increase the danger of injustice and oppression.
For to the order and instructions of the chief may be added the
private resentment of the baily, which may make up a double
weight against the supposed criminal.

I have not, I must own, been accustomed to hear trials in
these courts; but have been often told that one of these bailies
in particular seldom examines any but with raging words and
rancour: and if the answers made are not to his mind, he
contradicts them by blows; and one time even to the knocking
down of the poor wretch who was examined. Nay further, I
have heard say of him, by a very credible person, that a
Highlander of a neighbouring clan, with whom his own has been
long at variance, being to be brought before him, he declared
upon the accusation, before he had seen the party accused, *that
the very name should hang him*.

I have not mentioned this violent and arbitrary proceeding
as though I knew or thought it usual in those courts; but to
show how little mankind in general are to be trusted with a
lawless power, to which there is no other check or control but
good sense and humanity, which are not common enough to

restrain every one who is invested with such power, as appears
by this example.

The baily of regality in many cases takes upon him the same
state as the chief himself would do. As for one single instance:

When he travels in time of snow, the inhabitants of one
village must walk before him to make a path to the next; and
so on to the end of his progress. And in a dark night they light
him from one inhabited place to another, which are mostly far
distant, by carrying blazing sticks of fir.

Formerly the power assumed by the chief in remote parts
was perfectly despotic, of which I shall only mention what was
told me by a near relation of a certain attainted lord, whose
estate (that was) lies in the northern Highlands. But hold – this
moment, upon recollection, I have resolved to add to it an
example of the arbitrary proceeding of one much less powerful
than the chief, who nevertheless thought he might dispose of
the lives of foreigners at his pleasure. As to the first, – the father
of the late earl above-mentioned having a great desire to get a
fellow apprehended, who was said to have been guilty of many
atrocious crimes, set a price upon his head of one hundred and
twenty crowns (a species of Scots coin in those days), I suppose
about fivepence or sixpence; and of his own authority gave
orders for taking him alive or dead: that the pursuers, thinking
it dangerous to themselves to attempt the securing him alive
shot him and brought his head and one of his hands to the chief
and immediately received the promised reward. The other is as
follows:

I remember to have heard, a good while ago, that in the
time when prince George of Denmark was lord high admiral of
England, some Scots gentlemen represented to him, that
Scotland could furnish the navy with as good timber for masts
and other uses as either Sweden or Norway could do, and at a
much more reasonable rate.

This succeeded so far, that two surveyors were sent to examine
into the allegations of their memorial.

Those gentlemen came first to Edinburgh, where they staid
some time to concert the rest of their journey, and to learn from
the inhabitants their opinion concerning the execution of their

commission; among whom there was one gentleman that had some acquaintance with a certain chieftain in a very remote part of the Highlands, and he gave them a letter to him.

They arrived at the laird's house, declared the cause of their coming, and produced their credentials, which were a warrant and instructions from the prince; but the chieftain, after perusing them, told them he knew nothing of any such person: they then told him he was husband to queen Anne; and he answered, he knew nothing of either of them; 'But,' says he, 'there came hither, some time ago, such as you from Ireland, as spies upon the country; and we hear they have made their jests upon us among the Irish.'

'Now,' says he, 'you shall have one hour; and if in that time you can give me no better account of yourselves than you have hitherto done, I'll hang you both upon that tree.' Upon which his attendants showed great readiness to execute his orders; and in this perplexity he abruptly left them, without seeing the Edinburgh letter; for of that they made but little account, since the authority of the prince, and even the queen, were to him of no consequence: but afterwards, as they were walking backwards and forwards in the garden counting the minutes, one of them resolved to try what the letter might do: this was agreed to by the other as the last resort; but in the hurry and confusion they were in, it was not for some time to be found, being worked into a corner of the bearer's usual pocket, and so he passed to another, &c.

Now the hour is expired, and the haughty chieftain enters the garden; and one of them gave him the letter: this he read, and then turning to them, said, 'Why did not you produce this at first? If you had not had it, I should most certainly have hanged you both immediately.'

The scene being thus changed, he took them into his house, gave them refreshment, and told them they might take a survey of his woods the next morning, or when they thought fit.

LETTER XXV

It is often said, that some of the lairds of those [western]

islands take upon them the state of monarchs; and thence thei
vassals have a great opinion of their power.

Among other stories told of them, there is one pretty wel
known in the north of Scotland; but whether true, or feignee
as a ridicule upon them, I do not know. For, notwithstandin;
the Lowland Scots complain of the English for ridiculing othe
nations, yet they themselves have a great number of standin;
jokes upon the Highlanders.

They say a Spanish ship being stranded upon the coast o
Barra (a very small island to the south of Lewes), the chie
(M'Neil) called a council out of his followers (which I thin.
they say were about fifty in number), in order to determin
what was to be done with her. That in the course of th
consultation one of the members proposed, 'If she was ladei
with wine and brandy, she should be confiscated as an illici
trader upon the coast; but if she was freighted with othe
merchandise, they should plunder her as a wreck.'

Upon this, one of the council, more cautious than the res
objected, that the king of Spain might resent such treatment o
his subjects: but the other replied, 'We have nothing to do wit
that. M'Neil and the king of Spain will adjust the matte
between themselves.'

THOMAS PENNANT

Thomas Pennant was born at Downing, near Holywell in Flintshire, in 1726. He was educated at a small school at Wrexham and at Queen's College, Oxford. In 1754 he made a tour of Ireland, but – 'such was the conviviality of the country' – kept only an imperfect journal. In 1755 he began a correspondence with Linnaeus, and two years later was elected a member of the Royal Society of Uppsala. About 1761 he began one of his most important works, *The British Zoology*, of which the first volume was published in 1766 and the fourth and final volume in 1768. In 1765 he visited the Continent, stayed with Buffon and met Voltaire. On his return to England he was elected a Fellow of the Royal Society.

Pennant's next important publication was his *Tour in Scotland* which appeared in 1771, describing a journey made in 1769. This publication was a success, and according to Pennant himself 'the remotest part of North Britain' was thenceforward *inondée* with southern visitors.' In 1772 he made a second journey, this time travelling mostly by sea and visiting the west coast and many of the islands.

During the 1770s Pennant made tours in various parts of England and in Wales, but from about 1777 he began, according to his own account, to lose his taste for travelling. He preferred, instead, to make 'imaginary tours.' In 1781 he published his own favourite work, the *History of Quadrupeds*; in 1782 his *Journey from Chester to London*; and in 1784 there appeared his *Arctic Zoology*, giving 'a condensed view of the progress of discovery' along the northern coasts of Europe, Asia and America; some of the information for this book he received from Sir Joseph Banks, to whom the 1772 *Tour* is dedicated. In 1790 came *Of London*, a book twice reprinted in three years, and composed, according to its author, 'from the observations of perhaps half my life.' And in 1793 there was published *The Literary Life of the late Thomas Pennant Esq., By Himself*. Five years later Pennant died at Downing. Twice married, he had three children who reached adult age.

Pennant was one of the most eminent naturalists of the eighteenth century. As a traveller he had, in the words of Dr Johnson, 'greater variety of enquiry than almost any man,' and his books were widely read. The 1769 *Tour in Scotland* went into five editions between 1771 and 1790, and the 1772 *Tour* (less interesting to the public because the west coast and islands were so much less accessible) was re-published in 1790. Of all eighteenth century travellers in the Highlands, only Dr Johnson wrote an equally interesting book.

Pennant : 1769

———————◆▶—————————

JULY 27. Perth is large, and in general well-built; two of the
streets are remarkably fine; in some of the lesser are yet a few
wooden houses in the old style; but as they decay, the magistrates prohibit the rebuilding them in the old way. There is but
one parish, which has two churches, besides meetings for
separatists, who are very numerous. One church, which
belonged to a monastery, is very ancient: not a vestige of the
rest is now to be seen; for the disciples of that rough apostle
Knox, made a general desolation of every edifice that had given
shelter to the worshippers of the church of *Rome*: it being one of
his maxims, to pull down the nests, and then the Rooks would
fly away.

The flourishing state of *Perth* is owing to two accidents: the
first, that of numbers of *Cromwel's* wounded officers and soldiers
chusing to reside here, after he left the kingdom, who introduced
a spirit of industry among the people: the other cause was the
long continuance of the Earl of *Mar's* army here in 1715, which
occasioned vast sums of money being spent in the place. But
this town, as well as all *Scotland*, dates its prosperity from the
year 1745; the government of this part of *Great Britain* having
never been settled till a little after that time. The rebellion was
a disorder violent in its operation, but salutary in its effects.

The trade of *Perth* is considerable. It exports annually one
hundred and fifty thousand pounds worth of linnen, from
twenty four to thirty thousand bolls of wheat and barley to
London and *Edinburgh*, and about the same in cured salmon. That
fish is taken there in vast abundance; three thousand have been
caught in one morning, weighing, one with another, sixteen
pounds; the whole capture, forty eight thousand pounds. The
fishery begins at St. *Andrew's* Day, and ends *August* 26th., old

style. The rents of the fisheries amount to three thousand pounds *per annum*.

I was informed that smelts come up this river in *May* and *June*.

There has been in these parts a very great fishery of pearl got out of the fresh-water mussels. From the year 1761 to 1764, 10,000*l.* worth were sent to *London*, and sold from 10*s.* to 1*l.* 16*s. per* ounce. I was told that a pearl has been taken there that weighed thirty three grains. But this fishing is at present exhausted, from the avarice of the undertakers: it once extended as far as *Loch-Tay*.

|| Cross the *Tay* on a temporary bridge; the stone bridge which is to consist of nine arches, being at this time unfinished, the largest arch is seventy six feet wide; when complete, it promises to be a most magnificent structure. The river here is very violent, and admits of scarce any navigation above; but ships of eighty or ninety tons come as far as the town.

|| The country is good, full of barley, oats, and flax in abundance; but after a few miles travelling, is succeeded by a black heath. Ride through a beautiful plantation of pines, and after descending an easy slope, the plain beneath suddenly contracts itself into a narrow glen. The prospect before me strongly marked the entrance into the *Highlands*, the hills that bounded it on each side being lofty and rude. On the left was *Birnam* Wood, which seems never to have recovered the march which its ancestors made to *Dunsinane*: I was shewn at a great distance a high ridge of hills, where some remains of that famous fortress (*Macbeth's* castle) are said yet to exist.

The pass into the *Highlands* is awefully magnificent; high, craggy, and often naked mountains present themselves to view, approach very near each other, and in many parts are fringed with wood, overhanging and darkening the *Tay*, that rolls with great rapidity beneath. After some advance in this hollow, a most beautiful knowl, covered with pines, appears in full view, and soon after, the town of *Dunkeld*, seated under and environed by crags, partly naked, partly wooded, with summits of a vast height. Lay at *Inver*, a good inn, on the West side of the river.

|| J U L Y 28. The town of *Dunkeld* is small, and has a small

The market-cross at Inverness, surrounded by rich and poor; the figure with a gun looks like an officer in the Independent Companies

Women washing linen,
a common sight in Scotland in the eighteenth century

linnen manufacture. Much company resorts here, in the summer months, for the benefit of drinking goats' milk and whey: I was informed here, that those animals will eat serpents; as it is well known that stags do.

After a ride of two miles along a narrow strait, amidst trees, and often within sight of the *Tay*, was driven by rain into a fisherman's hut, who entertained me with an account of his business: said he paid ten pounds *per ann.* for the liberty of two or three miles of the river; sold the first fish of the season at three-pence a pound; after that, got three shillings *per* fish. The houses in these parts began to be covered with broom, which lasts three or four years: their insides mean, and very scantily furnished; but the owners civil, sensible, and of the quickest apprehensions.

‖ J U L Y 29. *Loch-Tay* abounds with Pike, Perch, Eels, Salmon, Charr, and Trout; of the last, some have been taken that weighed above thirty pounds. Of these species, the *Highlanders* abhor Eels, and also Lampreys, fancying from the form, that they are too nearly related to serpents.

The North side is less wooded, but more cultivated. The vast hill of *Laurs*, with beds of snow on it, through great part of the year, rises above the rest, and the still loftier mountain of *Benmor* closes the view far beyond the end of the lake. All this country abounds with game, such as Grous, Ptarmigans, Stags, and a peculiar species of Hare, which is found only on the summits of the highest hills, and never mixes with the common kind, which is frequent enough in the vales: is less than the common Hare; its limbs more slender; its flesh more delicate: is very agile and full of frolick when kept tame; is fond of honey and caraway comfits, and prognosticates a storm by eating its own dung: in a wild state does not run an end, but seeks shelter under stones as soon as possible. During summer its predominant color is grey: about *September* it begins to assume a snowy whiteness, the alteration of color appearing about the neck and rump, and becomes entirely white, except the edges and tips of the ears: in *April* it again resumes its grey coat.

The *Ptarmigans* inhabit the very summits of the highest mountains, amidst the rocks, perching among the grey stones, and during summer are scarcely to be distinguished from them, by reason of their color. They seldom take long flights, but fly about like pigeons; are silly birds, and so tame as to suffer a stone to be flung at them without rising. It is not necessary to have a dog to find them. They taste so like a Grous, as to be scarce distinguishable. During winter, their plumage, except a few feathers on the tail, are of a pure white, the color of the snow, in which they bury themselves in heaps, as a protection from the rigorous air.

Royston Crows, called here Hooded Crows, and in the *Erse*, *Feannag*, are very common, and reside here the whole year. They breed in all sorts of trees, not only in the *Highlands*, but even in the plains of *Murray*: lay six eggs; have a shriller note than the common sort; are much more mischievous; pick out the eyes of lambs, and even of horses, when engaged in bogs; but, for want of other food, will eat cranberries, and other mountain berries.

Ring Ouzels breed among the hills, and in autumn descend in flocks to feed on the berries of the wicken trees.

Sea Eagles breed in ruined towers, but quit the country in winter? the black Eagles continue there the whole year.[1]

‖ J U L Y 30. Went to divine service at *Kinmore* church, which, with the village, was re-built, in the neatest manner, by the present Lord *Breadalbane*: they stand beautifully on a small headland, projecting into the lake. His Lordship permits the inhabitants to live rent-free, on condition they exercise some trade, and keep their houses clean: so that, by these terms, he not only saves the expence of sending, on every trifling occasion, to *Perth* or *Crief*, but has got some as good workmen, in common trades, as any in his Majesty's dominions.

The church is a remarkably neat plain building, with a very handsome tower steeple. The congregation was numerous, decent, attentive, still; well and neatly clad, and not a ragged or slovenly person among them. There were two services, one in *English*, the other in *Erse*. After the first, numbers of people, of both sexes, went out of church, and seating themselves in the church-yard, made, in their motly habits, a gay and picturesque

[1] The punctuation of this sentence is as in the original. A.J.Y.

appearance. The devotion of the common people of *Scotland*, on the usual days of worship, is as much to be admired, as their conduct at the sacrament in certain places is to be censured. It is celebrated but once in a year; when there are some times three thousand communicants, and as many idle spectators. Of the first, as many as possible crowd on each side of a long table, and the elements are sometimes rudely shoven from one to another; and in certain places, before the day is at an end, fighting and other indecencies ensue. It has often been made a season for debauchery; and to this day, *Jack* cannot always be persuaded to eat his meat like a christian.

Every Sunday a collection is made for the sick or necessitous; for poor's rates are unknown in every country parish in *Scotland*. Notwithstanding the common people are but just rouzed from their native indolence, very few beggars are seen in *North Britain*: either they are full masters of the lesson of being content with a very little; or, what is more probable, they are possessed of a spirit that will struggle hard with necessity before it will bend to the asking of alms.

‖ JULY 31. Rode to *Glen-Lion;* went by the side of the river that gives name to it. It has now lost its antient title of *Duie*, or *Black*, given it on acount of a great battle between the *Mackays* and the *Macgregors*; after which, the conquerors are said to have stained the water with red, by washing in it their bloody swords and spears. On the right is a rocky hill, called *Shi-hallen*, or the Paps. Enter *Glen-Lion* through a strait pass: the vale is narrow, but fertile; the banks of the river steep, rocky, and wooded; through which appears the rapid water of the *Lion*. On the North is a round fortress, on the top of the hill; to which, in old times, the natives retreated, on any invasion. A little farther, on a plain, is a small *Roman* camp, called by the Highlanders *Fortingal*, or the Fort of the Strangers: themselves they style *Na fian*, or descendents of *Fingal*. In *Fortingal* church-yard are the remains of a prodigious yew-tree, whose ruins measured fifty-six feet and a half in circumference.

‖ Return South, and come at once in sight of *Loch-Tay*. The day very fine and calm, the whole scene was most beautifully repeated in the water. I must not omit that on the North side of this lake is a most excellent road, which runs the whole length of it, leading to *Teindrum*, and *Inveraray*, in *Argyle-shire*, and is the route which travellers must take, who make what I call the *petit tour* of Scotland.[1] This whole road was made at the sole expence of the present Lord *Breadalbane;* who, to facilitate the travelling, also erected thirty two stone bridges over the torrents that rush from the mountains into the lake. They will find the whole country excell in roads, partly military, partly done by statute labor, and much by the munificence of the great men.

I was informed, that Lord *Breadalbane's* estate was so extensive that he could ride a hundred miles an end on it, even as far as the West Sea, where he has also some islands. These great properties are divided into districts, called *Officiaries*; a ground officer presides over each, and has three, four, or five hundred men under his care. He superintends the duties due from each to their Lord, such as fetching peat, bringing coal from Crief, etc. which they do, at their own expence, on horses' backs, travelling in strings, the tail of one horse being fastened by a cord, which reaches to the head of the next: the horses are little, and generally white or grey; and as the farms are very small, it is common for four people to keep a plough between them, each furnishing a horse, and this is called a horse-gang.

The North side of *Loch-Tay* is very populous; for in sixteen square miles are seventeen hundred and eighty six souls: on the other side, about twelve hundred. The country, within these thirty years, manufactures a great deal of thread. They spin with rocks,[2] which they do while they attend their cattle on the hills; and, at the four fairs in the year, held at *Kinmore*, above sixteen hundred pounds worth of yarn is sold out of *Breadalbane* only: which shews the great increase of industry in these parts; for less than forty years ago there was not the lest trade in this

[1] Which comprehends the route I have described; adding to it, from *Taymouth*, along the road, on the side of the lake, to *Killin*, 16 miles; from thence to *Teindrum*, 20; *Glenorchie*, 12; *Inveraray*, 16; *Luss*, on the banks of *Loch-Lomond*, 30; *Dunbarton*, 12; *Glasgow*, 15; *Sterling*, 31; *Edinburgh*, by *Hopetoun House*, 35; a tract unparalleled, for the variety and frequency of fine and magnificent scenery.

[2] Rocks: distaffs. A.J.Y.

article. The yarn is bought by persons who attend the fairs for that purpose, and sell it again at *Perth*, *Glasgow*, and other places, where it is manufactured into cloth.

Much of this may be owing to the good sense and humanity of the chieftain; but much again is owing to the abolition of the feudal tenures, or vassalage; for before that was effected (which was done by the influence of a Chancellor[1] whose memory *Scotland* gratefully adores for the service) the Strong oppressed the Weak, the Rich the Poor. Courts indeed were held, and juries called; but juries of vassals, too dependent and too timid to be relied on for the execution of true justice.

AUGUST 1. Leave *Taymouth*; ford the *Lion*, and ride above it thro' some woods. On the left bursts out a fine cascade, in a deep hollow, covered with trees: at a small distance to the West is *Castle Garth*, a small castle seated like *Castle Campbell*, between two deep glens. Keep ascending a steep hill, but the corn country continues for a while: the scene then changes for a wild, black, and mountainous heath. Descend into *Rannoch*, a meadowy plain, tolerably fertile; the lake of the same name extends from East to West; is about eleven miles long, and one broad: the Northern bank appears very barren; part of the Southern finely covered with a forest of pine and birch, the first natural woods I had seen of pines: rode a good way into it, but observed no trees of any size, except a birch sixteen feet in circumference: the ground beneath the trees is covered with heath, bilberries, and dwarf arbutus, whose glossy leaves make a pretty appearance. This place gives shelter to black game, and Roes . . .

Near these woods is a saw-mill, which is rented from the Government; and the tenant is obliged to work 150 tuns of timber annually, paying eighteen shillings and six-pence *per* tun. The deal, which is the red sort, is sold in plank to different parts of the country, carried on horses' backs, for the trees are now grown so scarce as not to admit of exportation.

The lake affords no other fish than Trouts, small Chars, and Bull Trouts; the last, as I was informed, are sometimes taken

[1] Earl of Hardwick, (sic.) who may be truly said to have given to the *North Britons* their great charter of liberty.

of the length of four feet and a half. Many water fowl breed in the birns or little streams that trickle into the lake; among others, different sort of Grebes, and Divers: I was told of one which the inhabitants call *Fur-bhuachaille*, that makes a great noise before storms, and by their description find it to be the speckled Diver, *Br. Zool.* 2nd. ed. II 414. No rats have hitherto been observed in this country.

This country was once the property of *Robertson* of *Struan*, who had been in the rebellion of 1715; had his estate restored, but in 1745 rebelling a second time, the country was burnt, and the estate annexed to the crown. He returned a few years after, and died as he lived, a most abandoned sot; notwithstanding which, he had a genius for poetry, and left behind him a volume of elegies, and other pieces, in some of which he elegantly laments the ravages of war among his vassals, and the loss of his favorite scenes, and in particular his fountain *Argentine*.

The country is perfectly highland; and in spite of the intercourse this and the neighbouring parts have of late years had with the rest of the world, it still retains some of its antient customs and superstitions: they decline daily, but lest their memory should be lost, I shall mention several that are still practised, or but very lately disused in the tract I had passed over. Such a record will have this advantage when the follies are quite extinct, in teaching the unshackled and enlightened mind the difference between the pure ceremonies of religion, and the wild and anile flights of superstition.

The belief in spectres still exists; of which I had a remarkable proof while I was in the county of *Breadalbane*. A poor visionary, who had been working in his cabbage-garden, imagined that he was raised suddenly into the air, and conveyed over a wall into an adjacent corn-field; that he found himself surrounded by a crowd of men and women, many of whom he knew to have been dead some years, and who appeared to him skimming over the tops of the unbended corn, and mingling together like bees going to hive: that they spoke an unknown language and with a hollow sound: that they very roughly pushed him to and fro; but on his uttering the name of GOD, all vanished but a female sprite, who seizing him by the shoulder obliged him to promise an assignation, at that very hour, that day sevenight: that he then found that his hair was all tied in double knots, and that he had almost lost the use of his speech: that he kept his word with the spectre, whom he soon saw come floating thro' the air towards him: that he spoke to her, but she told him at that time she was in too much haste to attend to him, but bid him go away, and no harm should befall him; and so the affair rested when I left the country. But it is incredible the mischief these *Aegri Somnia* did in the neighbourhood: the friends and relations of the deceased, whom the old Dreamer had named, were in the utmost anxiety at finding them in such bad company in the other world: the almost extinct belief of the old idle tales began again to gain ground, and the good minister will have many a weary discourse and exhortation before he can eradicate the absurd ideas this idle story has revived.

In this part of the country the notion of witchcraft is quite lost: it was observed to cease almost immediately on the repeal of the witch act;[1] a proof what a dangerous instrument it was in the hands of the vindictive, or of the credulous.

Among the superstitious customs these are the most singular. A *Highlander* never begins anything of consequence on the day of the week on which the 3d of *May* falls, which he styles *La Sheachanna na bleanagh*, or the dismal day.

On the 1st of *May*, the herdsmen of every village hold their *Bel-tein*, a rural sacrifice. They cut a square trench on the ground, leaving the turf in the middle; on that they make a fire of wood, on which they dress a large caudle of eggs, butter, oatmeal and milk; and bring, besides the ingredients of the caudle, plenty of beer and whisky; for each of the company must contribute something. The rites begin with spilling some of the caudle on the ground, by way of libation: on that, every one takes a cake of oatmeal, upon which are raised nine square nobs, each dedicated to some particular being, the supposed preserver of their flocks and herds, or to some particular animal, the real destroyer of them: each person then turns his face to the fire, breaks off a knob, and flinging it over his shoulders, says *This I give to thee, preserve thou my horses; this to thee, preserve*

[1] Which was not till the year 1736.

thou my sheep; and so on. After that, they use the same ceremony to the noxious animals: *This I give to thee, O Fox! spare thou my lambs; this to thee, O hooded Crow! this to thee, O Eagle!*

When the ceremony is over, they dine on the caudle; and after the feast is finished, what is left is hid by two persons deputed for that purpose; but on the next *Sunday* they re-assemble, and finish the reliques of the first entertainment.

On the death of a Highlander, the corps being stretched on a board, and covered with a coarse linnen wrapper, the friends lay on the breast of the deceased a wooden platter, containing a small quantity of salt and earth, separate and unmixed; the earth, an emblem of the corruptible body; the salt, an emblem of the immortal spirit. All fire is extinguished where a corps is kept; and it is reckoned so ominous for a dog or cat to pass over it, that the poor animal is killed without mercy.

The *Late-wake* is a ceremony used at funerals. The evening after the death of any person, the relations and friends of the deceased meet at the house, attended by a bagpipe or fiddle; the nearest of kin, be it wife, son, or daughter, opens a melancholy ball, dancing and greeting, i.e. crying violently at the same time; and this continues till day-light; but with such gambols and frolicks among the younger part of the company, that the loss which occasioned them is often more than supplied by the consequences of that night. If the corps remains unburied for two nights, the same rites are renewed. Thus, *Scythian*-like, they rejoice at the deliverance of their friends out of this life of misery.

‖ August 2. Left *Carrie*, the house of Mr *Campbell*, factor for the *Struan* estate, where I had a very hospitable reception the preceding night. Went due East; passed over a bridge cross the *Tumel*, which discharges itself out of Loch-Rannoch. Not far off were some neat small houses, inhabited by veteran soldiers who were settled here after the peace of 1748; had land, and three pounds in money given, and nine pounds lent, to begin the world with. In some few places this plan succeeded; but in general, was frustrated by the dissipation of these new colonists, who could by no means relish an industrious life; but as soon as the money was spent, which seldom lasted long, left their tenements to be possessed by the next comer.

|| Ascend a very steep and high hill through a great birch wood; a most picturesque scene, from the pendent form of the boughs waving with the wind from the bottom to the utmost summits of the mountain. On attaining the top, had a view of the beautiful little *Straith*, fertile and prettily wooded, with the river in the middle, forming numbers of quick meanders, then suddenly swelling into a lake, that fills the vale from side to side; is about three miles long, and retains the name of the river. After riding along a black moor, in sight of vast mountains, arrive at *Blair*, or *Athol* House, seated on an eminence above a plain, watered by the *Gary*, an outrageous stream, whose ravages have greatly deformed the valley, by the vast beds of gravel which it has left behind. The house was once fortified, and held a siege against the Rebels in 1746; but at present is much reduced in height, and the inside highly finished by the noble owner. The most singular piece of furniture is a chest of drawers made of broom, most elegantly striped in veins of white and brown. This plant grows to a great size in *Scotland*, and furnishes pieces of the breadth of six inches.

Near the house is a fine walk surrounding a very deep glen finely wooded, but in dry weather deficient in water at the bottom; but on the side of the walk on the rock is a small crystalline fountain, inhabited at that time by a pair of *Naiads*, in form of golden fish. In a spruce fir was a hang-nest of some unknown bird, suspended at the four corners to the boughs; it was open at top, an inch and a half in diameter, and two deep; the sides and bottom thick, the materials moss, worsted, and birch bark, lined with hair and feathers. The streams afford the *Parr*,[1] a small species of Trout, seldom exceeding eight inches in length, marked on the sides with nine large bluish spots, and on the lateral line with small red ones.

No traveller should omit visiting *Yorke Cascade*, a magnificent cataract, amidst most suitable scenery, about a mile distant from the house.

This country is very mountainous, has no natural woods

[1] In modern usage, a young salmon before it becomes a smolt. A.J.Y.

except of birch; but the vast plantations that begin to cloath the hills will amply supply these defects. There is a great quantity of oats raised in this neighborhood, and numbers of black cattle reared, the resources of the exhausted parts of *South Britain.*

Visit the pass of *Killicrankie*, about five miles South of *Blair*: near the Northern entrance was fought the battle between the Viscount *Dundee* and General *Mackay*, in which the first was killed in the moment of victory. The pass is extremely narrow, between high mountains, with the Gary running beneath in a deep, darksome, and rocky channel, over-hung with trees, forming a scene of horrible grandeur. The road through this strait is very fine, formed by the soldiery lent by the Government, who have six-pence *per* day from the country besides their pay. About a mile beyond the pass, Mr *Robertson's* of *Faskally* appears like fairy ground amidst these wild rocks, seated in a most beautiful meadow, watered by the river *Tumel*, surrounded with pretty hills finely wooded.

The Duke of *Athol's* estate is very extensive, and the country populous: while vassalage existed, the chieftain could raise two or three thousand fighting men, and leave sufficient at home to take care of the ground. The forests, or rather chases (for they are quite naked) are very extensive, and feed vast numbers of Stags, which range, at certain times of the year, in herds of five hundred. Some grow to a great size: I have heard of one that weighed 18 stone, *Scots*, or 314 lb. exclusive of head, entrails and skin. The hunting of these animals was formerly after the manner of an *Eastern* monarch. Thousands of vassals surrounded a great tract of country, and drove the Deer to the spot where the Chieftains were stationed, who shot them at their leisure . . .

‖ AUGUST 3. Set out for the county of *Aberdeen*; ride East-ward over a hill into *Glen-Tilt*, famous in old times for producing the most hardy warriors; is a narrow glen, several miles in length, bounded on each side by mountains of an amazing height; on the South is the great hill of *Ben y glo*, whose base is thirty-five miles in circumference, and whose summit towers far above the others. The sides of many of these mountains is covered with fine verdure, and are excellent sheep-walks: but entirely woodless. The road is the most dangerous and the most horrible I ever travelled: a narrow path, so rugged that our horses often were obliged to cross their legs, in order to pick a secure place for their feet; while, at a considerable and precipitous depth beneath, roared a black torrent, rolling through a bed of rock, solid in every part but where the *Tilt* had worn its antient way. Salmon force their passage even as high as this dreary stream, in spite of the distance from the sea, and the difficulties they have to encounter.

Ascend a steep hill, and find ourselves on an *Arrie*, or tract of mountain which the families of one or two hamlets retire to with their flocks for pasture in summer. Here we refreshed ourselves with some goats' whey, at a *Sheelin* or *Bothay*, a cottage made of turf, the dairy-house, where the Highland shepherds, or graziers, live with their herds and flocks, and during the fine season make butter and cheese. Their whole furniture consists of a few horn-spoons, their milking utensils, a couch formed of sods to lie on, and a rug to cover them. Their food oat-cakes, butter or cheese, and often the coagulated blood of their cattle spread on their bannocks. Their drink milk, whey, and sometimes, by way of indulgence, whisky. Such dairy-houses are common to most mountainous countries: those in *Wales* are called *Vottys*, or Summer-houses; those on the *Swiss* alps, *Sennes*.

Dined on the side of *Loch-Tilt*, a small piece of water, swarming with Trouts. Continued our journey over a wild, black, moory, melancholy tract. Reached *Brae-mar;* the country almost instantly changed, and in lieu of dreary wastes, a rich vale, plenteous in corn and grass, succeeded. Cross the *Dee* near its head, which, from an insignificant stream, in the course of a very few miles, increases to the size of a great river, from the influx of numbers of other waters: and is remarkable for continuing near fifty miles of its course, from *Invercauld* to within six miles of *Aberdeen*, without any sensible augmentation. The rocks of *Brae-mar*, on the East, are exceedingly romantic, finely wooded with pine. The cliffs are very lofty, and their front most rugged and broken, with vast pines growing out of their fissures.

On the North side of the river lies *Dalmore*, distinguished by the finest natural pines in *Europe*, both in respect to the size of the trees and the quality of the timber. Single trees have been sold out of it for six guineas: they were from eighty to ninety feet high, without a collateral branch, and four feet and a half in diameter at the lower end. The wood is very resinous, of a dark red color, and very weighty. It is preferable to any brought from *Norway*, and being sawn into plank on the spot brings annually to the proprietor a large revenue. On the opposite side of the river is the estate of *Inverey*, noted also for its pines, but of a size inferior to those of *Dalmore*. When the river is swelled with rains, great floats of timber from both these estates are sent down into the Low Countries.

‖ The views from the skirts of the plain, near *Invercauld*, are very great; the hills that immediately bound it are cloathed with trees, particularly with birch, whose long and pendent boughs, waving a vast height above the head, surpass the beauties of the weeping willow.

The Southern extremity is pre-eminently magnificent; the mountains form there a vast theatre, the bosom of which is covered with extensive forests of pines: above, the trees grow scarcer and scarcer, and then seem only to sprinkle the surface after which vegetation ceases, and naked summits of a surprizing height succeed, many of them topped with perpetual snow and, as a fine contrast to the scene, the great cataract of *Garval bourn*, which seems at a distance to divide the whole, foam amidst the dark forest, rushing from rock to rock to a vast distance.

Some of these hills are supposed to be the highest part of *Great Britain*: their height has not yet been taken, but the conjecture is made from the descent of the *Dee*, which runs from *Brae-mar* to the sea, above seventy miles, with a most rapid course.

In this vale the Earl of *Mar* first set up the Pretender's standard on the 6th of *September* 1715; and in consequence drew the destruction his own, and several of the most noble families of *North Britain*.

Rode to take a nearer view of the environs; crossed the *Dee* on a good stone-bridge, built by the Government, and entered on excellent roads into a magnificent forest of pines of many miles extent. Some of the trees are of a vast size; I measured several that were ten, eleven, and even twelve feet in circumference, and near sixty feet high, forming a most beautiful column, with a fine verdant capital. These trees are of a great age, having, as is supposed, seen two centuries. Their value is considerable; Mr *Farquharson* informed me, that by sawing and retailing them, he has got for eight hundred trees five-and-twenty shillings each: they are sawed in an adjacent saw-mill, into plank ten feet long, eleven inches broad, and three thick, and sold for two shillings apiece.

Near this antient forest is another, consisting of smaller trees, almost as high, but very slender; one grows in a singular manner out of the top of a great stone, and notwithstanding it seems to have no other nourishment than what it gets from the dews, is above thirty feet high.

The prospect above these forests is very extraordinary, a distant view of hills over a surface of verdant pyramids of pines.

This whole tract abounds with game: the Stags at this time were ranging in the mountains; but the little Roebucks were perpetually bounding before us; and the black game often sprung under our feet. The tops of the hills swarmed with *Grous* and *Ptarmigans*. Green Plovers, Whimbrels, and Snow-flecks breed here: the last assemble in great flocks during winter, and collect so closely in their eddying flight, as to give the sportsman opportunity of killing numbers at a shot. Eagles, Peregrine Falcons, and Goshawks breed here: the Falcons in rocks, the Goshawks in trees: the last pursues its prey an end, and dashes through every thing in pursuit; but if it misses its quarry, desists from following it after two or three hundred yards flight. These birds are proscribed; half a crown is given for an eagle, a shilling for a hawk, or hooded crow.

Foxes are in these parts very ravenous, feeding on roes, sheep, and even she goats.

Rooks visit these vales in autumn, to feed on the different sort of berries; but neither winter nor breed here.

I saw flying in the forests, the greater Bulfinch of Mr

Edwards,[1] tab. 123, 124, the *Loxia enucleator* of *Linnaeus,* whose food is the seed of pine cones; a bird common to the North of *Europe* and *America.*

On our return passed under some high cliffs; with large woods of birch intermixed. This tree is used for all sorts of implements of husbandry, roofing of small houses, wheels, fuel; the Highlanders also tan their own leather with the bark; and a great deal of excellent wine is extracted from the live tree. Observed among these rocks a sort of projecting shelf, on which had been a hut, accessible only by the help of some thongs fastened by some very expert climbers, to which the family got, in time of danger, in former days, with their most valuable moveables.

The houses of the common people in these parts are shocking to humanity, formed of loose stones, and covered with clods, which they call *devots,* or with heath, broom, or branches of fir: they look, at a distance, like so many black mole-hills. The inhabitants live very poorly, on oatmeal, barley-cakes, and potatoes; their drink whisky, sweetened with honey. The men are thin, but strong; idle and lazy, except employed in the chace, or any thing that looks like amusement; are content with their hard fare, and will not exert themselves farther than to get what they deem necessaries. The women are more industrious, spin their own husbands' cloaths, and get money by knitting stockings, the great trade of the country. The common women are in general most remarkably plain, and soon acquire an old look, and by being much exposed to the weather without hats, such a grin, and contraction of the muscles, as heighten greatly their natural hardness of features: I never saw so much plainness among the lower rank of females: but the *ne plus ultra* of hard features is not found till you arrive among the fish women of *Aberdeen.*

Tenants pay their rent generally in this country in money except what they pay in poultry, which is done to promote the breed, as the gentry are so remote from any market. Those that rent a mill pay a hog or two; an animal so detested by the

[1] George Edwards (1694–1773), author of *History of Birds,* published 1743 1764.

Highlanders, that very few can be prevailed on to taste it, in any shape. Labor is here very cheap, the usual pay being fifty shillings a year, and two pecks of oatmeal a week.

Pursued my journey East, along a beautiful road by the river side, in sight of the pine forests. The vale now grows narrow, and is filled with woods of birch and alder. Saw on the road side the seats of gentlemen, high built, and once defensible. The peasants cultivate their little land with great care to the very edge of the stony hills. All the way are vast masses of granite, the same which is called in *Cornwall*, Moor-stone.

The Glen contracts, and the mountains approach each other. Quit the *Highlands*, passing between two great rocks, called the Pass of *Bollitir*, a very narrow strait, whose bottom is covered with the tremendous ruins of the precipices that bound the road. I was informed, that here the wind rages with great fury during winter, and catching up the snow in eddies, whirls it about with such impetuosity, as makes it dangerous for man or beast to be out at that time. Rain also pours down sometimes in deluges, and carries with it stone and gravel from the hills in such quantity, that I have seen the effects of these *spates*, as they are called, lie cross the roads, as the *avelenches*, or snow-falls, do those of the *Alps*. In many parts of the *Highlands* were *hospitia* for the reception of travellers, called by the *Scotch*, *Spittles*, or ospitals: the same were usual in *Wales*, where they are styled *spytty*; and in both places were maintained by the religious houses: as similar *Asylums* are to this day supported in many parts of the *Alps*.

This pass is the Eastern entrance into the Highlands. The country now assumes a new face: the hills grow less; but the land more barren, and is chiefly covered with heath and rock. The edges of the *Dee* are cultivated, but the rest only in patches, among which is generally a groupe of small houses. There is also a change of trees, oak being the principal wood, but even that is scarce.

On the South side of the river is *Glen-Muik*, remarkable for a fine cataract formed by the river *Muik*, which after running for a considerable way along a level moor, at once falls down a perpendicular rock of a semicircular form, called the *Lin of*

Muik, into a hole of so great a depth worn by the weight of water, as to be supposed by the vulgar to be bottomless.

Refreshed my horses at a hamlet called *Tullich,* and looking West, saw the great mountain *Laghin y gair,* which is always covered with snow.

Almost opposite to the village of *Tullich* is *Pananich,* noted for the mineral water discovered a few years ago, and found to be very beneficial in rheumatic and scrophulous cases, and complaints of the gravel. During summer great numbers of people afflicted with those disorders resort there to drink the waters, and for their reception, several commodious houses have already been built.

|| AUGUST 16. Passed over *Culloden Moor,* the place that *North Britain* owes its present prosperity to, by the victory of *April* 16, 1746. On the side of the Moor are the great plantations of *Culloden* House, the seat of the late *Duncan Forbes,* a warm and active friend to the house of *Hanover,* who spent great sums in its service, and by his influence, and by his persuasions, diverted numbers from joining in rebellion; at length he met with a cool return, for his attempt to sheath, after victory, the unsatiated sword. But let a veil be flung over a few excesses consequential of a day, productive of so much benefit to the united kingdoms.

The young adventurer lodged here the evening preceding the battle; distracted with the aversion of the common men to discipline, and the dissensions among his officers, even when they were at the brink of destruction, he seemed incapable of acting, could be scarcely persuaded to mount his horse, never came into the action, as might have been expected of a prince who had his last stake to play, but fled ingloriously to the old traitor *Lovat,* who, I was told, did execrate him to the person who informed him that he was approaching as a fugitive, foreseeing his own ruin as the consequence.

The Duke of *Cumberland,* when he found that the barges of the fleet attended near the shore for the safety of his person, in case of a defeat, immediately ordered them away, to convince his men of the resolution he had taken of either conquering or perishing with them.

The battle was fought contrary to the advice of some of the

Highland carts

Faskally;
'the situation of this place is extremely romantic'

Braemar Castle;
a square tower, built in 1628 'to curb the
discontented chieftains'

most sensible men in the rebel army, who advised the retiring into the fastnesses beyond the *Ness*, the breaking down the bridge of *Inverness*, and defending themselves amidst the mountains. They politically urged that *England* was engaged in bloody wars foreign and domestic, that it could at that time ill spare its troops; and that the Government might, from that consideration, be induced to grant to the insurgents their lives and fortunes, on condition they laid down their arms. They were sensible that their cause was desperate, and that their ally was faithless; yet it might be long before they could be entirely subdued; therefore drew hopes from the sad necessity of our affairs at that season: but this rational plan was superseded by the favorite faction in the army, to whose guidance the unfortunate adventurer had resigned himself.

After descending from the Moor, got into a well-cultivated country; and after riding some time under low but pleasant hills, not far from the sea, reach

INVERNESS, finely seated on a plain, between the firth of the same name and the river *Ness*: the first, from the narrow strait of *Ardersier*, instantly widens into a fine bay, and again as suddenly contracts opposite *Inverness*, at the ferry of *Kessock*, the pass into *Ross-shire*. The town is large and well built, and very populous, being the last of any note in *North Britain*. On the North is *Oliver*'s Fort, a pentagon; but only the form remains to be traced by the ditches and banks. Near it is a very considerable rope manufacture. On an eminence South of the town is old *Fort George*, which was taken and blown up by the Rebels: it had been no more than a very antient castle, the place where *Boethius* says that *Duncan* was murdered: from thence is a most charming view of the *Firth*, the passage of *Kessock*, the river *Ness*, the strange-shaped hill of *Tomman heurich*, and various groupes of distant mountains.

|| Cross the *Ness* on a bridge of seven arches, above which the tide flows for about a mile.

Proceed North; have a fine view of the Firth, which now widens again from Kessock into a large bay some miles in length. The hills slope down to the water-side, and are finely cultivated; but the distant prospect is of rugged mountains of a stupendous height, as if created as guards to the rest of the island from the fury of the boisterous North.

Ride close to the water-edge thro' woods of alder; pass near several houses of the *Fraziers*, and reach

Castle Dunie, the site of the house of their chieftain *Lord Lovat*.

The old house, which was very mean, was burnt down in 1746; but a neat box, the residence of the hospitable factor, is built in its stead on a high bank well wooded, over the pretty river *Bewley*, or *Beaulieu*. The country, for a certain circuit, is fertile, well cultivated, and smiling. The bulk of Lord *Lovat*'s estate was in these parts; the rest, to the amount of 500l. *per annum*, in *Straitherick*. He was a potent chieftain, and could raise about 1,000 men: but I found his neighbours spoke as unfavorably of him, as his enemies did in the most distant parts of the kingdom. His property is one of the annexed estates, i.e settled unalienably on the crown, as all the forfeited fortunes in the Highlands are: the whole value of which brought in at that time about 6,000l. *per annum*, and those in the Lowlands about the same sum; so that the power and interest of a poor twelve thousand *per annum* terrified and nearly subverted the constitution of these powerfull kingdoms.

The profits of these estates are lodged in the hands of Trustees who apply their revenue for the founding of schools for the instruction of children in spinning; wheels are given away to poor families, and flax-seed to farmers. Some money is given in aid of the roads, and towards building bridges over the torrents; by which means a ready intercourse is made to parts before inaccessible to strangers. And in 1753, a large sum was spent on an *Utopian* project of establishing colonies (on the forfeited estates) of disbanded soldiers and sailors: comfortable houses were built for them, land and money given, and some lent; but the success by no means answered the intentions of the projectors.

|| AUGUST 17. Pass through *Dingwall*, a small town, the capital of *Ross-shire*, situated near the head of the Firth of *Cromartie*: the Highlanders call it *Inner-Feorain, Feoran* being the name of the river that runs near it into the Firth. An antient cross, and an obelisk over the burying-place of the Earls of

Cromartie's family, were all I saw remarkable in it. In the year 1400 *Dingwall* had its castle, subject to *Donald*, Lord of the Isles, and Earl of *Ross*: after that *regulus* was weakened by the battle of *Harlaw*, his territories were invaded; and this castle reduced to the power of the crown of *Scotland* by the Duke of *Albany*.

Ride along a very good road cut on the side of a hill, with the country very well cultivated above and below, with several small woods interspersed near the water's edge. There is a fine view of almost the whole bay, the most capacious and secure of any in *Great Britain*; its whole navy might lie there with ease, and ships of two hundred tuns may sail up above two-thirds of its length, which extends thirty miles, from the *Sutters* of *Cromartie* to a small distance beyond *Dingwall*: the entrance is narrow; the projecting hills defend this fine bay from all winds; so it justly merits the name given it of *Portus salutis*.

|| Ride along a tedious black moor to *Tain*, a small town on the Firth of *Dornoch*; distinguished for nothing but its large square tower, decorated with five small spires. Here was also a collegiate church, founded in 1481 by *Thomas* Bishop of *Ross*. Captain *Richard Franks*, an honest *Cavalier*, who during the usurpation made an angling peregrination from the banks of the *Trent* to *John a Groat's* house, calls Tain 'as exemplary as any place for justice, that never uses gibbet or halter to hang a man, but sacks all their malefactors so swims them to their graves'. The place appeared very gay at this time; for all the gaudy finery of a little fair was displayed in the shew of hard ware, printed linnens, and ribbands. Kept along the shore for about two miles, through an open corn country; and crossing the great ferry, in breadth near two miles, thro' a rapid tide, and in a bad boat, land in the county of *Sutherland*, *Cattu* of the Highlanders; and in less than an hour reach its capital

DORNOCH, a small town, half in ruins; once the residence of the Bishops of *Cathness*, and, like *Durham*, the seat of Ecclesiastics: many of the houses still are called after the titles of those that inhabited them: the Bishop lodged in the castle: the Dean's house is at present the inn. The cathedral was in form of a cross; built by *Gilbert Moray*, who died Bishop of *Cathness* in

1245: it is now a ruin, except part, which is the present church.
On the doors and window-shutters were painted (as is common
in many parts of *North Britain*) white tadpole-like figures on a
black ground, designed to express the tears of the country for
the loss of any person of distinction . . .

‖ AUGUST 21. Dine at the good minister's of *Cannesby*. On
my return saw at a distance the *stacks* of *Dungsby*, a vast insulated
rock, over-topping the land, and appearing like a great tower.

Passed near the seat of a gentleman not long deceased; the
last who was believed to be possessed of the *second sight*. Originally he made use of the pretence, in order to render himself
more respectable with his clan; but at length, in spite of fine
abilities, was made a dupe to his own artifices, became possessed
with a serious belief of the faculty, and for a considerable
number of years before his death was made truely unhappy by
this strange opinion, which originally arose from the following
accident. A boat of his was on a very tempestuous night at sea
his mind, filled with anxiety at the danger his people were in
furnished him with every idea of the misfortune that really
befell them: he suddenly starting up, pronounced that his men
would be drowned, for that he had seen them pass before him
with wet garments and dropping locks. The event was corres
pondent, and he from that time grew confirmed in the reality
of spectral predictions.

There is another sort of divination, called *Sleinanachd*, or
reading the *speal-bone*, or the blade-bone of a shoulder of
mutton well scraped. When Lord *Loudon* was obliged to retrea
before the Rebels to the isle of *Skie*, a common soldier, on the
very moment the battle of Culloden was decided, proclaimed
the victory at that distance, pretending to have discovered th
event by looking through the bone.

I heard of one instance of second sight, or rather of foresight
which was well attested, and made much noise about the tim
the prediction was fulfilled. A little after the battle of *Presto*
Pans, the president, *Duncan Forbes*, being at his house of *Cullode*
with a nobleman, from whom I had the relation, fell int
discourse on the probable consequences of the action: after
long conversation, and after revolving all that might happen

Mr *Forbes*, suddenly turning to a window, said, *All these things may fall out; but depend on it, all these disturbances will be terminated on this spot.*

Returned the same road. Saw multitudes of *Gannets*, or *Soland* Geese, on their passage Northward: they went in small flocks from five to fifteen in each, and continued passing for hours: it was a stormy day; they kept low and near the shore; but never passed over the land, even when a bay intervened, but followed (preserving an equal distance from the shore) the form of the bay, and then regularly doubled the Capes. I saw many parties make a sort of halt for the sake of fishing; they soared to a great height, then darting down headlong into the sea, made the water foam and spring up with the violence of their descent; after which they pursued their route.

|| *Cathness* may be called an immense morass, mixed with some fruitful spots of oats and barley, much coarse grass, and here and there some fine, almost all natural, there being as yet very little artificial. At this time was the hay harvest both here and about *Dunrobin*, the hay on this rough land is cut with very short scythes, and with a brisk and strong stroke. The country produces and exports great quantities of *oatmeal*, and much whisky is distilled from the barley; the great thinness of inhabitants throughout Cathness enables them to send abroad much of its productions. No wheat had been raised this year in the county; and I was informed that this grain is sown here in the spring, by reason of the wet and fury of the winters.

The county is supposed to send out, in some years, 2,200 head of cattle; but in bad seasons, the farmer kills and salts numbers for sale. Great numbers of swine are reared here: they are short, high-backed, long-bristled, sharp, slender and long-nosed; have long erect ears, and most savage looks, and are seen tethered in almost every field. The rest of the commodities of *Cathness* are butter, cheese, tallow, hides, the oil and skins of seals, and the feathers of geese.

Here are neither barns nor granaries; the corn is thrashed out, and preserved in the chaff in bykes, which are stacks in shape of bee-hives, thatched quite round, where it will keep good for two years.

Much salmon is taken at *Castle-hill, Dunet, Wick,* and *Thurso.*
The miraculous draught at the last place is still talked of; not
less than 2,500 being taken at one tide, within the memory of
man. At a small distance from *Sinclair* castle, near *Staxigo* creek,
is a small herring fishery, the only one on the coast: Cod and
other white fish abound here; but the want of ports on this
stormy coast is an obstacle to the establishment of fisheries on
this side the country.

In the month of *November,* numbers of Seals are taken in the
vast caverns that open into the sea and run some hundred
yards under ground. Their entrance is narrow, their inside
lofty and spacious. The Seal-hunters enter these in small boats
with torches, which they light as soon as they land, and then
with loud shouts alarm the animals, which they kill with clubs
as they attempt to pass. This is a hazardous employ; for should
the wind blow hard from sea, these adventurers are inevitably
lost.

Much lime-stone is found in this country, which when burnt
is made into a compost with turf and sea plants. The tender sex
(I blush for the *Cathnessians*) are the only animals of burden:
they turn their patient backs to the dunghills, and receive in
their *keises,* or baskets, as much as their lords and masters think
fit to fling in with their pitchforks, and then trudge to the fields
in droves of sixty or seventy. The common people are kept here
in great servitude, and most of their time is given to their
Lairds, an invincible impediment to the prosperity of the
county.

Of the ten parishes in Cathness, only the four that lie S.E.
speak *Erse*; all the others speak *English,* and that in greater
purity than most parts of *North Britain.*

Inoculation is much practised by an ingenious physician (Dr
Mackenzie, of *Wick*) in this county, and also the Orkneys, with
great success, without any previous preparation. The success
was equally great at *Sanda,* a poor isle, where there was no sort
of fuel but what was got from dried cow-dung: but in all these
places the small-pox is very fatal in the natural way. Other
diseases in *Cathness* are colds, coughs, and very frequent palsies.

‖ A U G U S T 30. *Boethius* relates, that in his time *Inverness* was greatly frequented by merchants from *Germany*, who purchased here the furs of several sorts of wild beasts; and that wild horses were found in great abundance in its neighborhood: that the country yielded a great deal of wheat and other corn, and quantities of nuts and apples. At present there is a trade in the skins of Deer, Roes, and other beasts, which the Highlanders bring down to the fairs. There happened to be one at this time: the commodities were skins, various necessaries brought in by the Pedlars, coarse country cloths, cheese, butter and meal; the last in goat-skin bags; the butter lapped in cawls, or leaves of the broad *alga* or tang; and great quantities of birch wood and hazel cut into lengths for carts, etc. which had been floated down the river from *Loch-Ness*.

The fair was a very agreeable circumstance, and afforded a most singular groupe of Highlanders in all their motly dresses. Their *brechcan*, or plaid, consists of twelve or thirteen yards of a narrow stuff, wrapt round the middle, and reaches to the knees: it is often fastened round the middle with a belt, and is then called *brechcan-feill*; but in cold weather, is large enough to wrap round the whole body from head to feet; and this often is their only cover, not only within doors, but on the open hills during the whole night. It is frequently fastened on the shoulders with a pin often of silver, and before with a brotche (like the *fibula* of the *Romans*) which is sometimes of silver, and both large and extensive; the old ones have very frequently mottos.

The stockings are short, and are tied below the knee. The *cuaran* is a sort of laced shoe made of a skin with the hairy side out, but now seldom worn. The *truis* were worn by the gentry, and were breeches and stockings made of one piece.

The color of their dress was various, as the word *breaccan* implies, being dyed with stripes of the most vivid hues: but they sometimes affected the duller colors, such as imitated those of the Heath in which they often reposed; probably from a principle of security in time of war . . .

The *feil-beg*, i.e. little plaid, also called *kelt*, is a sort of short petticoat reaching only to the knees, and is a modern substitute for the lower part of the plaid, being found to be less cumbersome, especially in time of action, when the Highlanders used to tuck their *breachan* into their girdle. Almost all have a great pouch of badger and other skins, with tassels dangling before. In this they keep their tobacco and money.

Their antient arms were the *Lochaber* ax, now used by none but the town-guard of *Edinburgh;* a tremendous weapon, better to be expressed by a figure than words.

The broad-sword and target; with the last they covered themselves, with the first reached their enemy at a great distance. These were their antient weapons, as appears by *Tacitus;* but since the disarming act, are scarcely to be met with; partly owing to that, partly to the spirit of industry now rising among them, the Highlanders in a few years will scarce know the use of any weapon.

|| It will be fit to mention here the method the Chieftains took formerly to assemble the clans for any military expedition. In every clan there is a known place of rendezvous, styled *Carn a whin*, to which they must resort on this signal. A person is sent out full speed with a pole burnt at one end and bloody at the other, and with a cross at the top, which is called *Crosh-tarie* the cross of shame, or the fiery cross; the first from the disgrace they would undergo if they declined appearing; the second from the penalty of having fire and sword carried thro' their country, in case of refusal. The first bearer delivers it to the next person he meets, he running full speed to the third, and so on. In the late rebellion, it was sent by some unknown disaffected hand thro' the county of *Breadalbane*, and passed thro' a tract of thirty two miles in three hours, but without effect.

The women's dress is the *kirch*, or a white piece of linnen pinned over the foreheads of those that are married, and round the hind part of the head, falling behind over their necks. The single women wear only a ribband round their head, which they call a snood. The *tonnag* or plaid, hangs over their shoulders, and is fastened before with a brotche; but in bad weather is drawn over their heads: I have also observed during divine service that they keep drawing it forward in proportion as their attention increases; insomuch as to conceal at last their whole face, as if it was to exclude every external object that might interrupt their devotion. In the county of *Breadalbane* many wear, when in high dress, a great pleated stocking of an enormous length, called *ossan preassach*: in other respects, their dress resembles that of women of the same rank in *England*: but their condition is very different, being little better than slaves to our sex.

The manners of the native Highlanders may justly be expressed in these words: indolent to a high degree, unless roused to war, or to any animating amusement; or I may say, from experience, to lend any disinterested assistance to the distressed traveller, either in directing him on his way, or affording their aid in passing the dangerous torrents of the Highlands: hospitable to the highest degree, and full of generosity: are much affected with the civility of strangers, and have in themselves a natural politeness and address, which often flows from the meanest when least expected. Thro' my whole tour I never met with a single instance of national reflection! their forbearance proves them to be superior to the meanness of retaliation: I fear they pity us; but I hope not indiscriminately. Are excessively inquisitive about your business, your name, and other particulars of little consequence to them: most curious after the politicks of the world, and when they can procure an old newspaper, will listen to it with all the avidity of Shakespear's blacksmith. Have much pride, and consequently are impatient of affronts, and revengefull of injuries. Are decent in their general behaviour; inclined to superstition, yet attentive to the duties of religion, and are capable of giving a most distinct account of the principles of their faith. But in many parts of the Highlands, their character begins to be more faintly marked; they mix more with the world, and become daily less attached to their chiefs: the clans begin to disperse themselves through different parts of the country, finding that their industry and good conduct afford them better protection (since the due execution of the laws) than any their chieftain can afford; and the chieftain tasting the sweets of advanced rents, and the benefits of industry, dismisses from his table the crowds of retainers, the former instruments of his oppression and freakish tyranny.

‖ SEPTEMBER 2. After a small interval arrive on the banks of *Loch-Lochy*, a fine piece of water, fourteen miles long, and from one to two broad. The distant mountains on the North were of an immense height; those on the South had the appearance of sheep-walks. The road is continued on the side of the lake about eight miles. On the opposite shore was *Achnacarrie*, once the seat of *Cameron* of *Lochiel*, but burnt in 1746. He was esteemed by all parties the honestest and most sensible man of any that embarked in the pernicious and absurd attempt of that and the preceding year, and was a melancholy instance of a fine understanding and a well-intending heart, over-powered by the unhappy prejudices of education. By his influence he prevented the Rebels from committing several excesses, and even saved the city of *Glasgow* from being plundered, when their army returned out of *England*, irritated with their disappointment, and enraged at the loyalty that city had shewn. The Pretender came to him as soon as ever he landed. *Lochiel* seeing him arrive in so wild a manner, and so unsupported, entreated him to desist from an enterprize from which nothing but certain ruin could result to him and his partizans. The Adventurer grew warm, and reproached *Lochiel* with a breach of promise. This affected him so deeply, that he instantly went and took a tender and moving leave of his lady and family, imagining he was on the point of parting with them for ever. The income of his estate was at that time, as I was told, not above 70l. *per annum*, yet he brought fourteen hundred men into the field.

The waters of this lake form the river *Lochy*, and discharge themselves into the Western sea, as those of *Loch-Oich* do through *Loch-Ness* into the Eastern. About the beginning of this lake enter *Lochaber*; stop at *Low-bridge*, a poor house; travel over a black moor for some miles; see abundance of cattle, but scarce any corn. Cross

High-bridge, a fine bridge of three arches flung over the torrent *Spean*, founded on rocks; two of the arches are 95 feet high. This bridge was built by General *Wade*, in order to form a communication with the country. These publick works were

at first very disagreeable to the old Chieftains, and lessened
their influence greatly; for by admitting strangers among them,
their clans were taught that the Lairds were not the first of men.
But they had another reason much more solid: *Lochaber* had
been a den of thieves; and as long as they had their waters,
their torrents and their bogs, in a state of nature, they made
their excursions, could plunder and retreat with their booty
in full security. So weak were the laws in many parts of *North
Britain*, till after the late rebellion, that no stop could be put to
this infamous practice. A contribution, called the *Black-meal*,
was raised by several of these plundering chieftains over a vast
extent of country; whoever payed it had their cattle ensured,
but those who dared to refuse were sure to suffer. Many of
these free-booters were wont to insert an article, by which they
were to be released from their agreement, in case of any civil
commotion: thus, at the breaking out of the last rebellion, a
M'Gregor, who had with the strictest honor (till that event)
preserved his friends' cattle, immediately sent them word, that
from that time they were out of his protection, and must now
take care of themselves. *Barrisdale* was another of this class,
chief of a band of robbers who spread terror over the whole
country: but the Highlanders at that time esteemed the open
theft of cattle, or the making a *creach* (as they call it), by no
means dishonorable; and the young men considered it as a
piece of gallantry, by which they recommended themselves to
their mistresses. On the other side there was often as much
bravery in the pursuers; for frequent battles ensued, and much
blood has been spilt on these occasions. They also shewed great
dexterity in tracing the robbers, not only through the boggy
land, but over the firmest ground, and even over places where
other cattle had passed, knowing well how to distinguish the
steps of those that were wandering about from those that were
driven hastily away by the Free-booters.

From the road had a distant view of the mountains of *Arisaig*,
beyond which were *Moydart, Kinloch,* etc. At the end of *Loch-
hiel* the Pretender first set up his standard in the wildest place
that imagination can frame: and in this sequestered spot,
amidst antient prejudices, and prevaling ignorance of the

blessings of our happy constitution, the strength of the rebellion lay.

|| The great produce of *Lochaber* is cattle, that district alone sends out annually 3000 head; but if a portion of *Inverness-shire* is included, of which this property is part, the number is 10,000. There are also a few horses bred here, and a very few sheep; but of late several have been imported. Scarce any arable land, for the excessive wet which reigns here almost totally prevents the growth of corn, and what little there is fit for tillage sets at ten shillings an acre. The inhabitants of this district are therefore obliged, for their support, to import six thousand bolls of oatmeal annually, which cost about 400ol.; the rents are about 300ol. *per annum;* the return for their cattle is about 750ol.; the horses may produce some trifle; so that the tenants must content themselves with a very scanty subsistence, without the prospect of saving the lest against unforseen accidents. The rage of raising rents has reached this distant country: in *England* there may be reason for it (in a certain degree) where the value of lands is increased by accession of commerce, and by the rise of provisions: but here (contrary to all policy) the great men begin at the wrong end, with squeezing the bag, before they have helped the poor tenant to fill it, by the introduction of manufactures. In many of the isles this already shews its unhappy effect, and begins to depopulate the country; for numbers of families have been obliged to give up the strong attachment the *Scots* in general have for their country, and to exchange it for the wilds of *America*.

The houses of the peasants in *Lochaber* are the most wretched that can be imagined; framed of upright poles, which are wattled; the roof is formed of boughs like a *wigwam*, and the whole is covered with sods; so that in this moist climate their cottages have a perpetual and much finer verdure than the rest of the country.

Salmons are taken in these parts as late as *May*; about 5 tons are caught in the season. These fish never appear so early on this coast as on the Eastern.

Phinocs are taken here in great numbers, 1500 having been taken at a draught. They come in *August*, and disappear i

November. They are about a foot long, their colour grey, spotted with black, their flesh red; rise eagerly to a fly. The fishermen suppose them to be the young of what they call a great *Trout*, weighing 30 lb. which I suppose is the *Grey*.

SEPTEMBER 4. Left *Fort William*, and proceeded South along the military road on the side of a hill, an awefull height above *Loch-Leven*, a branch of the sea, so narrow as to have only the appearance of a river, bounded on both sides with vast mountains, among whose winding bottoms the tide rolled in with solemn majesty. The scenery begins to grow very romantic; on the West side are some woods of birch and pines: the hills are very lofty, many of them taper to a point; and my old friend, the late worthy Bishop *Pocock*, compared the shape of one to mount *Tabor*. Beneath them is *Glen-Co*, infamous for the massacre of its inhabitants in 1691, and celebrated for having (as some assert) given birth to *Ossian*; towards the North is *Morven*, the country of his hero *Fingal*.

'The scenery[1] of this valley is far the most picturesque of any in the Highlands, being so wild and uncommon as never fails to attract the eye of every stranger of the lest degree of taste or sensibility. The entrance to it is strongly marked by the craggy mountain of *Buachal-ety*, a little West of the *King's house*. All the other mountains of *Glen-Co* resemble it, and are evidently but naked and solid rocks, rising on each side perpendicularly to a great height from a flat narrow bottom, so that in many places they seem to hang over, and make approaches, as they aspire, towards each other. The tops of the ridge of hills on one side are irregularly serrated for three or four miles, and shot in places into spires, which forms the most magnificent part of the scenery above *Ken-Loch-Leven*. In the middle of the valley is a small lake, and from it runs the river *Coan*, or *Cona*, celebrated in the works of *Ossian*. Indeed no place could be more happily calculated than this for forming the taste and inspiring the genius of such a poet.

The principal native animals on the mountains of *Glen-Co* are, Red Deer, *Alpine* Hares, Foxes, Eagles, Ptarmigans, and a

---

[1] I am indebted to Mr *John Stuart of Killin* for the description of this curious valley, having only had a distant view of it.

few moor-fowl. It is remarkable that the common Hare was never seen either here, in *Glen-Creran*, or *Glen-Ety*, till the military roads were made. The Partridge is a bird but lately known here, and is still rare. There are neither rats nor vipers.

In *Glen-Co* are six farms, forming a rent of 241l. *per annum*; the only crops are oats, bear and potatoes. The increase of oats is three bolls and a half from one; of bear four or five. But the inhabitants cannot subsist upon their harvest: about three hundred pounds worth of meal is annually imported. They sell about seven hundred pounds worth of black cattle; but keep only sheep and goats for the use of private families, neither butter or cheese is made for sale. The men servants are paid in kind; and commonly married.

Glen-Co lies in the united parish of *Lismore* and *Appin*, and contains about four hundred inhabitants, who are visited occasionally by a preacher from *Appin*.'

Leave on the left a vast cataract, precipitating itself in a great foaming sheet between two lofty perpendicular rocks, with trees growing out of the fissures, forming a large stream, called the water of *Boan*.

Breakfast at the little village of *Kinloch-Leven* on most excellent minced stag, the only form I thought that animal good in.

Near this village is a single farm fourteen miles long, which lets for only 35l. *per annum;* and from the nature of the soil, perhaps not very cheap.

Saw here a *Quern*, a sort of portable mill, made of two stones about two feet broad, thin at the edges, and a little thicker in the middle. In the centre of the upper stone is a hole to pour in the corn, and a peg by way of handle. The whole is placed on a cloth; the grinder pours the corn into the hole with one hand, and with the other turns round the upper stone with a very rapid motion, while the meal runs out at the sides on the cloth. This is rather preserved as a curiosity, being much out of use at present. Such are supposed to be the same with what are common among the *Moors*, being the simple substitute of a mill.

Immediately after leaving *Kinloch-Leven* the mountains soar to a far greater height than before; the sides are covered with wood, and the bottoms of the glens filled with torrents that roar amidst the loose stones. After a ride of two miles begin to ascend the *black mountain*, in *Argyleshire*, on a steep road, which continues about three miles almost to the summit, and is certainly the highest publick road in *Great Britain*. On the other side the descent is scarce a mile, but is very rapid down a zigzag way. Reach the *King's* house, seated in a plain; it was built for the accomodation of his Majesty's troops, in their march through this desolate country, but is in a manner unfurnished.

Pass near *Loch-Talla*, a long narrow piece of water, with a small pine wood on its side. A few weather-beaten pines and birch appear scattered up and down, and in all the bogs great numbers of roots, that evince the forest that covered the country within this half century. These were the last pines which I saw growing spontaneously in *North Britain*. The pine forests are become very rare: I can enumerate only those on the banks of *Loch-Rannoch*, at *Invercauld*, and *Brae-mar*; at *Coygach* and *Dirry-Monach*: the first in *Straithnavern*, the last in *Sutherland*. Those about *Loch-Loyn*, *Glen-Moriston*, and *Straith-Glas*; a small one near *Loch-Garrie*, another near *Loch-Arkig*, and a few scattered trees above *Kinloch-Leven*, all in *Inverness-shire*; and I was also informed that there are very considerable woods about *Castle Grant*. I saw only one species of Pine in those I visited; nor could I learn whether there was any other than what is vulgarly called the *Scotch Fir*, whose synonyms are these:

Pinus sylvestris foliis brevibus glaucis, conis parvis albentibus. Raii[1] hist. Pl. 1401. syn. stirp. Br. 442.

Pinus sylvestris. Gerard's herb. 1356. Lin. sp. Pl. 1418. Flora Angl. 361.[2]

Pin d'Ecosse, ou de Geneve. Du Hamel Traité des Arbres. II. 125, No. 5.[3]

Fyrre, Strom. Sondmor. 12.[4]

Most of this long day's journey from the *black mountain* w

John Ray, *Historia Plantarum* (1685–1704).
John Gerard, *The Herball or generall historie of plants* (1597).
Duhamel du Monceau, *Traité des Arbres* (1755).
Hans Ström, *Physisk og oeconomisk Beskrivelse över Fogderiet Söndmör* (1762–766).

truely melancholy, almost one continued scene of dusky moors
without arable land, trees, houses, or living creatures, fo
numbers of miles. The names of the wild tracts I passed throug!
were *Euachil-ety*, *Corricha-ba*, and *Bendoran*.

The roads are excellent; but from *Fort William* to *Kinloch
Leven* very injudiciously planned, often carried far about, an(
often so steep as to be scarce surmountable; whereas had th
engineer followed the track used by the inhabitants, thos
inconveniences would have been avoided.

These roads, by rendering the highlands accessible, contri
buted much to their present improvement, and were owing t(
the industry of our soldiery; they were begun in 1723, unde
the directions of Gen. *Wade*, who, like another *Hannibal*, force(
his way through rocks supposed to have been unconquerable
many of them hang over the mighty lakes of the country, an(
formerly afforded no other road to the natives than the paths o
sheep or goats, where even the Highlander crawled wit!
difficulty, and kept himself from tumbling into the far subjacen
water by clinging to the plants and bushes of the rock. Man·
of these rocks were too hard to yield to the pick-ax, and th
miner was obliged to subdue their obstinacy with gunpowder
and often in places where nature had denied him footing, an(
where he was forced to begin his labors, suspended from abov
by ropes on the face of the horrible precipice. The bog
and moors had likewise their difficulties to overcome; but al
were at length constrained to yield to the perseverance of ou
troops.

In some places I observed, that, after the manner of th
Romans, they left engraven on the rocks the names of the regi
ment each party belonged to, who were employed in thes
works; nor were they less worthy of being immortalized tha
the *Vexillatio's* of the Roman legions; for civilization was th
consequence of the labours of both.

These roads begin at *Dunkeld*, are carried on thro' the note·
pass of *Killicrankie*, by *Blair*, to *Dalnacardoch*, *Dalwhinie*, and ove
the *Coryarich*, to *Fort Augustus*. A branch extends from thenc
Eastward to *Inverness*, and another Westward, over *High-bridg(*
to *Fort William*. From the last, by *Kinloch-Leven*, over the *Blac*

Column on the coast of Caithness

Inveraray, the seat of the Duke of Argyle;
the castle 'stands very pleasantly, considering the mountainous country
in which it is situated'

General view of Iona

Inside the cathedral of Iona

Mountain, by the King's house, to *Tyendrum*; and from thence, by *Glen-Urqhie*, to *Inveraray*, and so along the beautifull boundaries of *Loch-Lomond*, to its extremity.

Another road begins near *Crief*, passes by *Aberfeldy*, crosses the *Tay* at *Tay-bridge*, and unites with the other road at *Dalnacardoch;* and from *Dalwhinie* a branch passes through *Badenoch* to *Inverness*.

These are the principal military roads; but there may be many others I may have over-looked.

‖ SEPTEMBER 5. Pass between hills finely planted with several sorts of trees, such as *Weymouth* pines, etc. and after a picturesque ride, reach

Inveraray; the castle the principal seat of the Dukes of *Argyle*, chief of the *Campbells;* was built by Duke *Archibald*; is quadrangular with a round tower at each corner, and in the middle rises a square one glazed on every side to give light to the staircase and galleries, and has from without a most disagreeable effect. In the attic story are eighteen good bed-chambers: the ground-floor was at this time in a manner unfurnished, but will have several good apartments. The castle is built of a coarse *lapis ollaris*, brought from the other side of *Loch-Fine*, and is the same kind with that found in *Norway*, of which the King of *Denmark's* palace at *Copenhagen* is built. Near the new castle are some remains of the old.

This place will in time be very magnificent: but at present the space between the front and the water is disgraced with the old town, composed of the most wretched hovels that can be imagined. The founder of the castle designed to have built a new town on the west side of the little bay the house stands on: he finished a few houses, a custom-house, and an excellent inn: his death interrupted the completion of the plan, which, when brought to perfection, will give the place a very different appearance to what it now bears.

From the top of the great rock *Duniquaich* is a fine view of the castle, the lawn sprinkled with fine trees, the hills covered with extensive plantations, a country fertile in corn, bordering the Loch, and the Loch itself covered with boats. The trees on the lawn about the castle are said to have been planted by the Earl of *Argyle*: they thrive greatly; for I observed beech from nine to twelve feet and a half in girth, pines nine, and a lesser maple between seven and eight.

But the busy scene of the herring-fishery gave no small improvement to the magnificent environs of *Inveraray*. Every evening some hundreds of boats in a manner covered the surface of *Loch-Fine*, an arm of the sea, which from its narrowness and from the winding of its shores, has all the beauties of a fresh-water lake: on the week-days, the chearfull noise of the bagpipe and dance echoes from on board: on the sabbath, each boat approaches the land, and psalmody and devotion divide the day; for the common people of the North are disposed to be religious, having the example before them of a gentry untainted by luxury and dissipation, and the advantage of being instructed by a clergy, who are active in their duty, and who preserve respect, amidst all the disadvantages of a narrow income.

|| SEPTEMBER 7. Crossed over an elegant bridge of three arches upon the *Aray*, in front of the castle, and kept riding along the side of the Loch for about seven miles: saw in one place a shoal of herrings, close to the surface, perfectly piled on one another, with a flock of Gulls, busied with this offered booty. After quitting the water-side the road is carried for a considerable way through the bottoms of naked, deep and gloomy glens. Ascend a very high pass with a little loch on the top, and descend into *Glen-Crow*, the seat of melancholy seldom cheared with the rays of the sun. Reach the end of *Loch-Long*, another narrow arm of the sea, bounded by high hills, and after a long course terminates in the *Firth* of *Clyde*.

Near this place see a house, very pleasantly situated, belonging to Colonel *Campbell*, amidst plantations, with some very fertile bottoms adjacent. On ascending a hill not half a mile further, appears

LOCH LOMOND. *North-Britain* may well boast of its waters, for so short a ride as thirty miles presents the traveller with the view of four most magnificent pieces. *Loch-Aw*, *Loch-Fine*, *Loch Long*, and *Loch-Lomond*. Two indeed are of salt-water; but, by their narrowness, give the idea of fresh-water lakes. It is an idle observation of travellers, that seeing one is the same with seeing all of these superb waters; for almost every one I visited has its proper characters.

‖ The country from *Luss* to the Southern extremity of the lake continually improves; the mountains sink gradually into small hills; the land is highly cultivated, well planted, and well inhabited. I was struck with rapture at a sight so long new to me: it would have been without alloy, had it not been dashed with the uncertainty whether the mountain virtue, hospitality, would flourish with equal vigor in the softer scenes I was on the point of entering on; for in the *Highlands* every house gave welcome to the traveller.

Highland hospitality

Pennant : 1772

J UNE 25. In the evening . . . steer towards *Campbeltown*, but make very little way, by reason of the stillness of the night.

‖ J UNE 26. *Campbeltown* is now a very considerable place, having risen from a petty fishing town to its present flourishing state in less than thirty years. About the year 1744 it had only two or three small vessels belonging to the port: at present there are seventy-eight sail, from twenty to eighty tuns burthen, all built for, and employed in, the herring fishery; and about eight hundred sailors are employed to man them. This town in fact was created by the fishery; for it was appointed the place of rendezvous for the busses; two hundred and sixty have been seen in the harbour at once; but their number declines since the ill-payment of the bounty. I do not know the gradual increase of the inhabitants here; but it is computed that there are seven thousand in the town and parish.

‖ Notwithstanding the quantity of bear raised, there is often a sort of dearth; the inhabitants being mad enough to convert their bread into poison, distilling annually six thousand bolls of grain into whisky. This seems a modern liquor, for in old times the distillation was from thyme, mint, anise, and other fragrant herbs; and ale was much in use with them. The former had the same name with the usquebaugh, or *water of life;* but, by *Boethius's* account, it was taken with moderation.

The Duke of *Argyle*, the principal proprietor of this country, takes great pains in discouraging the pernicious practice; and obliges all his tenants to enter into articles, to forfeit five pounds and the still, in case they are detected in making this *liqueur d'enfer*; but the trade is so profitable that many persist in it, to the great neglect of manufactures. Before this business got ground, the women were accustomed to spin a great deal of yarn (for much flax is raised in these parts) but at present they employ themselves in distilling, while their husbands are in the field.

Rural economy is but at a low ebb here: his grace does all in his power to promote that most useful of arts, by giving a certain number of bolls of burnt lime to those who can shew the largest and best fallow; and allowing ten *per cent* out of the rents to such farmers as lay out ready money in solid improvements; for example, in inclosing, and the like. The duke also shews much humanity in another instance, by permitting his tenants, in the places of his estates where stags inhabit, to destroy them with impunity; resigning that part of the ancient chieftains magnificence, rather than beasts of chace should waste the bread of the poor.

|| At night am admitted freeman of *Campbeltown*, and, according to the custom of the place, consult the ORACLE of the BOTTLE about my future voyage, assisted by a numerous company of brother burgesses.

JUNE 28. Leave *Campbeltown* with a full sense of all the civilities received there. Ride over a plain about five miles wide. See on the road side a great wheel, designed for the raising water from the neighboring collieries. The coal is eight feet thick, dips one yard in five, and points N.E. by N.W; is sold on the bank for four shillings per tun; but sufficient is not yet raised for the use of the country.

|| Dine at a tolerable house at *Bar*; visit the great cave of *Bealach-a'-chaochain*, near the shore. Embark in a rotten, leaky boat, and passing through six miles of rippling sea, find late at night our vessel safe at anchor, under the East side of the isle of Gigha.

JUNE 30. Land in *Jura*, at a little village, and see to the right on the shore the church, and the minister's *Manse*. Ride Westward about five miles to *Ard-fin*, the residence of Mr *Campbel*, seated above the sound of *Ilay*.

Jura the most rugged of the *Hebrides*, is reckoned to be about thirty-four miles long, and in general ten broad, except along the sound of *Ilay*: is composed chiefly of vast mountains, naked and without the possibility of cultivation. Some of the South, and a little of the western sides only are improveable: as is natural to be supposed, this island is ill peopled, and does not contain above seven or eight hundred inhabitants; having been a little thinned by the epidemic migrations.

‖ The produce is about three or four hundred head of cattle, sold annually at 3l. each, to graziers who come for them. About a hundred horses are also sold annually: here are a few sheep with fleeces of most excellent fineness, and numbers of goats. In good seasons sufficient bear and oats are raised as will maintain the inhabitants: but they sometimes want, I suppose from the conversion of their grain into whisky. But the chief food of the common people is potatoes and fish, and shell fish. It is to be feared that their competence of bread is very small. Bear produces four or five fold; oats three fold.

‖ Sloes are the only fruits of the island. An acid for punch is made of the berries of the mountain ash: and a kind of spirit is also distilled from them.

Necessity hath instructed the inhabitants in the use of native dyes. Thus the juice of the tops of heath boiled supplies them with a yellow; the roots of the white water lilly with a dark brown. Those of the yellow water *iris* with a black: and the *Gallium verum*, *Ru* of the islanders with a very fine red, not inferior to that from *Madder*.

‖ The women are very prolific, and very often bear twins. The inhabitants live to a great age, and are liable to very few distempers. Men of ninety work; and there is now living a woman of eighty who can run down a sheep. The account given by *Martin* of *Gillouir Mac-Crain*, was confirmed to me. His age exceeded that of either *Jenkins* or *Par*; for he kept a hundred and eighty christmasses in his own house, and died in the reign of *Charles* I. Among the modern instances of longevity I forgot to mention *John Armour*, of *Campbeltown*, aged one hundred and four, who was a cockswain in our navy, at the time of the peace of *Utrecht*; and within these three years was stout enough to go out a shooting.

‖ JULY 1. Ride along the shore of the sound: take boat at the ferry, and go a mile more by water: see on the Jura side some sheelins or summer huts for goatherds, who keep here a flock of eighty for the sake of the milk and cheeses. The last are made without salt, which they receive afterwards from the ashes of sea tang, and the tang itself which the natives lap it in.

Land on a bank covered with sheelins, the habitations of some peasants who attend the herds of milch cows. These formed a grotesque groupe; some were oblong, many conic, and so low that entrance is forbidden, without creeping through the little opening, which has no other door than a faggot of birch twigs, placed there occasionally: they are constructed of branches of trees, covered with sods; the furniture a bed of heath, placed on a bank of sod; two blankets and a rug; some dairy vessels; and above, certain pendant shelves, made of basket work, to hold the cheese, the produce of the Summer. In one of the little conic huts, I spied a little infant asleep, under the protection of a faithful dog.

Cross, on foot, a large plain of ground, seemingly improveable, but covered with deep heath, and perfectly in a state of nature. See the *artic-gull*, a bird unknown in *South-Britain*, which breeds here on the ground: it was very tame, but, if disturbed, flew about like the lapwing, but with a more flagging wing. After a walk of four miles, reach the *Paps*: left the lesser to the South East, preferring the ascent of the greatest, for there are three; *Beinn-a-chaolais*, or, the mountain of the sound; *Beinn-sheunta*, or, the hallowed mountain; and *Beinn-an-òir*, or, the mountain of gold. We began to scale the last; a task of much labor and difficulty; being composed of vast stones, slightly covered with mosses near the base, but all above bare, and unconnected with each other . . . Gain the top, and find our fatigues fully recompenced by the grandeur of the prospect from this sublime spot: *Jura* itself afforded a stupendous scene of rock, varied with little lakes innumerable. From the west side of the hill ran a narrow stripe of rock, terminating in the sea, called, the slide of the old hag. To the South appeared *Ilay*, extended like a map beneath us; and beyond that, the North of *Ireland*; to the West, *Gigha* and *Cara*, *Cantyre* and *Arran*, and the Firth of *Clyde*, bounded by Airshire; an amazing tract of mountains to the N.E. as far as *Ben-Lomond*; *Skarba* finished the Northern view; and over the Western ocean was scattered *Colonsay* and *Oronsay*,

Mull, Iona, and its neighbouring groups of isles; and still further
the long extents of *Tirey* and *Col* just apparent.

On the summit are several lofty *cairns*, not the work of
devotion, but of idle herds, or curious travellers. Even this vast
heap of stones was not uninhabited: a hind passed along the
sides full speed, and a brace of *Ptarmigans* often favoured us
with their appearance, even near the summit.

‖ JULY 8. Steer to the North West; but our course greatly
delayed by calms: take numbers of grey gurnards in all depths
of water, and find young herrings in their stomachs.

Towards evening arrive within a sight of *Iona*, and a tremendous chain of rocks, lying to the South of it, rendered more
horrible by the perpetual noise of breakers. Defer our entrance
into the *Sound* till day-light.

About eight of the clock in the morning very narrowly escape
striking on the rock *Bonirevor*, apparent at this time by the
breaking of a wave: our master was at some distance in his
boat, in search of sea fowl, but alarmed with the danger of his
vessel, was hastening to its relief; but the tide conveyed us out
of reach of the rock, and saved him the trouble of landing us;
for the weather was so calm as to free us from any apprehensions
about our lives. After tiding for three hours, anchor in the
sound of *Iona*, in three fathoms of water, on a white sandy
bottom; but the safest anchorage is on the East side, between a
little isle and that of *Mull*: this sound is three miles long and one
broad, shallow, and in some parts dry at the ebb of spring-
tides: is bounded on the East by the island of *Mull*; on the West
by that of *Iona*, the most celebrated of the *Hebrides*.

Multitudes of gannets were now fishing here: they precipitated
themselves from a vast height, plunged on their prey at least
two fathom deep, and took to the air again as soon as they
emerged. Their sense of seeing must be exquisite; but they are
often deceived, for Mr *Thompson* informed me, that he had
frequently taken them by placing a herring on a hook, and
sinking it a fathom deep, which the gannet plunges for and is
taken.

The view of *Iona* was very picturesque: the East side, or that
which bounds the sound, exhibited a beautiful variety; an

extent of plain, a little elevated above the water, and almost covered with the ruins of the sacred buildings, and with the remains of the old town, still inhabited. Beyond these the island rises into little rocky hills, with narrow verdant hollows between (for they merit not the name of vallies) and numerous enough for every recluse to take his solitary walk, undisturbed by society.

|| The soil is a compound of sand and comminuted sea shells, mixed with black loam; is very favorable to the growth of bear, natural clover, crowsfoot and daisies. It is in perpetual tillage, and is ploughed thrice before the sowing: the crops at this time made a promising appearance, but the seed was commited to the ground at very different times; some, I think, about the beginning of *May*, and some not three weeks ago. Oats do not succeed here; but flax and potatoes come on very well. I am informed that the soil in *Col*, *Tir-I*, and North and South *Uist*, is similar to that in *Iona*.

The tenants here *run-rig*, and have the pasturage in common. It supports about a hundred and eight head of cattle, and about five hundred sheep. There is no heath in this island: cattle unused to that plant give bloody milk; which is the case with the cattle of *Iona* transported to *Mull*, where that vegetable abounds; but the cure is soon effected by giving them plenty of water. Servants are paid here commonly with a fourth of the crop, grass for three or four cows and a few sheep.

The number of inhabitants is about a hundred and fifty: the most stupid and the most lazy of all the islanders; yet many of them boast of their descent from the companions of St *Columba*.

A few of the more common birds frequent this island: wild geese breed here, and the young are often reared and tamed by the natives.

The beautiful *Sea-Bugloss* makes the shores gay with its glaucous leaves and purple flowers. The *Eryngo*, or sea-holly, is frequent; and the fatal *Belladonna* is found here.

|| *Iona* derives its name from a *Hebrew* word, signifying a dove, in allusion to the name of the great saint, *Columba*, the founder of its fame. This holy man, instigated by his zeal, left his native country, *Ireland*, in the year 565, with the pious design of

preaching the gospel to the *Picts*. It appears that he left his native soil with warm resentment, vowing never to make a settlement within sight of that hated island. He made his first trial at *Oronsay*, and on finding that place too near to *Ireland*, succeeded to his wish at *Hy*, for that was the name of *Iona* at the time of his arrival. He repeated here the experiment on several hills, erecting on each a heap of stones; and that which he last ascended is to this day called *Carnan-chul-reb-Eirinn*, or, the eminence of the back turned to *Ireland*.

Columba was soon distinguished by the sanctity of his manners; a miracle that he wrought so operated on the *Pictish* king, *Bradeus*, that he immediately made a present of the little isle to the saint. It seems that his majesty had refused *Columba* an audience; and even proceeded so far as to order the palace gates to be shut against him; but the saint, by the power of his word, instantly caused them to fly open.

‖ Columba led here an exemplary life, and was highly respected for the sanctity of his manners for a considerable number of years. He is the first on record who had the faculty of *second-sight*, for he told the victory of *Aidan* over the *Picts* and *Saxons* on the very instant it happened. He had the honor of burying in his island *Convallus* and *Kinnatil*, two kings of *Scotland*, and of crowning a third. At length, worn out with age, he died, in *Iona*, in the arms of his disciples.

‖ After the death of St *Columba*, the island received the name of *Y-columb-cill*, or, the isle of the cell of *Columba*. In process of time the island itself was personified, and by a common blunder in early times converted into a saint, and worshipped under the title of St *Columb-killa*.

‖ Took boat and landed on the spot called the *Bay of Martyrs*, the place where the bodies of those who were to be interred in this holy ground, were received, during the period of superstition.

Walked about a quarter of a mile to the South, in order to fix on a convenient spot for pitching a rude tent, formed of oars and sails, as our day residence, during our stay on the island.

‖ Having settled the business of our tent, return through the town, consisting at present of about fifty houses, mostly very nean, thatched with straw of bear pulled up by the roots, and bound tight on the roof with ropes made of heath. Some of the houses that lie a little beyond the rest seemed to have been better constructed than the others, and to have been the mansions of the inhabitants when the place was in a flourishing state, but at present are in a very ruinous condition.

Visit every place in the order that they lay from the village. The first was the ruin of the nunnery, filled with canonesses of St *Augustine*, and consecrated to St *Oran*. They were permitted to live in community for a considerable time after the reformation, and wore a white gown; and above it a rotchet of fine linnen.

The church was fifty-eight feet by twenty: the roof of the east end is entire, is a pretty vault made of very thin stones, bound together by four ribs meeting in the centre. The floor is covered some feet thick with cow-dung; this place being at present the common shelter for the cattle; and the islanders are too lazy to remove this fine manure, the collection of a century, to enrich their grounds.

With much difficulty, by virtue of fair words, and a bribe, prevale on one of these listless fellows to remove a great quantity of this dung-hill; and by that means once more expose to light the tomb of the last prioress. Her figure is cut on the face of the stone; an angel on each side supports her head; and above them is a little plate and a comb. The prioress occupies only one half of the surface: the other is filled with the form of the virgin *Mary*, with head crowned and mitred; the child in her arms; and, to denote her *Queen of Heaven*, a sun and moon appear above.

‖ This nunnery could never have been founded (as some assert) in the days of St *Columba*, who was no admirer of the fair sex: in fact, he held them in such abhorrence, that he detested all cattle on their account, and would not permit a cow to come within sight of his sacred walls; because, '*Sfar am i bo, bu'dh bean, 'Sfar am bi bean, bi'dh mallacha*: 'Where there is a cow, there must be a woman; and where there is a woman, there must be mischief.'

Advance from hence along a broad paved way, which is

continued in a line from the nunnery to the cathedral: another branches from it to the *Bay of Martyrs*: and a third, narrower than the others, points towards the hills.

|| Arrive at *Reilig ourain*, or the burying place of *Oran*: a vast enclosure; the great place of interment for the number of monarchs who were deposited here; and for the potentates of every isle, and their lineage; for all were ambitious of lying in this holy spot. The place is in a manner filled with grave-stones, but so overgrown with weeds, especially with the common butter-bur, that very few are at present to be seen.

|| The chapel of St *Oran* stands in this space, which legend reports to have been the first building attempted by St *Columba*: by the working of some evil spirit, the walls fell down as fast as they were built up.

After some consultation it was pronounced, that they never would be permanent till a human victim was buried alive: *Oran*, a companion of the saint, generously offered himself, and was interred accordingly: at the end of three days St *Columba* had the curiosity to take a farewel look at his old friend, and caused the earth to be removed: to the surprize of all beholders *Oran* started up, and began to reveal the secrets of his prison-house; and particularly declared, that all that had been said of hell was a mere joke. This dangerous impiety so shocked *Columba*, that, with great policy, he instantly ordered the earth to be flung in again: poor *Oran* was overwhelmed, and an end for ever put to his prating. His grave is near the door, distinguished only by a plain red stone.

|| The cathedral lies a little to the north of this enclosure: is in the form of a cross. The length from east to west is a hundred and fifteen feet. The breadth twenty three. The length of the transept seventy. Over the centre is a handsome tower: on each side of which is a window with stone work of different forms in every one.

On the south side of the chancel are some Gothic arche supported by pillars, nine feet eight inches high, including the capitals; and eight feet nine inches in circumference. The capitals are quite peculiar; carved round with various superstitious figures, among others is an angel weighing of souls.

The altar was of white marble veined with grey, and is vulgarly supposed to have reached from side to side of the chancel; but Mr *Sacheveral*,[1] who saw it when almost entire, assures us, that the size was six feet by four.

The demolition of this stone was owing to the belief of the superstitious; who were of opinion that a piece of it conveyed to the possessor success in whatever he undertook. A very small portion is now left; and even that we contributed to diminish.

‖ The monastery lies behind the cathedral. It is in a most ruinous state; a small remnant of a cloister is left. In a corner are some black stones, held so sacred, but for what reason I am ignorant, that it was customary to swear by them: perhaps from their being neighbours to the tutelar saint, whose grave is almost adjacent.

‖ Proceed on our walk. To the west of the convent is the abbot's mount, overlooking the whole. Beneath seem to have been the gardens, once well cultivated, for we are told that the monks transplanted from other places herbs both esculent and medicinal.

Beyond the mount are the ruins of a kiln, and a granary: and near it was the mill. The lake or pool that served it lay behind; is now drained, and is the turbery, the fuel of the natives: it appears to have been once divided, for along the middle runs a raised way, pointing to the hills. They neglect at present the conveniency of a mill, and use only *querns*.

North from the granary extends a narrow flat, with a double dike and foss on one side, and a single dike on the other. At the end is a square containing a *cairn* and surrounded with a stone dike. This is called a burial place: it must have been in very early times contemporary with other *cairns*, perhaps in the days of *Druidism*. For bishop *Pocock* mentions, that he had seen two stones seven feet high, with a third laid across on their tops, an evident *Cromleh*: he also adds, that the *Irish* name of the island was *Inish Drunish*; which agrees with the account I have somewhere read, that *Iona* had been the seat of *Druids* expelled by *Columba*, who found them there.

William Sacheverell, author of *An Account of the Isle of Man, with a Voyage I-Columb-Kill* (1702). A.J.Y.

Before I quit this height, I must observe, that the whole of their religious buildings were covered on the north side by dikes, as a protection from the northern invaders, who paid little regard to the sanctity of their characters.

|| At present, this once celebrated seat of learning is destitute of even a school-master; and this seminary of holy men want even a minister to assist them in the common duties of religion.

JULY 10. Cross the island over a most fertile elevated track to the S. West side, to visit the landing place of St *Columba*; a small bay, with a pebbly beach, mixed with variety of pretty stones. . . A vast tract near this place was covered with heaps of stones, of unequal sizes: these, as is said, were the penances of monks who were to raise heaps of dimensions equal to their crimes: and to judge by some, it is no breach of charity to think there were among them enormous sinners.

|| JULY 11. At eight of the clock in the morning, with the first fair wind we yet had, set sail for the sound: the view of *Iona*, its clustered town, the great ruins, and the fertility of the ground, were fine contrasts, in our passage to the red granite rocks of *Mull*.

Sail under the vast mountains of *Rum*, and the point of *Bredon*, through a most turbulent sea, caused by the clashing of two adverse tides. See several small whales, called here *Pollacks* that when near land are often chaced on shore by boats: they are usually about ten feet long, and yield four gallons of oil. At seven o'clock in the evening find ourselves at anchor in four fathom water, in the snug harbour of the isle of CANNAY.

|| As soon as we had time to cast our eyes about, each shore appeared pleasing to humanity; verdant, and covered with hundreds of cattle: both sides gave a full idea of plenty, for the verdure was mixed with very little rock, and scarcely any heath: but a short conversation with the natives soon dispelled this agreeable error; they were at this very time in such want that numbers, for a long time had neither bread nor meal for their poor babes: fish and milk was their whole subsistence at this time: the first was a precarious relief, for, besides the uncertainty of success, to add to their distress, their stock of

fish-hooks was almost exhausted; and to ours, that it was not in our power to supply them. The rubbans, and other trifles I had brought, would have been insults to people in distress. I lamented that my money had been so uselessly laid out; for a few dozens of fish-hooks, or a few pecks of meal, would have made them happy.

The crops had failed here the last year: but the little corn sown at present had a promising aspect: and the potatoes the best I had seen: but these were not fit for use. The isles I fear annually experience a temporary famine; perhaps from improvidence, perhaps from eagerness to encrease their stock of cattle, which they can easily dispose of to satisfy the demands of their landlords, or the oppression of an agent. The people of *Canny* export none, but sell them to the numerous busses who put into this *Portus Salutis* on different occasions.

The cattle are of a middle size, black, long legged, and have thin staring manes from the neck along the back, and up part of the tail. They look well, for in several parts of the island they have good warm recesses to retreat to in winter. About sixty head are exported annually.

‖ Here are very few sheep: but horses in abundance. The chief use of them in this little district is to form an annual cavalcade of *Michaelmas*. Every man on the island mounts his horse unfurnished with saddle, and takes behind him either some young girl, or his neighbour's wife, and then rides backwards and forwards from the village to a certain cross, without being able to give any reason for the origin of this custom. After the procession is over, they alight at some public house, where, strange to say, the females treat the companions of their ride. When they retire to their houses an entertainment is prepared with primaeval simplicity: the chief part consists of a great oat cake, called *Struan-Micheil*, or *St Michael's* cake, composed of two pecks of meal, and formed like the quadrant of a circle: it is daubed over with milk and eggs, and then placed to harden before the fire.

Matrimony is held in such esteem here, that an old maid or old batchelor is scarcely known; such firm belief have they in the doctrine of the ape-leading disgrace in the world below. So, to avoid that danger the youth marry at twenty; the lasses at seventeen. The fair sex are used here with more tenderness than common, being employed only in domestic affairs, and never forced into the labors of the field. Here are plenty of poultry and of eggs.

Abundance of cod and ling might be taken; there being a fine sand-bank between this isle and the rock *Heisker*, and another between *Skie* and *Barra*; but the poverty of the inhabitants will not enable them to attempt a fishery.

‖ The length of the island is about three miles; the breadth near one: its surface hilly. This was the property of the bishop of the isles, but at present that of Mr *Macdonald* of *Clan-Ronald*. His factor, a resident-agent, rents most of the island, paying two guineas for each *penny-land*; and these he sets to the poor people at four guineas and a half each; and exacts, besides this, three days labor in the quarter from each person. Another head tenant possesses other penny-lands, which he sets in the same manner, to the impoverishing and very starving of the wretched inhabitants.

The *penny-lands* derive their name from some old valuation. The sum requisite to stock one is thirty pounds: it maintains seven cows and two horses; and the tenant can raise on it eight bolls of small black oats, the produce of two; and four of bear from half a boll of seed; one boll of potatoes yields seven. The two last are manured with sea tang.

The arable land in every farm is divided into four parts, and lots are cast for them at *Christmas*: the produce, when reaped and dried, is divided among them in proportion to their rents; and for want of mills is ground in the quern. All the pasture is common, from *May* to the beginning of *September*.

It is said that the factor has in a manner banished sheep, because there is no good market for them; so that he does his best to deprive the inhabitants of cloathing as well as food. At present they supply themselves with wool from *Rum*, at the rate of eight-pence the pound.

All the cloathing is manufactured at home: the women not only spin the wool, but weave the cloth: the men make their

Dunvegan Castle, Isle of Skye, seat of the MacLeods;
in continuous occupation by the same family for the last
seven centuries

Ben Lomond, 'piercing the very clouds'

Gannet. This bird lives on the sea, and when fishing
dives on its prey from a great height

own shoes, tan the leather with the bark of willow, or the roots of the *tormentilla erecta*, and in defect of wax-thread, use split thongs.

About twenty tuns of kelp are made in the shores every third year.

Sickness seldom visits this place: if any disorder seizes them the patient does no more than drink whey, and lie still. The small-pox visits them about once in twenty years.

All disputes are settled by the factor, or, if of great moment, by the justices of the peace in *Skie*.

This island, *Rum*, *Muck*, and *Egg*, form one parish. *Cannay* is inhabited by two hundred and twenty souls; of which all, except four families, are *Roman Catholics*; but in the whole parish there is neither church, manse nor school: there is indeed in this island a catechist, who has nine pounds a year from the royal bounty. The minister and the popish priest reside in *Egg*, but by reason of the turbulent seas that divide these isles, are very seldom able to attend their flocks. I admire the moderation of their congregations, who attend the preaching of either indifferently as they happen to arrive. As the *Scotch* are oeconomists in religion, I would recommend to them the practice of one of the little *Swiss* mixed cantons, who, through mere frugality, kept but one divine; a moderate honest fellow, who, steering clear of controversial points, held forth to the *Calvinist* flock on one part of the day, and to his *Catholic* on the other. He lived long among them much respected, and died lamented.

The protestant natives of many of the isles observe *Yule* and *Pasch*, or *Christmas* and *Easter*; which among rigid presbyterians is esteemed so horrid a superstition, that I have heard of a minister who underwent a censure for having a goose to dinner on *Christmas* day; as if any one day was more holy than another, or to be distinguished by any external marks of festivity.

In popish times here was probably a resident minister; for here are to be seen the ruins of a chapel, and a small cross.

Much rain and very hard gales the whole night; the weather being, as it is called in these parts, broken.

|| JULY 13. A continuation of bad weather. At half an hour after one at noon, loose from *Cannay*, and after passing with a

favorable gale through a rolling sea, in about two hours, anchor in the

Isle of R u m,

in an open bay, about two miles deep, called *Loch-Sgriosard*, bounded by high mountains, black and barren: at the bottom of the bay is the little village *Kinloch*, of about a dozen houses, built in a singular manner, with walls very thick and low, with the roofs or thatch reaching little beyond the inner edge, so that they serve as benches for the lazy inhabitants, whom we found sitting on them in great numbers, expecting our landing, with that avidity for news common to the whole country.

Entered the house with the best aspect, but found it little superior in goodness to those of *Ilay*; this indeed had a chimney and windows, which distinguished it from the others, and denoted the superiority of the owner: the rest knew neither windows nor chimnies; a little hole on one side gave an exit to the smoke: the fire is made on the floor beneath; above hangs a rope, with the pot-hook at the end to hold the vessel that contains their hard fare, a little fish, milk, or potatoes. Yet beneath the roof I entered, I found an address and politeness from the owner and his wife that were astonishing: such pretty apologies: for the badness of the treat, the curds and milk that were offered; which were tendered to us with as much readiness and good will, as by any of old *Homer's* dames, celebrated by him in his *Odyssey* for their hospitality. I doubt much whether their cottages or their fare was much better; but it must be confessed that they might be a little more cleanly than our good hostess.

Rum, or *Ronin* as it is called by the D e a n,[1] is the property of Mr *Macleane*, of *Coll;* a landlord mentioned by the natives with much affection. The length is about twelve miles; the breadth six; the number of souls at this time three hundred and twenty five; of families only fifty-nine, almost all protestant. The head of families, with their wives, were at this time all alive, except five, three widowers and two widows. They had with them a hundred and two sons and only seventy-six daughters: this

[1] Dean Monro, author of *Western Isles of Scotland and genealogies of the clan* (1549). A.J.Y.

disproportion prevales in *Cannay*, and the other little islands; in order, in the end, to preserve a ballance between the two sexes; as the men are, from their way of life, so perpetually exposed to danger in these stormy seas, and to other accidents that might occasion a depopulation, was it not so providentially ordered.

The island is one great mountain, divided into several points; the highest called *Aisgobhall*. About this bay, and towards the East side, the land slopes towards the water side; but on the South West forms precipices of a stupendous height. The surface of *Rum* is in a manner covered with heath, and in a state of nature: the heights rocky. There is very little arable land, excepting about the nine little hamlets that the natives have grouped in different places; near which the corn is sown in diminutive patches, for the tenants here *run-rig* as in *Cannay*. The greatest farmer holds five pounds twelve shillings a year, and pays his rent in money. The whole of the island is two thousand marks.[1]

The little corn and potatoes they raise is very good; but so small is the quantity of bear and oats, that there is not a fourth part produced to supply their annual wants: all the subsistence the poor people have besides, is curds milk and fish. They are a well made and well-looking race, but carry famine in their aspect. Are often a whole summer without a grain in the island; which they regret not on their own account, but for the sake of their poor babes. In the present oeconomy of the island, there is no prospect of any improvement. Here is an absurd custom of allotting a certain stock to the land; for example, a farmer is allowed to keep fourteen head of cattle, thirty sheep, and six mares, on a certain tract called a *penny-land*. The person who keeps more is obliged to repair out of his superfluity any loss his neighbour may sustain in his herds or flocks.

A number of black cattle is sold, at thirty or forty shillings per head, to graziers, who come annually from *Skie*, and other places. The mutton here is small, but the most delicate in our dominions, if the goodness of our appetites did not pervert our judgment: the purchase of a fat sheep was four shilling and sixpence: the natives kill a few, and also of cows, to salt for

[1] A *Scotch* mark is little more than thirteen-pence-farthing.

winter provisions. A few goats are kept here: abundance of mares and a necessary number of stallions; for the colts are an article of commerce, but they never part with the fillies.

JULY 14. Notwithstanding this island has several streams, here is not a single mill; all the molinary operations are done at home: the corn is *graddan'd*, or burnt out of the ear, instead of being thrashed: this is performed two ways; first, by cutting off the ears, and drying them in a kiln, then setting fire to them on a floor, and picking out the grains, by this operation rendered as black as coal. The other method is more expeditious, for the whole sheaf is burnt, without the trouble of cutting off the ears: a most ruinous practice, as it destroys both thatch and manure, and on that account has been wisely prohibited on some of the islands . . .

‖ The *quern* or *bra* is made in some of the neighbouring counties, in the mainland, and costs about fourteen shillings. This method of grinding is very tedious: for it employs two pair of hands four hours to grind only a single bushel of corn. Instead of a hair sieve to sift the meal the inhabitants here have an ingenious substitute, a sheep's skin stretched round a hoop, and perforated with small holes made with a hot iron. They knead their bannock with water only, and bake or rather toast it, by laying it upright against a stone placed near the fire.

For want of lime they dress their leather with calcined shells: and use the same method of tanning it as in *Cannay*.

The inhabitants of *Rum* are people that scarcely know sickness: if they are attacked with a dysentery they make use of a decoction of the roots of the *Tormentilla erecta* in milk. The small-pox has visited them but once in thirty-four years, only two sickened, and both recovered. The measles come often.

It is not wonderful that some superstitions should reign in these sequestered parts. Second sight is firmly believed at this time. My informant said that *Lauchlan Mac-Kerran* of *Cannay* had told a gentleman that he could not rest for the noise he heard of the hammering of nails into his coffin: accordingly the gentleman died within fifteen days.

Molly Mac-leane (aged forty) has the power of foreseeing events through a well scraped blade bone of mutton: some time ago she took up one and pronounced that five graves were soon to be opened: one for a grown person; the other four for children; one of which was to be of her own kin: and so it fell out. These pretenders to second sight, like the *Pythian* priestess, during their inspiration fall into trances, foam at the mouth, grow pale, and feign to abstain from food for a month, so over-powered are they by the visions imparted to them during their paroxysms.

‖ JULY 15. The weather grows more moderate; at one o'clock at noon sail from *Rum*, with a favourable and brisk gale, for the isle of *Skie*. Soon reach the point of *Slate*, at the south end, a division of that great island, a mixture of grass, a little corn and much heath. Leave on the right the point of *Arisaig*. Pass beneath *Ormadale* in *Skie*, a seat beautifully wooded, gracing most unexpectedly this almost tree-less tract. A little farther to the West opens the mouth of *Loch-in-daal*, a safe harbour, and opposite to it on the main-land, that of *Loch-Jurn*, or the lake of *Hell*, with black mountains of tremendous height impending above.

‖ JULY 16. Land at a point called the *Kyle*, or passage, where about four-score horses were collected to be transported *à la nage* to the opposite shore, about a mile distant. They were taken over by fours, by little boats, a pair on each side held with halters by two men, after being forced off a rock into the sea. We undertook the conveyance of a pair. One a pretty grey horse, swam admirably; the other was dragged like a log; but as soon as it arrived with in scent of its companions before landed, revived, disengaged itself, and took to the shore with great alacrity. Some very gentleman-like men attended these animals; and with great politeness offered their services.

Among the crowd was a lad *erectis auribus*, his ears had never been swaddled down, and they stood out as nature ordained; and I dare say his sense of hearing was more acute by this liberty.

The horned cattle of *Skie* are swam over, at the narrow passage of *Kul-ri*, at low water; six, eight, or twelve are passed over at a time, tied with rope, fastened from the horn of one to its tail, and so to the next; the first is fastened to a boat, and thus are conveyed to the opposite shore. This is the great pass into the island, but is destitute even of a horse-ferry.

JULY 17. At five in the morning quit our situation, and, passing thro' a narrow and short sound, arrive in another fine expanse, beautifully land-locked by the mainland (part of *Ross-shire*), the islands of *Rona* and *Croulin*, *Rasa*, distinguished by the high hillock, called *Dun-canna*; *Scalpa*, and the low verdant isle of *Pabay*, in old times the seat of assassins.[1] *Skie* shows a verdant slope for part of its shore: beyond soar the conic naked hills of *Straith*, and still farther, the ragged heights of *Blaven*.

See, behind us, the ruins of the castle, and the entrance of the bay we had left, the openings into the great lochs *Kisserne* and *Carron*, and, as a back-ground, a boundless chain of rugged mountains. The day was perfectly clear, and the sea smooth as a mirror, disturbed but by the blowing of two whales, who entertained us for a considerable space by the jet d'eaux from their orifices.

‖ The country is divided by low banks of earth, and, like the other islands, has more corn than pasturage. In my walk to *Kilchrist*, the church of the parish of *Strath*, saw on the road-side vast strata of limestone and stonemarle, the former grey, the last white, and in many parts dissolved into an impalpable powder, and ready to the hands of the farmer. It is esteemed a fine manure, but better for corn than grass.

‖ On my return am entertained with a rehearsal I may call it of the *Lunghadh*, or, *walking of cloth*, a substitute for the fulling-mill: twelve or fourteen women, divided into two equal numbers, sit down on each side of a long board, ribbed length-ways, placing the cloth on it: first they begin to work it backwards and forwards with their hands, singing at the same time as the quern: when they have tired their hands, every female uses her feet for the same purpose, and six or seven pair of naked feet are in the most violent agitation, working one against the other: as by this time they grow very earnest in their labours, the fury of the song rises; at length it arrives to such a pitch,

[1] In the time of the Dean all these little isles were full of woods at present quite naked.

that without breach of charity you would imagine a troop of female *daemoniacs* to have been assembled.

They sing in the same manner when they are cutting down the corn, when thirty or forty join in chorus. The subject of the songs at the *Luaghadh*, the *Quern*, and on this occasion, are sometimes love, sometimes panegyric, and often a rehearsal of the deeds of the antient heroes, but all the tunes slow and melancholy.

Singing at the *Quern* is now almost out of date since the introduction of water-mills. The laird can oblige his tenants, as in *England*, to make use of this more expeditious kind of grinding; and empowers the miller to search out and break any *Querns* he can find, as machines that defraud him of the toll.

Walk up *Beinn-na-caillich*, or, the hill of the old hag; one of those picturesque mountains that made such a figure from the sea. After ascending a small part, find its sides covered with vast loose stones, like the paps of *Jura*, the shelter of ptarmigans: the top flat and naked, with an artificial *cairn*, of a most enormous size, reported to have been the place of sepulture of a gigantic woman in the days of Fingal. The prospect to the West was that of desolation itself; a savage series of rude mountains, discolored, black and red, as if by the rage of fire. Nearest, joined to this hill by a ridge, is *Beinn-na-grian*, or the mountain of the SUN; perhaps venerated in antient times. *Mal-more*, or the round mountain, appears on the North. The serrated tops of *Blaven* affect with astonishment; and beyond them, the clustered height of *Quillin*, or the mountain of Cuchullin, like its antient hero, *stood like a hill that catches the clouds of heaven.* The deep recesses between these *Alps*, in times of old, *possessed the sons of the narrow vales, the hunters of deer;* and to this time are inhabited by a fine race of stags.

|| J U L Y 22. S K I E is the largest of the *Hebrides*, being above sixty measured miles long; the breadth unequal, by reason of the numbers of lochs that penetrate far on both sides. It is supposed by some to have been the Eastern *Aebudae* of the antients; by others, to have been the *Dumna*. The modern name is of *Norwegian* origin, derived from *Ski*, a mist; and from the clouds (that almost constantly hang on the tops of its lofty hills)

was styled, *Ealand skianach*, or, the cloudy island. No epithet could better suit the place, for, except in the summer season, there is scarcely a week of fair weather; the summers themselves are also generally wet, and seldom warm.

The westerly winds blows here more regularly than any other, and arriving charged with vapour from the vast *Atlantic*, never fails to dash the clouds it wafts on the lofty summits of the hills of Cuchullin, and their contents deluge the island in a manner unknown in other places. What is properly called the rainy season commences in *August:* the rains begin with moderate winds; which grow stronger and stronger till the autumnal *equinox*, when they rage with incredible fury.

The husbandman then sighs over the ruins of his vernal labours: sees his crops feel the injury of climate: some laid prostrate; the more ripe corn shed by the violence of the elements. The poor foresee famine, and consequential disease: the humane tacksmen agonize over distresses, that inability, not want of inclination, deprive them of the power of remedying. The nearer calls of family and children naturally first excite their attention: to maintain and to educate are all their hopes, for that of accumulating wealth is beyond their expectation: so the poor are left to Providence's care: they prowl like other animals along the shores to pick up limpets and other shell-fish, the casual repasts of hundreds during part of the year in these unhappy islands. Hundreds thus annually drag through the season a wretched life: and numbers, unknown, in all parts of the western highlands (nothing local is intended) fall beneath the pressure, some of hunger, more of the putrid fever, the epidemic of the coasts, originating from unwholesome food, the dire effects of necessity. Moral and innocent victims! who exult in the change, first finding that place *where the wicked cease from troubling, and where the weary are at rest.*

The farmer labors to remedy this distress to the best of his power, but the wetness of the land late in spring prevents him from putting into the ground the early seed of future crops, bear and small oats: the last are fittest for the climate: they bear the fury of the winds better than other grain, and require less manure, a deficiency in this island. Poverty prevents him from making experiments in rural oeconomy: the ill success of a few made by the more opulent, determines him to follow the old tract, as attended with more certainty, unwilling, like the dog in the fable, to grasp at the shadow and lose the substance, even poor as it is.

The produce of the crops very rarely are in any degree proportioned to the wants of the inhabitants: golden seasons have happened, when they have had superfluity; but the years of famine are as ten to one. The helps of the common years are Potatoes: it is difficult to say whether the discovery of *America* by the *Spaniards* has contributed to preserve more lives by the introduction of this vegetable; or to have caused more to perish by the insatiable lust after the pretious metals of the new world.

The difficulties the farmer undergoes in this bad climate are unknown in the South: there he sows his seed, and sees it flourish beneath a benign sun and secured from every invasion. Here a wet sky brings a reluctant crop: the ground, inclosed only with turf mounds, accessible to every animal: A continual watch employs numbers of his people: some again are occupied in repairing the damages sustained by their houses from storms the preceding year: others are laboring at the turberies, to provide fuel to keep off the rigor of the severe season: or in fencing the natural (the only) grasses of the country to preserve their cattle from starving; which are the true and proper staple of these islands.

The quantity of corn raised in tolerable seasons in this island, is esteemed to be about nine thousand bolls. The number of mouths to consume them near thirteen thousand: migration, and depression of spirit, the last a common cause of depopulation, having since the year 1750 reduced the number from fifteen thousand to between twelve and thirteen: one thousand having crossed the *Atlantic*, others sunk beneath poverty, or in despair, ceased to obey the first great command, Encrease and Multiply.

In that year the whole rent of Skie was three thousand five hundred pounds. By an unnatural force some of the rents are now doubled and trebled. People long out of all habit of industry, and used to the convivial tables of their chieftains, were unable instantly to support so new a burden: in time not very long preceding that, they felt the return of some of their rents: they were enabled to keep hospitality; to receive their chieftain with a well covered board; and to feed a multitude of poor. Many of the greater tacksmen were of the same blood with their chieftains; they were attached to them by the ties of consanguinity as well as affection: they felt from them the first act of oppression, as *Caesar* did the wound from his beloved *Brutus*.

The high advance of the price of cattle is a plea for the high advance of rents; but the situation of the tacksman here is particular, he is a gentleman, and boasts the same blood with his laird: (of five hundred fighting men that followed *Macleod* in 1745 in his Majesty's army, four hundred were of his kindred) has been cherished by him for a series of years often with paternal affection: has been used to such luxuries as the place affords: and cannot instantly sink from a good board to the hard fare of the common farmer. When the chieftain riots in all the luxuries of *South Britain*, he thinks himself entitled to share a due degree of the good things of this life, and not to be forever confined to the diet of *Brochan* or the compotation of *Whisky*. During the feudal reign their love for their chieftain induced them to bear many things, at present intolerable. He was their pride and their glory: they strained every nerve in support of him, in the same manner as the *French* through vanity, refuse nothing to aggrandize their *Grand Monarque*.

Resentment drove many to seek a retreat beyond the *Atlantic*: they sold their stock, and in numbers made their first essay. They found, or thought they found, while their passions were warm, an happy change of situation: they wrote in terms savouring of romance, an account of their situation: their friends caught the contagion: and numbers followed: and others were preparing to follow their example. The tacksmen from a motive of independency; the poor from attachment, and from excess of misery. Policy and humanity, as I am informed, have of late checked this spirit so detrimental to the public. The wisdom of legislature may perhaps fall on some methods to conciliate the affections of a valuable part of the community:

it is unbecoming my little knowledge of the country to presume to point out the methods. It is to be hoped the head will, while time permits, recollect the use of the most distant members.

The proper products of this and all the *Hebrides*, are men and cattle: the use of the first in an island which the late war felt at last its deficiency, need not be insisted on. In respect to cattle, this in particular bears the pre-eminence of having the largest breed of all the highlands. The greater tenants keep their cattle during winter in what are called *winter-parks*, the driest and best ground they have: here they are kept till *April*, except the winter proves very hard, when they are foddered with straw: in *April* the farmer turns them to the moor-grass (cotton-grass) which springs first, and at night drives them into the dry grounds again.

The poorer tenants, who have no winter parks, are under the necessity of keeping the cattle under the same roof with themselves during night; and often are obliged to keep them alive with the meal designed for their families. The cows are often forced, through want of other food, to have recourse to the shores, and feed on the sea-plants at low water: by instinct they will, at ebb of tide, hasten from the moors, notwithstanding they are not within sight of the sea.

|| There is certainly much ill management in the direction of the farms: a tacksman of fifty pounds a year often keeps twenty servants; the laziest of creatures, for not one will do the least thing that does not belong to his department. Most of them are married, as in *Ilay*. Their common food is *Brochan*, a thick meal-pudding, with milk, butter or treacle; or a thinner sort, called *Easoch*, taken with their bannocs. This number of servants seemed to answer the retainers in great families before that pernicious custom was abolished by *Henry* VII; in feudal times they were kept here for the same bad end. The cause is now no more, but the habit cannot suddenly be shaken off: charity forbids one to wish it, till some employ is thought of for them; otherwise, like the poor cottagers before-mentioned, starving must be their portion.

Cattle is at present the only trade of the island: about four thousand are annually sold, from forty shillings to three pounds a head. The loss sustained in *Skie* by the severity of the last winter, and the general failure of the crops the preceding season, amounted to five thousand; perhaps in some measure owing to the farms being over-stocked.

About two hundred and fifty horses are purchased from hence every year.

Here are no sheep but what are kept for home consumption, or for the wool for the cloathing of the inhabitants. Hogs are not introduced here yet, for want of proper food for those animals.

About three hundred tuns of kelp are made here annually, but it is thought not to answer, as it robs the land of so much manure.

There are not above two or three slated houses in the island; the general thatch is fern, root and stalk, which will last above twenty years.

‖ A wild species of magic was practised in the district of *Trotterness*, that was attended with a horrible solemnity: a family who pretended to oracular knowledge practiced these ceremonies. In this country is a vast cataract, whose waters falling from a high rock, jet so far as to form a dry hollow beneath, between them and the precipice. One of these impostors was sowed up in the hide of an ox, and, to add terror to the ceremony, was placed in this concavity: the trembling enquirer was brought to the place, where the shade, and the roaring of the waters, encreased the dread of the occasion. The question is put, and the person in the hide delivers his answer, and so ends this species of divination styled *Taghairm*.

But all these idle tales are totally exploded, and good sense and polished manners prevale, instead of that barbarity which in 1598 induced *James* VI to send here a new colony to civilize the natives; who were so little disposed to receive their instructors, that his majesty was in the end obliged to desist from his design.

JULY 24. After a most tempestuous night, loose from our harbour at two o'clock at noon. Go through a narrow channel at the North end, a rock lying in the middle. Have to the West a view of *Fisher's* rock; and to the North a strange chain of rocky

les, very singular in their appearance, and varying in their
rms in the process of our course. The highest is called *Bordh-*
or-mhic-leod, or *Macleod's* great table. Another is called *Flada.*
In the first Mr *Thompson* took in our absence the little *petrel*,
hich with numbers of others were lurking beneath the loose
ones, and betrayed themselves by their loud twittering. These
re the least of palmipeds; the dread of mariners who draw a
ertain presage of a storm from their appearance; for they
ways collect in numbers at the approach of a tempest beneath
he stern; running along the waves in the wake of the ship,
ith a swiftness incredible . . .

|| Have a full view of the isle of *Lewis*, the *Lodhus* of the
orwegians: and off it a groupe of little isles called *Siant*, or
hant, and somewhat to the north of those is the fine harbour
nd town of Stornaway. It was my intention to have steered for
hat port, but was dissuaded from it by the accounts I had from
he gentlemen of *Skie*, that a putrid fever raged there with great
iolence.

Direct our course for *Loch Broom*, in the county of *Ross*. An
asy breeze carries us off the cape *Ruth an ri*, in the maps *Row-*
e. About eight o'clock in the morning of

JULY 25. Find ourselves near a considerable number of
nall isles, with a most dreary appearance, miscalled the
mmer islands. Within is a great bay six miles broad and eight
eep, bounded by vast and barren mountains, patched with
ow. The wind chops about and blows very fresh, so that after
any teizing tacks, about nine o'clock in the evening drop
nchor under isle *Martin*, in the bottom of the bay, which is
re called *Loch Kinnard*. To the South is a hill which we landed
n, and ascended, and saw on the other side great loch *Broom*,
· *Braon*, narrow, of a vast depth, and running many miles up
e country. At its head receives a river frequented by salmon
April.

This parish is one of the largest on the mainland of *Scotland*,
eing thirty-six miles long and twenty broad. It has in it seven
aces of worship, three catechists,[1] and about two thousand

A catechist is one who goes from house to house to instruct the people in
e principles of religion, and in the catechisms, approved in the general

examinable persons: but is destitute of a parochial school. None
of the people except the gentry understand *English*. The country
is inhabited by the *Mackenzies*, even quite from *Kintail*, whose
chieftain is the earl of *Seaforth*.

It is a land of mountains, a mixture of rock and heath, with
a few flats between them producing bear and black oats, but
never sufficient to supply the wants of the inhabitants.

Cattle are the great support of the country, and are sold, to
graziers who come for them even as far as from *Craven* in
Yorkshire, at the rate of thirty shillings to three pounds a head.
A great deal of butter and cheese is sold to the busses. Land is
set here by the *Davoch* or half *Davoch*; the last consists of ninety
six *Scotch* acres of arable land, such as it is, with a competent
quantity of mountain and grazing ground. This maintains sixty
cows and their followers, and is rented for fifty-two pounds a
year. To manage this the farmer keeps eight men and eight
women servants, and an overseer, who are all paid partly in
money, partly in kind. The common servants have thirty
shillings per annum, house, garden, six bolls of meal and shoes.
The dairy maids thirteen shillings and four pence and shoes;
the common drudges six and eight pence and shoes.

The tender cattle are housed during winter. The common
manure of the country is dung, or sea-wrack.

JULY 27. Still on board. The weather very bad.

JULY 28. Land at the bottom of the bay, in

R O S S - S H I R E .

Procure horses. Observe some houses built for the veteran
soldiers and sailors; but as usual, all deserted. Proceed up
Strath-Kennard, which with *Coygach* that bounds the north side
of the bay is a forfeited estate, and unalterably annexed to the
crown. The commissioners give all possible encouragement to
the tenants; and have power to grant longer leases than the
lairds are inclined to do, which keeps the people under the
government contented, and banishes from their minds all
thoughts of migration.

Kindness and hospitality possess the people of these parts. We

assembly; are appointed by its committee, and are supported out of her
majesty's bounty.

carce passed a farm but the good woman, long before our
approach, sallied out and stood on the road side, holding out
o us a bowl of milk or whey.

Ascend a very high mountain, and pass through a birch
wood, over a pretty little loch: various other woods of the same
kind were scattered over the bottoms; but the trees were small.
Roots of pines filled all the moors, but I saw none of those
trees standing. Pass under some great precipices of limestone,
mixed with marble: from hence a most tremendous view of
mountains of stupendous height, and generally of conoid forms.

never saw a country that seemed to have been so torn and
convulsed: the shock, whenever it happened, shook off all that
vegetates: among these aspiring heaps of barrenness, the sugar-
loaf hill of *Suil-bhein* made a conspicuous figure: at their feet
he blackness of the moors by no means assisted to chear our
ideas. Enter *Assynt*, in

SUTHERLAND:

Ride by *Loch-Camlach*; enjoy some diversity of the scene, for it
was prettily decorated with little wooded islands. Reach *Led-
eg*, where we obtained quarters, and rough hospitality, from
. gigantic and awful landlady; a spouse fit for *Fin-mac-cuil*
himself, was he in the land of the living.

This country is environed with mountains; and all the strata
near their base, and in the bottom, are composed of white
marble, fine as the *Parian*; houses are built with it, and walls
raised; burnt, it is the manure of the country; but oftener
nature dissolves, and presents it ready prepared to the lazy
farmer.

This tract seems the residence of sloth; the people almost
torpid with idleness, and most wretched; their hovels most
miserable, made of poles wattled and covered with thin sods.
There is not corn raised sufficient to supply half the wants of
the inhabitants: climate conspires with indolence to make
matters worse; yet there is much improveable land here in a
state of nature: but till famine pinches they will not bestir
themselves: they are content with little at present, and are
thoughtless of futurity; perhaps on the motive of *Turkish*
vassals, who are oppressed in proportion to their improvements.

Dispirited and driven to despair by bad management, crowds were now passing, emaciated with hunger, to the Eastern coast, on the report of a ship being there loaden with meal. Numbers of the miserables of this country were now migrating: they wandered in a state of desperation; too poor to pay, they madly sell themselves, for their passage, preferring a temporary bondage in a strange land, to starving for life on their native soil.

|| *Assynt* parish contains between three and four thousand souls; and sends out five hundred head of cattle annually; and about two or three lasts of salmon are taken every year in the water of *Innard*, on the coast.

|| JULY 28. It was our design on leaving the ship to have penetrated by land as far as the extremity of the island, but was informed that the way was impassable for horses three miles farther, and that even a highland foot-messenger must avoid part of the hills by crossing an arm of the sea. Return the same road through a variety of bog, and hazardous rock, that nothing but our shoe-less little steeds could have carried us over. At length we arrive safely on board the ship,

> A wond'rous token
> Of heaven's kind care, with necks unbroken.

Found in our harbour some busses, just anchored, in expectation of finding the shoals of herrings usually here at this season; but at present were disappointed: a few were taken sufficient to convince us of their superiority in goodness over those of the South: they were not larger, but as they had not wasted themselves by being in roe, their backs and the part next to the tail were double the thickness of the others, and the meat rich beyond expression.

|| The busses are from twenty to ninety tons burden, but the best size is eighty. A vessel of eighty tuns ought to take ten lasts or a hundred and twenty barrels of herrings, to clear expences the price of the fish to be admitted to be a guinea a barrel: a ship of this size ought to have eighteen men, and three boats one of twenty tons should have six men; and every five tons above, require an additional hand.

To every tun are two hundred and eighty yards of nets; so a vessel of eighty tuns carries twenty thousand square yards: each net is twelve yards long, and ten deep; and every boat takes out from twenty to thirty nets, and puts them together, so as to form a long train: they are sunk at each end of the train by a stone, which weighs it down to the full extent: the top is supported by buoys, made of sheeps-skin, with a hollow stick at the mouth, fastened tight; through this the skin is blown up, and then stopt with a peg, to prevent the escape of the air. Sometimes these buoys are placed at the top of the nets; at other times the nets are suffered to sink deeper, by the lengthening the cords fastened to them, every cord being for that purpose ten or twelve fathoms long. But the best fisheries are generally in more shallow water.

The nets are made at *Greenock*, in *Knapdale*, *Bute* and *Arran*; but the best are procured from *Ireland*, and, I think, from some part of *Caernarvonshire*.

The fishing is always performed in the night, unless by accident. The busses remain at anchor, and send out their boats a little before sun-set, which continue out, in Winter and Summer, till day-light; often taking up and emptying their nets, which they do ten or twelve times in a night in case of good success. During Winter it is a most dangerous and fatiguing employ, by reason of the greatness and frequency of the gales in these seas, and in such gales are the most successful captures; but by the providence of heaven the fishers are seldom lost; and, what is wonderful, few are visited with illness. They go out well prepared, with a warm great coat, boots and skin aprons, and a good provision of beef and spirits. The same good fortune attends the busses, who in the tempestuous season, and in the darkest nights, are continually shifting in these narrow seas from harbour to harbour.

Sometimes eighty barrels of herring are taken in a night by the boats of a single vessel. It once happened, in *Loch-Slappan*, in *Skie*, that a buss of eighty tuns might have taken two hundred barrels in one night, with ten thousand square yards of net; but the master was obliged to desist, for want of a sufficient number of hands to preserve the capture.

from the locals.

The herrings are preserved by salting, after the entrails are taken out; an operation performed by the country people, who get three-halfpence per barrel for their trouble; and sometimes, even in the Winter, can gain fifteen-pence a day. This employs both women and children, but the salting is only entrusted to the crew of the busses. The fish are laid on their backs in the barrels, and layers of salt between them. The entrails are not lost, for they are boiled into an oil: eight thousand fish will yield ten gallons, value at one shilling the gallon.

|| The barrels are made of oak staves, chiefly from *Virginia*; the hoops from several parts of our own island, and are made either of oak, birch, hazel, or willow: the last from *Holland*, liable to a duty.

|| The herrings in general are exported to the *West-Indies*, to feed the negroes, or to *Ireland*, for the *Irish* are not allowed to fish in these seas. By having a drawback of five-pence a barrel, and by re-packing the fish in new barrels of twenty-eight gallons, they are enabled to export them to our colonies at a cheaper rate than the *Scots* can do.

The trade declines apace; the bounty, which was well paid, originally kept up the spirit of the fishery; but for the last six years the arrears have been very injurious to several adventurers, who have sold out at thirty per cent loss, besides that of their interest.

|| *Loch-Broom* has been celebrated for three or four centuries as the resort of herrings. They generally appear here in *July*: those that turn into this bay are part of the brigade that detaches itself from the Western column of that great army that annually deserts the vast depths of the *arctic* circle, and come, heaven-directed, to the seats of population, offered as a cheap food to millions, whom wasteful luxury or iron-hearted avarice hath deprived, by enhancing the price, of the wonted supports of the poor.

The migration of these fish from their Northern retreat is regular: their visits to the Western isles and coasts, certain: but their attachment to one particular loch, extremely precarious. All have their turns; that which swarmed with fish one year, is totally deserted the following; yet the next loch to it be crowded with the shoals. These changes of place give often full employ to the busses, who are continually shifting their harbour in quest of news respecting these important wanderers.

|| The signs of the arrival of the herrings are flocks of gulls, who catch up the fish while they swim on the surface; and of gannets, who plunge and bring them up from considerable depths. Both these birds are closely attended to by the fishers.

In a fine day, when the fish appear near the surface, they exhibit an amazing brilliancy of colors; all the various coruscations that dart from the diamond, sapphire, and emerald, enrich their tract: but during night, *if they break*, i.e. play on the surface, the sea appears on fire, luminous as the brightest *phosphorus*.

During a gale, that part of the ocean which is occupied by the great shoals, appears as if covered with the oil that is emitted from them.

They seem to be greatly affected by lightening: during that phenomenon they sink towards the bottom, and move regularly in parallel shoals one above the other.

|| Before I leave this bay it must be observed, that there are here as in most of the lochs, a few, a very few of the natives who possess a boat and nets; and fish in order to sell the capture fresh to the busses: the utmost these poor people can attain to are the boat, and nets; they are too indigent to become masters of barrels, or of salt, to the great loss of the public as well as theirselves. . . .

JULY 29. Weigh anchor, and sail with a favorable breeze towards the mouth of the lay, with a design of returning South; but towards evening the wind changes, cold weather and hard adverse gales succeed, which oblige us to tack and anchor in the mouth of *Little Loch-Broom*, an arm of the sea, about seven miles long, and not half a mile broad, bounded by high mountains, covered in many parts with birch woods. The hill *Talloch-Essie* may vie with the highest I have seen.

For two hours amuse ourselves with taking with hand-lines abundance of cod, some dog-fish, and a curious ray.

The night was most tempestuous: our situation was disagreeable, as Mr *Thompson* thought our vessel would drive, and that he should be obliged to cut his cables, and put to sea; which, under the circumstances of a black night, a furious storm, and rocky narrows, did not contribute to the repose of fresh-water seamen.

JULY 30. The wind grows moderate: in weighing anchor discover on the cable several very uncommon *Asteriae*. No sooner was our anchor on board, but a furious squall arises, and blows in blasts like a hurricane, driving us before it at a vast rate, till we arrived within a mile of the bottom of the loch. Drop anchor, but without effect; are obliged to weigh again, while the furious gale engages an attention to the sails, and flings us into a double perplexity in this narrow strait, where for an hour our tacks were almost perpetual, and the vessel frequently in no small danger. The blasts from the mountains were tremendous, not only raising a vast sea, but catching up the waves in eddies, and raising them up in the air to a surprizing height. At length were relieved from our distress by a successful anchorage, under a high and finely wooded hill, in eight fathom water, but within a small distance of eighty.

Procure horses, by favor of Kenneth Mac-kenzie, Esq., of *Dundonnel*. Ride about a mile on the side of the hill, above the loch; arrive in a small but fertile plain, winding among the vast mountains, and adorned with a pretty river and woods of alder. Here we were rejoiced with the sight of enclosures long strangers to us: the hay was good, the bear and oats excellent; but the manner of manuring, called in these parts *tathing*, was very singular: many of the fields were covered with the boughs of alders, lately cut: these are left during the whole Winter to rot; in *March* the ground is cleared of the undecayed parts, and then ploughed. Fern is also used for the same end.

|| AUGUST 2. At seven in the morning, take a six-oared boat, at the east end of *Loch-Maree*: keep on the north shore beneath steep rocks, mostly filled with pines waving over our heads. Observe on the shore a young man of good appearance, hailing the boat in the *erse* language. I demanded what he wanted: was informed, a place in the boat. As it was entirely filled, was obliged to refuse his request. He follows us for two miles through every difficulty, and by his voice and gestures threatened

revenge. At length a rower thought fit to acquaint us, that he was owner of the boat, and only wanted admission in lieu of one of them. The boat was ordered to shore, and the master taken in with proper apologies and attempts to sooth him for his hard treatment. Instead of insulting us with abuse as a *Charon* of *South Britain* would have done, he instantly composed himself, and told us through an interpreter, that he felt great pride in finding that his conduct gained any degree of approbation.

Continue our course. The lake, which at the beginning was only half a mile broad, now, nearly half its length, widens into a great bay, bending towards the South, about four miles in breadth, filled with little isles, too much clustered and indistinct.

Land on that called *Inch-maree*, the favored isle of the saint, the patron of all the coast from *Applecross* to *Loch-broom*. The shores are neat and gravelly; the whole surface covered thickly with a beautiful grove of oak, ash, willow, wicken, birch, fir, hazel, and enormous hollies. In the midst is a circular dike of stones, with a regular narrow entrance: the inner part has been used for ages as a burial place, and is still in use. I suspect the dike to have been originally *Druidical*, and that the antient superstition of *Paganism* had been taken up by the saint, as the readiest method of making a conquest over the minds of the inhabitants. A stump of a tree is shewn as an altar, probably the memorial of one of stone; but the curiosity of the place is the well of the saint; of power unspeakable in cases of lunacy. The patient is brought into the sacred island, is made to kneel before the altar, where his attendants leave an offering in money: he is then brought to the well, and sips some of the holy water: a second offering is made; that done, he is thrice dipped in the lake; and the same operation is repeated every day for some weeks: and it often happens, by natural causes, the patient receives relief, of which the saint receives the credit. I must add, that the visitants draw from the state of the well an omen of the disposition of *St Maree*: if his well is full they suppose he will be propitious; if not, they proceed in their operations with fears and doubts: but let the event be what it will, he is held in high esteem: the common oath of the country is, by his name: if a traveller passes by any of his resting-places, they never neglect to leave an offering; but the saint is so moderate as not to put him to any expence: a stone, a stick, a bit of rag contents him.

This is the most beautiful of the isles; the others have only a few trees sprinkled over their surface.

‖ AUGUST 3. Ride about six miles South, and reach *Gairloch*; consisting of a few scattered houses, on a fine bay of the same name. Breakfast at *Flowerdale*; a good house, beautifully seated beneath hills finely wooded. This is the seat of Sir *Hector Mackenzie*, whose ancestor received a writ of fire and sword against the antient rebellious owners: he succeeded in his commission and received their lands for his pains.

The parish of *Gair-loch* is very extensive, and the number of inhabitants evidently encrease, owing to the simple method of life, and the convenience they have of drawing a support from the fishery. If a young man is possessed of a herring-net, a hand-line, and three or four cows, he immediately thinks himself able to support a family, and marries. The present number of souls are about two thousand eight hundred.

Herrings offer themselves in shoals from *June* to *January*: cod-fish abound on the great sand-bank, one corner of which reaches to this bay, and is supposed to extend as far as *Cape Wrath*; and South, as low as *Rona*, off *Skie*; with various branches all swarming with cod and ling. The fishery is carried on with long-lines, begins in *February* and ends in *April*. The annual capture is uncertain, from five to twenty-seven thousand. The natives at present labor under some oppressions, which might be easily removed, to the great advancement of this commerce. At present the fish are sold to some merchants from *Campbeltown*, who contract for them at two-pence farthing a-piece, after being cured and dried in the sun. The merchants take only those that measure eighteen inches from the gills to the setting on of the tail; and oblige the people to let them have two for one of all that are beneath that length. The fish are sent to *Bilboa*; ling has also been carried there, but was rejected by the *Spaniards*. This trade is far from being pushed to its full extent; is monopolized, and the poor fishers obliged to sell their fish at half the price to those who sell it to the merchants.

‖ AUGUST 6. Weigh anchor at eight o'clock in the morning,

and turn out with wind and tide adverse. After a struggle of three or four miles, put into *Loch-Jurn*, or the lake of hell, on the *Inverness* coast, and anchor about two o'clock near a little isle on the South side, four miles within the mouth. Land on the North side, three miles distant from our ship, and visit Mr *Macleod*, of *Arnisdale*. I shall never forget the hospitality of the house: before I could utter a denial, three glasses of rum, cordialized with jelly of bilberries, were poured into me by the irresistable hand of good Madam *Macleod*. Messrs *Lightfoot* and *Stuart* sallied out in high spirits to botanize: I descended to my boat, to make the voyage of the lake.

Steer S. East. After a small space the water widens into a large bay, bending to the South, which bears the name of *Barrisdale*: turn suddenly to the East, and pass through a very narrow strait, with several little isles on the outside; the water of a great depth, and the tide violent. For four miles before us the loch was strait, but of an oval form; then suddenly contracts a second time. Beyond that was another reach, and an instantaneous and agreeable view of a great fleet of busses, and all the busy apparatus of the herring fishery; with multitudes of little occasional hovels and tents on the shore, for the accomodation of the crews, and of the country people, who resort here at this season to take and sell herrings to the strangers. An unexpected sight, at the distance of thirteen miles from the sea, amidst the wildest scene in nature.

A little farther the loch suddenly turns due South, and has a very narrow inlet to a third reach: this strait is so narrow as to be fordable at the ebb of spring-tides; yet has within the depth of ten and seventy fathom; the length is about a mile, the breadth a quarter. About seven years ago it was so filled with herrings, that had crowded in, that the boats could not force their way, and thousands lay dead on the ebb.

The scenery that surrounds the whole of this lake has an *Alpine* wildness and magnificence; the hills of an enormous height, and for the most part cloathed with extensive forests of oak and birch, often to the very summits. In many places are extensive tracts of open space, verdant, and only varied with a few trees scattered over them: amidst the thickest woods aspire vast grey rocks, a noble contrast! nor are the lofty headlands a less embellishment; for through the trees that wave on their summit, is an awful sight of sky, and spiring summits of vast mountains.

On the South side, or the country of *Knoydart*, are vast numbers of pines, scattered among the other trees, and multitudes of young ones springing up. A conflagration had many years ago destroyed a fine forest; a loss which in a little time, it is to be hoped, will be repaired. Besides this, I can add some other pine forests to my former list: that near *Loch-maree*, *Abernethy*, and *Rothy-murchu*; both belonging to gentlemen of the name of *Grant*; *Glen-more*, the Duke of *Gordon's*; and *Glen-taner*, the property of Lord *Aboyne*. Our old botanists are silent about these British productions, till the time of Mr *Evelyn* and Mr *Ray*. This species of pine seems not to have been cultivated in *England*, till the former, as he says, received some seeds from that unhappy person, the late Marquis of *Argyle*: but *Speed*, in his chronicle, mentions the vast size of those on the banks of *Loch-Argicke*, and their fitness for masts, as appeared by the report from Commissioners sent there for that purpose, in the time of *James* VI. *Taylor*, the water-poet, speaks in high terms of those in *Brae-mar*, 'That there are as many as will serve to the end of the world, for all the shippes, carracks, hoyes, galleys, boates, drumlers, barkes and water craftes, that are now in the world, or can be these forty years.'

‖ In our return from the extremity of this sequestered spot, am most agreeably amused with meeting at least a hundred boats, rowing to the place we were leaving, to lay their nets; while the persons on shore were busied in lighting fires, and preparing a repast for their companions, against their return from their toilsome work.

So unexpected a prospect of the busy haunt of men and ships in this wild and romantic tract, afforded this agreeable reflection: that there is no part of our dominions so remote, so inhospitable, and so unprofitable, as to deny employ and livelihood to thousands; and that there are no parts so polished, so improved, and so fertile, but which must stoop to receive advantage from the dreary spots they so affectedly despise; and must be obliged to acknowledge the mutual dependency of part on part, howsoever remotely placed, and howsoever different in modes and manner of living.

|| Return to *Arnisdale*, and pass a most chearful evening. Mr *Lightfoot* returned happy in having found the *azalea procumbens*: Mr *Stuart* loaden with fine specimens of *amianthus* and black tale.

Return on board at midnight: the night most excessive dark; but every stroke of our oars, every progressive motion of our boat, flung a most resplendent glory around, and left so long and luminous a train in our wake, as more than compensated the want of stars in the firmament. This appearance was occasioned by myriads of noctilucous *Nereids*, that inhabit the ocean, and on every agitation become at certain times apparent, and often remain sticking to the oars, and, like glow-worms, give a fine light. Mr *Thompson* informed us, that they were most brilliant before rain and tempests. He was not deceived in his predictions.

There is not an instance of any country having made so sudden a change in its morals as this I have just visited, and the vast tract intervening between these coasts and Loch-ness. Security and civilization possess every part; yet thirty years have not elapsed since the whole was a den of thieves, of the most extraordinary kind. They conducted their plundering excursions with the utmost policy, and reduced the whole art of theft into a regular system. From habit it lost all the appearance of criminality: they considered it as laboring in their vocation; and when a party was formed for any expedition against their neighbor's property, they and their friends prayed as earnestly to heaven for success, as if they were engaged in the most laudable design.

The constant petition at grace of the old highland chieftains, was delivered with great fervor, in these terms: 'Lord! *Turn the world upside down, that christians may make bread out of it.*' The plain *English* of this pious request was, That the world might become, for their benefit, a scene of rapine and confusion.

They paid a sacred regard to their oath; but as superstition must, among a set of *Banditi*, infallibly supersede piety; each, like the distinct casts of *Indians*, had his particular object of veneration: one would swear upon his *dirk*, and dread the penalty of perjury; yet make no scruple of forswearing himself upon the bible: a second would pay the same respect to the name of his chieftain: a third again would be most religiously bound by the sacred book: and a fourth, regard none of the three, and be credited only if he swore by his crucifix. It was always necessary to discover the inclination of the person, before you put him to the test: if the object of his veneration was mistaken, the oath was of no signification.

The greatest robbers were used to preserve hospitality to those that came to their houses, and, like the wild *Arabs*, observed the strictest honor towards their guests, or those that put implicit confidence in them. The *Kennedies*, two common thieves, took the young Pretender under protection, and kept him with faith inviolate, notwithstanding they knew an immense reward was offered for his head. They often robbed for his support, and to supply him with linen they once surprized the baggage horses of one of our general officers. They often went in disguise to *Inverness* to buy provisions for him. At length, a very considerable time after, one of these poor fellows, who had virtue to resist the temptation of thirty thousand pounds, was hanged for stealing a cow, value thirty shillings.

The greatest crime among these felons was that of infidelity among themselves: the criminal underwent a summary trial and, if convicted, never missed of a capital punishment. The chieftain had his officers, and different departments of government; he had his judge, to whom he entrusted the decision of all civil disputes: but in criminal causes the chief, assisted perhaps by some favorites, always undertook the process.

The principal men of his family, or his officers, formed his council; where every thing was debated respecting their expeditions. Eloquence was held in great esteem among them for by that they could sometimes work on their chieftain to change his opinion; for, notwithstanding he kept the form of a council, he always reserved the decisive vote in himself.

When one man had a clame on another, but wanted power to make it good, it was held lawful for him to steal from his debtor as many cattle as would satisfy his demand, provided he sent notice (as soon as he got out of reach of pursuit) that he had them, and would return them, provided satisfaction was made on a certain day agreed on.

When a *creach* or great expedition had been made against distant herds, the owners, as soon as discovery was made, rose in arms, and with all their friends made instant pursuit, tracing the cattle by their track for perhaps scores of miles. Their nicety in distinguishing that of their cattle from those that were only casually wandering, or driven, was amazingly sagacious. As soon as they arrived on an estate where the track was lost, they immediately attacked the proprietor, and would oblige him to recover the track from his land forwards, or to make good the loss they had sustained. This custom had the force of law, which gave to the Highlanders this surprizing skill in the art of tracking.

It has been observed before, that to steal, rob and plunder with dexterity, was esteemed as the highest act of heroism. The feuds between the great families was one great cause. There was not a chieftain but that kept, in some remote valley in the depth of woods and rocks, whole tribes of thieves in readiness to let loose against his neighbors; when, from some public or private reason, he did not judge it expedient to resent openly any real or imaginary affront. From this motive the greater chieftain-robbers always supported the lesser, and encouraged no sort of improvement on their estates but what promoted rapine.

‖ August 12. Arrive in the beautiful bay of *Ard-maddie*, or the height of the *Wolves*. A house small, but elegant, stands in front, and the sides of the bay high, entirely cloathed with wood. Here I find the kindest welcome from my worthy acquaintance, Captain *Archibald Campbel*, tenant here to the Earl of *Breadalbane*; who, with the utmost friendship, during the voyage charged himself with the care of my groom and my horses. Here I also took leave of Mr *Archibald Thompson*; whose attention to the objects of my enquiries, obliging conduct throughout, and skill in his profession, demand my warmest acknowledgements. Thus ended this voyage of amusement, successful and satisfactory in every part, unless where embittered with reflections on the sufferings of my fellow-creatures. Gratitude forbids my silence respecting the kind reception I universally met with; or the active zeal of everyone to facilitate my pursuits; or their liberal communication of every species of information, useful or entertaining.

THOMAS THORNTON

Thomas Thornton was born in London in 1757, and was educated at Charterhouse and Glasgow University. His father, William Thornton of Thornville Royal (now Stourton) in Yorkshire, was for some years a Member of Parliament. In 1745 he raised a troop of volunteers, and was present at the Battle of Falkirk. Thomas Thornton succeeded to the estate in 1769, and some years later was appointed colonel of his father's old regiment, the West Riding militia. He resigned this position 'in disgust' in 1795, after being court-martialled and publicly reprimanded for having his soldiers draw him into camp in a triumphal carriage.

Thornton visited France prior to the Revolution, and returned to that country in 1802 with the intention of purchasing an estate there, but legal difficulties and then impending war frustrated his plan. During this visit, however, he was introduced to Napoleon, to whom he presented a pair of pistols, and he joined some French hunting parties. These experiences resulted in a book, *A Sporting Tour in France*, published in 1806. In 1805 he sold Thornville Royal to Lord Stourton, and lived in a succession of places in England. In the autumn of 1814 he landed in France, accompanied by a party of sportsmen and a pack of hounds, and is reported to have attracted 'a crowd of spectators' at Rouen. He soon returned to London, but after Waterloo went once more to France, hired the Château de Chambord, and purchased an estate at Pont-sur-Seine. On the strength of this he styled himself Prince de Chambord and Marquis de Pont. In 1821 he sold his estate, and latterly lived in lodgings in Paris, where he died in 1823.

Thornton is stated to have been twice married, but it is not clear that the first 'Mrs Thornton' was his legal wife. By his second wife he had a son, but by a will of 1818 he left almost all his property to Thornvillia Diana Thornton, his illegitimate daughter. His widow disputed the will on behalf of her son, and its validity was not upheld.

A man of very considerable wealth and of eccentric independence of mind, Thornton was a Whig, a Franco-phile, an admirer of women, a showman, and above all a sportsman. His sporting tour in the Highlands is supposed to have been undertaken in 1786, but in fact he seems to have been in Scotland almost every summer from 1782 to 1789. As has been pointed out by Michael Brander,[1] his *Tour*, not published until 1804, is a conflation of several expeditions to the Highlands and is chronologically and geographically confusing. Some of it may well have been written shortly before publication, and there are passages copied from both Pennant and Newte.[2] It was commented upon in not very favourable terms by Scott in the *Edinburgh Review*, and has been re-published only once, in Sir Herbert Maxwell's 'Sporting Library' in 1896. Nevertheless, Thornton provides for the most part a highly original picture of Speyside in the 1780s. He found a sportsman's paradise, and his narrative is as personal and vivid as many of the other eighteenth century tours to the Highlands are conventional and dull.

---

[1] Michael Brander, *Soho for the Colonel* (London 1961).
[2] Thomas Newte, *Tour in England and Scotland* (London 1791).

Thornton : 1804

JULY 3. Mr P(arkhurst)[1] having recovered from his fatigue, we trotted on briskly, not at all satiated with a succession of similar scenery, and arrived at Tarbat.

It has always been a rule with me, to defer giving my opinion of an inn till I have examined the most useful part, I mean the *inside*. The rooms here were small indeed, but they were clean, and we wanted nothing more: better linen I never saw, and every attention was shown us that the most finical traveller could wish for.

Having told the servant to get what the house afforded for supper, and it being only a little turned of six o'clock, we again strolled out. Mr Gerrard took the road for *Inverary*, in order to see Loch Long. Mr P. and myself, not cloyed with our day's sport, enquired where a boat could be procured, in which we might troll on the edge of the lake, in some safe harbour. We were soon shown a boatman's house, the master of which was at a *whisky shop*, they said, hard by. I quickly, therefore, adjusted my tackle, for we found it inconvenient to troll with two rods, as the snaps were continually catching each other; and, having taken out my hooks, and fastened on my bait, the proprietor of the boat made his appearance. I thought him *drunk*, but he walked pretty steadily, and, having got on board his vessel, which lay in a rivulet that ran into the lake, I followed him, and, jumping in, alighted on some faggots or hurdles, and found myself pretty handsomely splashed with the water, which they covered at the bottom of the boat. Mr P. followed more cautiously.

I was now adjusting my famous rod, and finding the boatman, a man apparently turned of seventy, very officious and trouble-some, and jumping about like a school-boy, I cautioned him to

[1] A gentleman who had accompanied the colonel from London. A.J.Y.

take care, and not come near the rod, and desired Mr P. to
attend to him, for there remained no doubt of his inebriety.
In spite of all my admonitions, and Mr P.'s vigilance, the old
gentleman, nevertheless, jumped upon the fourth piece of the
rod, and broke it. I think I was never so much mortified.
Without being a warm man, it would have been excusable to
have thrown him overboard, and have given him a good
ducking. Mr P. was more out of humour, if possible, than
myself: we soon, however, softened each other, and, looking at
the boatman, and his vessel very much resembling a condemned
west-country barge, and the furious tempest that blew on
the lake, readily acknowledged the accident an intervention
of Providence, and left the old gentleman not a little disappointed at the loss of the *siller* he had expected, and of the
different libations it would have afforded him of his favourite
whiskey.

‖ JULY 4. Day sultry . . .

‖ Arrived at *Glen Falloch*: inn very bad; here we took leave,
with regret, of our delightful companion, Loch Lomond; and,
passing through a pleasant vale, the pasturage incomparable,
as it had been for many miles, we proceeded for Cree in La
Roche,[1] over the most horrid country imaginable, and a still
worse road. A few struggling fir-trees, from their scarcity and
stinted appearance, gave a stronger idea of the wretched
poverty of this country than the total want of them would have
done.

At *Cree in La Roche* we dined, or rather attempted it; and Mr
Gerrard, from the meanness of the inn, had really rode past it,
but, conceiving this very possible to happen, I hailed him,
having kept a sharp look out for that purpose. He was all
astonishment; but uncomfortable as the house was, we found
good eggs, fresh barley bannocks, and tolerable porter, together
with some smoked salmon, which *Bruce* dressed; and, on the
whole, we did as well as we could; drank some good brandy
and water, and I, getting my tackle ready, fell to fishing, in the
river *Dochart*, which runs below Cree in La Roche, while the
horses were baiting after this severe stage.

[1] Presumably Crianlarich, near Loch Dochart. A.J.Y.

Yorke Cascade, near Blair Atholl

Roebuck; and White Hare.
'The roebuck is the most timid and innocent of all animals'

|| Though I have remarked, that the Highland roads, in general, are tolerably good, and do honour to the projectors, I must mention this stage as an exception. The water courses are made, in the most extraordinary manner, like ditches of about two feet deep and two broad, no trap for *springs* could be better conducted; I had taken every precaution human nature could devise, to prevent the inconveniency I had suffered from fore springs, in my former expeditions, by taking them off; never conceiving that the hind ones, which had now gone above three thousand miles, totally unimpared, could suffer; but I was mistaken. One of them, with a loud crash, gave way, and we were obliged to walk the remainder of the stage, to save the other. The road, in other respects, I mean for cavalry, is not bad.

We entered Killin about nine o'clock, passing over a bridge, from whence we saw, by the faint glimmerings of the moon, some singularly-broken rocks over which the water breaking, had a very extraordinary and pleasing effect.

KILLIN. – Though the inn at Cree in La Roche is bad, the traveller is here amply recompensed, I never saw a better inn than that at Killin; Lord Breadalbane, much to his credit, having taken great pains to make it very commodious. The landlord I found had been a neighbour of mine; a lively, honest Yorkshireman, who had frequently hunted with my hounds, and knew me perfectly well, as did also his wife, a neat active woman, who soon got us every thing we could wish for. Her husband, however, thought it absolutely necessary to deafen my ears with repeated *tallyhoes*, which I could very easily have dispensed with; for, how pleasantly soever they may have sounded at hunts, when on Ascham bog, they had no great music in them at Killin.

|| *Head of Loch Tay*, JULY 5. Day delightful. Having engaged our boatman, and prepared everything necessary for sailing down the charming Loch Tay, we took a short walk, before breakfast, to view the country around, and again gratified our curiosity, in examining the appearance of the broken rocks, which had made such an impression on us on entering the town the night before. The bridge itself is very well, but the

rapid Lyon, dashing over these obstructions, has a wonderful effect.

‖ The views up and down the lake, as we passed, were very beautiful; and we had the additional pleasure to see the carriage and servants always in view, hanging, as it were, above us, and constantly within call, had we either found any inconvenience in the vessel, from the wind being too boisterous, of which, however, we had little apprehension, or had there been a dead calm, which we at first feared; but as we advanced, a very refreshing breeze came from *Ben More*, and, gently swelling our canvas, we glided on exactly at the rate which suited us for trolling.

‖ Landed, and came to the inn at Kenmore.

Our boatman being called in, we wished to know what would satisfy him, and, at the same time, meant to give a couple of shillings to a man he had brought with him, without any order from us; and both of them, as I have observed, had fared very well on board. Unwilling to give what might not be thought adequate, I consulted the landlord, whose opinion was, that three shillings for the boatmen, as they had been found in provisions, would be very handsome, and two to take him back and that I might give the attendant what I pleased.

On considering that we had hired two men at Loch Lomond on their own terms, at *eighteen-pence* a-day each, during our stay there, though we had given them four shillings, with their victuals; it appeared to me, as the wages of this part of the country were at six-pence a day, that five shillings to the boat man, allowing him to give his companion what he thought proper, would be at least sufficient; but, unwilling to disappoint even his most sordid expectations, I gave him what silver I had, which was nine shillings and six-pence; when, to my no small mortification, he was dissatisfied, and behaved very unhandsomely. I therefore recommend it to gentlemen to make a previous agreement with every countryman whose services they may want, but in particular with a Highlander: many of them have but one idea, which is, that an Englishman is a walking mint, and they are never satisfied, should you give, as I have often done, four times as much as the man would have had from an inhabitant for executing the same business. He will still be discontented, and say he expected double the money he received. I am sorry to say that I have found this disposition too general; and, I must confess, I have been so much mortified by their want of generosity, that I have employed them as seldom as possible. In England this unsatisfied temper is undoubtedly to be met with, but it is by no means so general. A man whom I employ to walk for hounds, and other articles I may want, has gone a journey of fifty-seven miles in one day, and his constant pay is three shillings and six-pence a day only, to find himself in everything. A Highlander would think himself well paid with less from an inhabitant, but would not be contented with more than double from a stranger. They really fancy no person understands the value of money but themselves.

‖ J u l y 8. The morning foreboding a very warm day, and knowing our intended route to Blair would produce some heavenly views, we quitted Invar,[1] after taking a comfortable, solid breakfast, to enable us to endure the day's fatigue, not intending to dine till late.

We soon came to the ferry, but were prevented from crossing for some time, by a number of wild-looking horses, and their owners, little less wild than themselves, who were waiting there for a passage. The servants claimed the right they supposed we had of crossing first, and made a considerable *hubbub;* but as it appeared to me, that, in crossing a public ferry, no other precedence could be claimed than priority of application, or, as it is usually styled, 'first come first served', I desired them to desist, and highly amused myself with seeing the embarkation.

The men pulled and hauled in their horses, accoutred, in general, not with bridles, but *branks*,[2] which, when the rider or conductor wishes to stop his steed, he pulls, and, consequently, pinches the animal by the nose. This effect happening, I presume, to several of the *shelties* at the same time, a great confusion ensued, attended with much kicking from men and horses, and more noise, for all were equally engaged. So

[1] Across the Tay from Dunkeld. A.J.Y.
[2] Two pieces of wood, through which a halter runs, generally made of twisted birch.

ridiculous a situation, without any great danger, created infinite laughter from those on shore. We thought the over-setting of the boat, at one time, impossible to be avoided, but it was prevented, fortunately, by three of the horses, who had extricated themselves from their drivers, leaping, like goats, into the river, and dragging one [man], more obstinate than the rest, with them. The first horse swam to the opposite shore; the rest followed. The Highlander, thus emerged, might have run the risk of being drowned, had not a friend caught him by the kilt, as he floated near the boat. He was hauled in, and the remainder of the cargo landed without farther trouble.

We embarked next, and landed very quietly, and, finding the road level, moved on at a good pace. The soil was here chiefly a reddish gravel, and the sides of the declivities nearly covered with very fine beds of broom.

FASCALLY. The situation of this place is extremely romantic, and had been admired by us some time before we reached it. A scene near the bridge is particularly fine; and I could not help wondering how it escaped Mr Pennant, for it is certainly far superior to his view. The road from hence to Blair we found excellent, running along the banks of the Gary; it extends, for a very considerable way, and was made entirely at the expence of Lord Breadalbane, who, to facilitate the travelling, has erected, over the torrents that rush from the mountains into the lakes, a great number of stone bridges; Mr Pennant says, as many as *thirty-two*; but I did not count them.

Having arrived at the inn, which we found tolerably com-fortable, and dispatched a hasty dinner, we walked towards the castle . . .

The house itself rather deceived our expectations, with respect to its internal embellishments, though it is certainly very commodious. The walls are wonderfully thick, as all old castles are, but have been much reduced in height since the rebellion in 1746, when it was strongly fortified, and held out a close siege. I have heard many circumstances of this event when conversing with Mr C. a lieutenant, who attended my father's volunteers in the year 1745. This gentleman was taken prisoner by the rebels besieging this castle, by whom, being neglected, he with some others escaped and joined Sir Andrew Agnew, then blocked up in it with his troops, and has often mentioned the great spirit with which it was defended.

I remember to have heard him say, that, in order to save a favourite horse they had taken in with them, grass was pulled from the ramparts, where it grew in some quantity, and though the men, so employed, were frequently in danger of being shot, and very often fired at, they carried their point.

The most singular piece of furniture here is a chest of drawers made of broom, most elegantly striped in veins of white and brown. This plant grows to a great size in Scotland, and furnishes pieces of the breadth of six inches. We saw several guns belonging to his grace, chiefly rifles, which, we thought, in general, too unwieldy.

JULY 9. Morning delightful but very cold.

|| The *Falls of Brewer* are superior to Pennant's boasted York Cascade. Had he seen this, I am confident he never would have mentioned the other.

|| Set out the following morning at eleven, with the intention of killing some snipes, the servants, with our fishing-tackle, provisions, liquors, etc. following. Fished, and killed some very fine trout; but they did not rise eagerly. Attempted, though near three o'clock, to go to a famous lake, a Scotch mile further. Arrived here, and killed some fish; but they were little superior in size to the former, and, in quantity, inferior. We lost, by this means, a good deal of time, but killed, on our return, thirty trout and one char. One trout I saw coming at me, which I think might weigh five pounds, or thereabouts; but could not rise him.

Had not the evening foreboded rain, which now began to fall, I think I could easily have killed three dozen more, as they now began to rise freely; but were obliged to pack up our tackle, and return to the *auberge*, where we arrived about eight o'clock, and found dinner just ready; and, to give an idea how we starve in the Highlands, take the following table:

Hodge podge,
pudding, . . . greens,
trout and char,

roast mutton, excellent.

SECOND COURSE

Brandered chickens,

cold hams,

snipes,

Cheshire cheese . . . biscuits.

WINES.

Claret, good . . . Port, ditto,

limes, Jamaica rum, and

incomparable *porter* from *Calvert's*.

|| JULY 19. Morning fine, afternoon showery. Went to church, where I found a much thinner audience than I had ever remembered, and, conversing upon this subject with the Rothemurcos, and other gentlemen of the neighbourhood, they informed me, that the spirit of emigration had seized the people of these parts, and that many handicraftsmen and others, whose services I much wanted, had actually left the country. My shoemaker and carpenter were both gone, and with them many more: this fully accounted for the thin congregation.

The evening proved very tempestuous, and every persuasion was made use of by me, to induce my visitors, the Laird of Rothemurcos and Mr Cuming, to take such beds as I could give them, and to stay at Raits[1] till the morning, but without success; and these gentlemen, having fortified themselves with a few bottles of claret and a dram, which, in the Highlands, is thought necessary to keep out the cold, set off in defiance of the weather. I felt much for them, as they must have had a very unpleasant ride.

|| JULY 21. Day cold. I wished that Mr W. should see a roebuck before he left the country; but, though there were several in the neighbourhood, it was impossible to get a shot at one, on such short notice, and he had resolved to leave us this day. I thought, therefore, the following deception might answer every purpose. I had ordered a goat, as nearly the colour of a roebuck as possible, to be procured the night before from the mountains where they then were, directing the falconers to

[1] Thornton thus refers to the house at which he stayed. It was presumably near Raitts Burn, two miles east of Kingussie. A.J.Y.

place and tether him in the most inaccessible, obscure, and wild situation imaginable; which was done accordingly. The conversation, during supper, we had intentionally turned upon stags, roebucks, etc. till Mr W.'s imagination became so heated, that no doubt he dreamt, in the night, of nothing else.

We now sat down to breakfast, when, as privately agreed on, we received intelligence, that the herdsman had seen, early that morning, a roe and a roebuck among the rocks. The company were all eager to pursue them, and the rifles being prepared and loaded by me (as knowing the proper charge), some with powder and double wadding, others with ball only, which were, in the presence of Mr W. rammed down; every person, for fear of accident, had his post alloted him. Mr W. in compliment, as a stranger, and on the point of quitting us, was attended by the falconer, as the most intelligent person, with *Otter*, the deer dog, in a slip, and Mr Gerrard, whose curiosity was also not a little heightened. Thus they proceeded, being repeatedly cautioned, that, as their game was remarkable for quickness of sight and hearing, they must be prepared to fire immediately. After great care, seldom speaking, and never but in whispers, and making signs, on passing by some very likely places, the falconer pretended he heard a rustling; upon which, as they had been directed, the party fell flat upon the ground, cautiously crawling on; when Mr W. seeing an animal, and concluding it to be the game he so ardently sought for, judiciously and precipitately fired. From the struggle made by the animal, occasioned by the report, with which he was unacquainted, Mr W. imagining he had desperately wounded him, flew to seize him, but was repulsed by some strong and well-directed efforts of the goat's horns: this obliged him to call out loudly for the assistance of Otter, who, being slipped, rushed forward, but, in his hurry, did not discover the animal he was to attack, which was now almost covered and entangled in some strong junipers; but he soon came about, and, being properly fixed, he and Mr W. seized on their antagonist with great avidity, who soon ought to have convinced them, by his language, that the roebuck in question was unfortunately only a shaven goat.

Capt Waller and myself, who were standing on a very

dangerous precipice, at a considerable distance, might have paid dear for this joke, for I nearly fell off the rock, overcome with a fit of laughter, which this truly-comic and well-executed scheme had occasioned.

Mr W. for some time could not tell what to make of it, when he was complimented, in a strain of irony, on his great good fortune, etc. The jokes that went round, however, he bore with a pleasantry of temper so great and peculiar to himself, that, in the end, it totally disarmed the satirical remarks of the company: after dinner he was obliged to leave us, and we very much regretted the loss of his company, more especially as the weather during his stay had been so unfavourable for a keen sportsman in the midst of game.

‖ JULY 26. Day charming. Went to some lochs, which proved to be the lower *Guiacks*,[1] said to be six miles off, but turned out ten.

‖ The day was too calm; my guide and the herdsman, pretending they were good fishers; in this country they pretend to everything; I got my tackle adjusted, and fishing very fine, killed twenty-seven good trout; and, if I had had the boat in order, for there is one belonging to his Grace of Gordon, I might have killed one hundred.

‖ Saw the skeleton and jaws of a trout, destroyed, as I suppose, by an otter, which, at least, must have been ten pounds weight. Dined on the side of this beautiful sheet of water, as luxuriously as ever I did at Weltgie's or Letelliers.

On the top of these mountains, to the south, is what is called the Forest of Guiack, the property of his Grace of Gordon; and before it was disforested, six or seven years ago, four hundred head of deer might be seen at a time.

On my return to Raits, killed three grey plover: the hawks, were flown twice, and succeeded, and we found that *Claret* (procured as an addition to the pointers I had, and brought to Raits with infinite care and trouble) was really good for nothing, and though much pains were taken to reclaim him, he proved of no use.

[1] This may be a reference to Loch Gynack, one mile north of Kingussie. A.J.Y.

Returns of the day, twenty-seven trout, three grey plover, two snipes.

‖ AUGUST 7. *Loch Neiland*[1] is a most enchanting spot; the lake itself is not large, when compared with those we had already passed and explored; but every turn presents a fresh beauty. On the water stands an old castle, now in ruins, whose walls are, at least, eleven feet thick, and partly covered with ivy: these, with one or two old wild ash-trees, whose weather-beaten trunks resist, with all their force, the different blasts which, in time, must precipitate them into the lake, give additional lustre to this *coup d'oeil*. Nearly one half of this sheet of water to the north is bounded by some very fine, short, tender pasturage, and girded by an irregular wood of weeping birches, here and there exhibiting views of beautiful rocks, vieing with each other in the singularity of their shapes, and the natural elegance of their contrasted shades.

To the west is seen, over some plain, but rising, moors, the great mountains above Raits, amongst which will be easily distinguished the beautiful Croke Franc.[2]

To the south are discerned some very lofty, perpendicular mountains, rising directly out of an immense forest of the finest pines; and, to add to the wildness of this romantic scene, innumerable trees, of a prodigious size, appear torn up by the roots, in the strangest manner: this has been caused by the violence of the preceding winter's hurricane, from which my friend, Mr G. the proprietor, assures me, that he suffered a loss, amounting nearly to one thousand pounds.

To the north is a forest composed of firs and junipers, and filled with roebucks and stags, whose foliage may well be said, by its thickness, to be

> *Impenetrabile nullo astro . . .*

as is the delightful *Glenmore*, where, I believe, the trees are still larger than in Rothemurcos forest.

Trolled the lake, and killed thirteen fine pike.

‖ AUGUST 14. Day charming; went to church, and heard a very well-delivered sermon from Mr Anderson. This gentleman,

---

[1] This seems to be a shocking anglicisation of Loch an Eilein. A.J.Y.
[2] Probably Cnoc Fraing, five miles north of Kincraig. A.J.Y.

though a Lowlander, by absolute perseverance, has taught
himself the Erse language, in which he preaches a sermon, after
delivering one in English.

It appeared to me, that the men came here to eat tobacco,
and the women to sleep. I may venture to affirm, that a tax on
sleeping females at church would bring in, from this parish, a
pretty revenue.

‖ AUGUST 23. In the morning we found the wind as high
as the day before, which made me give up all thoughts of fishing.

Our plan for the day was as follows: I proposed to ascend the
dreadfully high mountains, which almost overhang Aberarder,
threatening by their appearance of falling, total perdition to
the town; there I hoped to kill a whitish hare, and some other
specimens of game which abound; also imagined I might obtain
some good views and gather some botanical plants, or choice
flowers . . . Having supplied ourselves with a flask of rum,
another of lime-juice, and some oat-cakes and cheese, we
proceeded, Mr Gerrard, at my request, though he had never
fished with the fly, took the charge of a rod, as we meant in the
evening to come by Corgarderder, said to be as wild as Glen
Ennoch,[1] and to have a lake at the foot of it, so full of trout
that the accounts we received exceeded all credibility. However, five or six had been taken, with as many hooks and flies
at one throw by Dr M'Pherson.

We walked *fifteen* miles, in point of ground, and fatigue equal
to *twenty*: it took us above four hours, though we were all
perhaps, as good walkers as any in Britain; and we only saw
one brood of white game, which induced me to depart from my
regulation to oblige Mr Gerrard. The situation was tolerably
safe for the hawks, as it lay under the wind, whereas, on the top
it blew a hurricane. The falcon flew her bird well, and killed
and, now having committed one trespass, we grew hardened in
iniquity, and killed two brace with the Duchess and the Devil
who took to them very keenly.

At a distance, on the verge of these barren rocks, we saw four
large stags, and regretted that we had no rifle, nor my stag
hound, which I had left at Aberarder; for, if we had been

[1] Glen Einich. A.J.Y.

properly provided, we might soon have brought one to bay. As we proceeded, we met with several charming scenes, and got a view of the almost-unpassable road over the Coriarich; also discerned, at a distance, Ben Nevis, and other hills, whose names are not known, and whose northern sides are covered with quantities of snow-drifts. I saw several flocks of golden plover, and killed a brace and a half. At two o'clock we dined on our scanty fare, and drank our punch at a spring, said to be the coldest in the kingdom. Mr Gerrard descended from the precipice to draw and to fish. I promised to call for him on my return, and, the day being now fine, we tried several *corrys* under wind, and found plenty of ptarmigants, also one white hare: but, unfortunately, though very near, I could not get a shot at her.

The mist came on at six o'clock, which obliged us to make the best of our way home, though said to be only *four* miles, lest we should lose ourselves on these inhospitable rocks and mountains. Surely such a descent was hardly ever passed by man. I repeatedly thought I should have broken my neck; nor did I get down the first half mile in less than an hour and forty minutes, the loose stones continually falling almost every step I took: I must here observe that, however still the day or night may be, scarce an instant passes without stones being seen or heard falling around you; this, one might naturally conceive, would fill up the valley, but it does not so happen: probably, indeed, in heavy rains, they are swept into the lake below, which will thereby, in time, become wider and shallower.

We looked carefully about the lake for Mr Gerrard, and, not seeing him, concluded he was gone home; but it was the distance that deceived us; for, at length, we discerned him, reduced to about nineteen inches in stature, and barely perceptible. In coming up to him, I very narrowly escaped breaking my legs, or a more fatal accident; for, leaping on a stone, in order to cross a brook, my feet slipped in such a manner, that, had I not sprung in the air, I must have fallen on some fragments of rock beneath; as it was, I hurt myself very much. The herdsman, without shoes, walked unhurt, with his horny feet, to my utter astonishment, over the angular, sharp rocks, whilst my feet, though, from experience, I had ordered the strongest bear-soles to my shoes, were severely cut and bruised, and both my ankles mangled with the stones that repeatedly fell upon them.

Mr Gerrard, having finished his different sketches, amused himself with fishing; and, as a proof how much trout abounded in this lake, in less than an hour he killed between two and three dozen: an expert angler might certainly have killed double the number in the same time.

‖ DULNON CAMP. AUGUST 26. Awakened by the gabbling of moor-cocks (and a very extraordinary circumstance), the calling of partridges at four in the morning. Looked out of my canvass retreat, and found the day very inauspicious, cloudy, and likely for rain; turned into my cot, and got a comfortable nap; breakfasted at nine; all having had a pleasant night's rest, and perfectly pleased with our tents, which are really much superior for comfort to any I ever saw, and do credit to that very ingenious man, Mr Trotter, of Frith-Street, whom I may well recommend, for this business, to any sportsman. We breakfasted on some of Mr Cartone's best tea, excellent cream from my old landlady (I must here say that their butter and cream are as neatly kept, and as clean as any in the world, which was not the case when I was here before), some good eggs, marmalade and currant jelly, wheat bread, biscuits, etc. the latter very good, and brought from Leith. At ten it began to clear up, and became a very fine day, but rather a want of wind. Killed forty-one birds and a brace of snipes.

Returns; forty-one moor game, two snipes, thirty-nine trout. Shot at the tent door before breakfast two old moor cocks.

AUGUST 27. Day delightful.

‖ The game on these moors is innumerable. In a mile long, and not half a one broad, I saw at least one thousand brace of birds.

On the front of the encampment, not above one hundred yards beyond the brook, arose that beautifully-even, immense hill, called Croke Franc, whose sides had plenty of Moor game, and on whose summit were found *ptarmigants* and *cairvanes*, and where I once saw a species of fox nearly white.

This hill was totally preserved untouched for Messrs Serle and Parkhurst, affording excellent hawking, easily to be obtained by the one, and commodious shooting for the other.

On our left, about two miles, we got a partial peep at the beautiful forest of Dulnon,[1] in which are plenty of stags and roebucks, also black game on its edges.

Returns of the day: shot two moor-game, hawks killed nine, trout twenty-seven.

|| SEPTEMBER 4. The dogs, in the course of this day, got upon something, I could not tell what, which they footed a considerable way, and by the bristles rising on their backs, I plainly perceived it was not game, but vermine. Conceived it to be a wild cat, or martin, which in these moors abound, and should have been particularly pleased to have got a shot at it, but it escaped me.

The wild cats here are very large, nearly the bulk of a middling-sized fox, remarkably fierce, and very destructive to game and lambs. Their brush is nearly as thick as that of the fox.

Repaired to camp, not a little pleased with the prospect of the next day being fine.

Returns; shot twenty-nine, hawks eight; total, thirty-seven.

SEPTEMBER 5. Day rather cloudy. Wishing to avoid severe walking, being rather lame, was desirous to vary scene, and take a day or two of that famous fishing I had had a taste of in Lawson's Gulph. On our return to Raits, notwithstanding the rain, we got some few shots, and the weather afterwards clearing up, determined to proceed towards our ground.

About three miles from camp, followed a vale so choked up with junipers, rocks, and water, that it was with difficulty we could make any road, even on our moor ponies.

At eleven we got to our beat, and the instant the dogs were uncoupled, they stood: the brood flushing, I singled out the cock, and finding this brood of a very desirable size for the tercel, we gave up the shooting, and uncoupled the hawking dogs; and posting the servants and horses, Mr Gerrard and

[1] Dulnain, north of Kingussie. A.J.Y.

myself, attended by Crosly, flew the tercel, which killed a brac
handsomely.

I then disposed of the hawks as follows: – I went on about hal
a mile before them, down wind, so that any birds coming from
me might be easily marked by Mr Gerrard or Crosly, and i
wounded, they would as easily take them, which, added to it
answering their purpose, would be an act of mercy; for, to
allow a wounded bird to draw out a miserable existence, wher
it can be any way prevented, is surely brutal; and I trust tha
other gentlemen make it a constant rule never to allow, i
possible, a wounded bird to live. Many an hour's sport have
given up for that purpose.

I never was better pleased with my dogs, they behave
wonderfully; ground very mossy and bad, but game plentiful
shot with great success till one o'clock when rain came on, an
forced us to take shelter under a rock, where we refreshe
ourselves, and Mr Gerrard joined me with the hawks. Seein
no prospect, however, of the day's holding fine for any lengt
of time, we made towards home; my gun never hung fire, an
though muffled up, I now and then got a shot, and when
found a fair blink, we took an occasional flight. As our encamp
ment lay down the wind, this did not impede us; we got
handsome wetting, but had good sport, and came home to
comfortable fire in the bothee; all our apparatus, for change c
dress, etc. the servants grown expert by practice, had mad
thoroughly warm, and dinner being hastened, to our grea
satisfaction, was soon ready.

Returns; shot forty-two, hawks nine; total fifty-one.

‖ SEPTEMBER 12. Morning gentle, warm rain, but calm.

‖ After a long and luxurious breakfast on Cartone's tea, egg
etc, we got out before one, the day being then very fine, an
continuing so, we parted, each taking fresh ground, and M
Drighorn his best dogs.

Early in the day, I tried the goss-hawk at a wounded bir
but, just as I expected, she took to the soor and we lost her
indeed, I feared irrecoverably. While Crosly looked for her,
shot with indifferent success, accommodating my ground, nc
following the most likely for game, but to assist him, an act c

fellow feeling; for, to a sportman, I do not know a more dreadful punishment, than that of searching for a lost hawk, or for a pack of hounds after being thrown out. Matt came up to us, while at dinner, bringing the falcon; we flew her twice, and then sent her home, that Crosly might be less engaged; and on looking again for the goss-hawk, he soon returned, having recovered her.

Of game I found an immense quantity, and, I am convinced, I could have killed any number: indeed I never shot better, nor killed so many, all our nets and my ammunition pocket being crammed full. At last I drove in three broods among some large junipers, certainly the most capital and luxurious of all shooting; this tempted me to take a double shot, and I killed both. Humanity then cried stop, would you destroy the whole race? No. I slung my gun, and, contemplating, joined Crosly, who was looking again for the goss-hawk. I had thrown her out a wounded old moor-game cock, which she had not seen; I then threw her out a strong polt, which, to my surprise, she raked with ease, and carried it into the junipers. Though I had determined, on no account, to fire at any moorgame, and cautiously avoided disturbing them, by following the edge of the beautifully and now gently purling Dulnon; an unfortunate snipe got up, I could not resist, and killed it.

‖ SEPTEMBER 22. Day very pleasant; but too calm for roebuck shooting, which I intended to attempt at Glenmore and Rothemurcos, having sent to Mr Stewart, the Duke of Gordon's head forester, to meet me; which he did accordingly; and the wind getting up with the day, I dispatched two servants to the boat, with such refreshments and apparatus as I should want, particularly my pike-tackle, in case my other amusements should prove unsuccessful.

Proceeded, in order to meet the above gentleman, and, after he had joined us, we found a covey of partridges; flew the tercel, which soon killed a brace, and then, leaving the hawks with Mr Parkhurst, went on with Mr Stewart, and soon got into the most likely harbours for both stag and roebuck, and, if I could have gotten within a hundred yards of either, I looked upon myself as pretty secure of success, having set my rifle very exactly.

I am generally as quick sighted as most sportsmen; but could not now see a roebuck which was within fifteen yards of me. My companion, who was behind me, saw it, and touched me with his pole; but two large, bushy fir-trees, between me and the animal, intercepted my view; for, though I looked very attentively, I could not get the least glimpse of him. It seems he made one bound, and there was an end of my chance; though it can scarce be called a chance; for, by his account of the small distance, if I had been so fortunate to get sight of him, he must have died.

Our search having been tedious, and the day warm, we were tempted by the vast quantity of bley berries under our feet; and, sitting down, did not barely eat, but absolutely devoured this cooling, delicious fruit, which certainly is very innocent, or we must both have felt the effects of making so free with it.

Understanding that my prospect for roebuck was more certain at Dulnon, and not having a single day to spare, I relinquished my plan of sleeping at Glenmore; and, though now near seven o'clock, and my road ten miles through the forest, I determined to get to Avemore,[1] taking Mr Stewart part of the way, still trying for our game, as we went over ground the most likely I ever saw; but, not finding any, to oblige him, before we parted, I shot at a mark on a large stone at the distance of eighty yards, which I hit, to his astonishment, and, in some degree, to mine, though I knew I could hit a crownpiece at a greater distance, having done it frequently.

Got to our inn at Avemore about ten, to the great joy of Mr Parkhurst, who had been rather out of spirits, from being left alone. He gave me an account of some good flights; of his sport in shooting, and that he had seen a roebuck near Lawson's Gulph.

Returns; Mr Parkhurst shot five moor-game; hawks killed four; ditto eight partridges.

The house being full, I gave up my bed to a *lady*, happy to find, on farther enquiry, that this act of civility had been shown to Mrs . . . , a Yorkshire lady, with whom I had the pleasure of being acquainted: had the landlord, who is certainly a most

[1] Aviemore. A.J.Y.

Loch Einich, some miles south of Aviemore

Isle of Inchmerin, Loch Lomond; Colonel Thornton shooting duck

Loch Awe, dominated for centuries by the Campbells

Inveraray, the new town under construction
early in the nineteenth century

unfit man for his station, informed me that she was an English lady, or mentioned her name in time, I should easily have induced her, in such a retired place as this, to have waved that form, though necessary elsewhere, and have prevailed on her to favour us with her company at supper.

The intelligence of the lady's name came too late; but gave me an opportunity of requesting permission to pay my compliments to her in the morning. I received for answer, that she was indispensably obliged to set out early, but if I could breakfast at the Gothic hour of six, she should be glad of my company.

SEPTEMBER 23. Day most desirable for my pursuit. Got up by six o'clock, and, after breakfast, went towards camp, expecting the Laird of M'Intosh, for whom the hawks were kept hooded, and almost ruined for want of Mr P. and Captain M'Intosh to shoot; they soon, however, met me with the pointers; for I had no wish to mix mine with such lewd dogs as Highland pointers are, and we afterwards separated, each following his own plan: and, now having given my bullet-gun to one of my servants, and my shot-gun to another, I ordered them to take a pointer, *in utrumque paratus*, either for roebuck or black-game, and to proceed on the road, where I should soon overtake them on horseback.

Setting out soon after, I met with the fox-hunter of this district, who not only undertook to procure me the certainty of a shot at a roebuck, but very obligingly attended me.

I trotted on, and he followed me on foot, running as fast as my shooting poney could amble.

When we came to the place where I expected to meet the servants, no tidings whatever could be obtained concerning them. We tried another road, but in vain. We then ascended a high mountain, in order to see and be seen; and, though, we could perceive several people distinctly, we could not discern any thing of our party, who were easily to be distinguished by their number and their white dogs in a lease. After a fruitless search, I gave up the pursuit, and confess I felt the disappointment the more, as the getting a roebuck, which I much wanted Mr Gerrard to draw, seemed morally certain, with such a guide, if I had had my gun.

I now changed my plan, and leaving the fox-hunter, turned back towards Avemore, intending to dine with my worthy friends, the Rothemurcos. Met Mr Parkhurst, who had quitted his companion with the hawks. Took a few flights with him, then went home, dressed, and proceeded. In my way, was highly pleased with passing by, and admiring some immense piles of fir-planks, ready for floating down the river, with the first fresh in the water.

Received with a most hearty welcome, and sat down to an excellent dinner.

On my return to Avemore in the evening, I had no guide to cross the ford, having dismissed the man sent to conduct me, thinking I could find my way very well; but the difference between day and night, not having been this way before, gave me some trouble. At length, coming to the river, in order to try my mare, (which seemed to me to know perfectly well what she was about), I laid the reins on her neck, and leaving her totally to herself, she brought me, exactly by the same road we had come in the morning, safe to Avemore. . . .

Returns; Mr Parkhurst shot one moor-game, three partridges; Captain M'Intosh, three brace and a half; hawks, with the Laird of M'Intosh, three brace; Crosly killed eleven trout.

SEPTEMBER 24. Morning horrid: in a short time it rather appeared to improve; and, as everything was fixed for breaking up the encampment, and all the cavalry come up, to remove our apparatus, our dairy-maid and cows gone, we set out, that is to say, Lawson and myself, leaving the gentlemen and cavalry to come at their leisure. We soon got a complete ducking: my Highland friends got also pretty handsomely soused, nor were the cavalry and their attendants better off; the whole party were like so many drowned rats.

Had the honour of four gentlemen, and three very handsome ladies, to dine with me; one of the latter was the great *belle* of Badenoch, whom I have had occasion to mention before.

Miss A.M'P. is really a very healthy, fine girl, perfectly easy and affable; and, having introduced myself to her again here, in the Scotch way,[1] I found her less coy.

[1] That is by saluting, or, in plain English, kissing her.

Instituted a whist party, which was to continue whilst I remained here, the company spending the evening.

SEPTEMBER 25. Went out at eleven, and, to vary the scene, killed fourteen partridges full grown, and three brace of snipes; and as hawks' meat, the [hawks'] palate being glutted with game,[1] by way of a *bon bouche*, killed them a carrion and two magpies. Tercels, seven partridges.

Ordered some hounds to be thrown into the wood at Raits, and soon unkenneled a fox,[2] which was murdered; he had done much damage among the sheep; tried for some roebucks, roused a brace and a half, but not coming near me, or Jones, who had *Orson* (the deer hound) ready to slip, but taking soil, they swam to an island, and, the water being much out, did not get either a shot or a hound.

Lawson coming from Raits early, saw three roebucks near the house. Dined at Rothermurcos, and passed the evening. I went there in hopes of meeting his Grace of Gordon, and of giving him my thanks for the civilities shown me and my party; but some material business prevented him from coming.

Mr Grant of Rothemurcos has built a very commodious house, not in the best situation, though his table, etc. is the most enviable in the world, as is his estate. He was an acquaintance of mine when I was here before.

As a proof that his table is well served, I will only mention that he has added, to every other luxury, what few possess, viz. roebucks, cairvauns, hare, black game, dottrel, white game, partridges, ducks, and snipes; salmon, pike, trout, char, par, lampreys and eels, all of which are in abundance upon his estate.

Ate some uncommonly fine char, fresh caught, much superior to any I had ever tasted before; they were absolutely a lump of fat. These fish, when fresh, have a taste something similar to that of a herring; a large pot of them Mr Grant was pleased to order to be sent me.

SEPTEMBER 26. Day very calm. Rose early, intending to

[1] A variety of food, which in a state of nature they constantly are procuring, is absolutely necessary to keep up their appetite; the first requisite in hawks.
[2] Foxes are very numerous, and extremely destructive to lambs and kids.

proceed on my journey to Gordon Castle, but, imagining that Forres would be far enough for the horses, and having forwarded the gig, I amused myself a few hours in trolling Loch Alva, and had excellent sport, killing five pike, one of which weighed fifteen pounds, the rest from six to nine pounds. After breakfast set out for Grantown, over a dreary moor; the road good, and not very hilly, but encumbered by some exceeding large stones, or fragments of rocks in the centre, which ought to be blown up, being extremely dangerous at night to the traveller. Within three miles of Grantown, the scene becomes more interesting, from the magnificence of the large woods, chequered with hanging banks of birch, amongst which arises, overtopping the whole, Castle Grant.

This castle is a very large building, partly ancient, partly modern, and conveys an idea of the weight of the old feudal chieftains.

I had the satisfaction to pass some days here, when I was in this country many years since, and never enjoyed more hospitable conviviality. The late Sir L. Grant was then living, a jovial companion and a worthy man, much esteemed and respected on these accounts, as well as for adapting himself to the manners of the people with whom he lived.

I was astonished to observe how very much all ranks of people were changed in their manners in the course of ten or twelve years. Luxury and effeminacy have proportionably found their way hither, and through the facility of intercourse with the South, by means of the high military roads, have almost totally destroyed the power of the chieftains.

|| The inn at Grantown is very neat and clean, and so cheap a bill I scarcely ever met with. Rain came on instead of a moist mist, which had fallen when I alighted: however, I resolved to proceed for Forres, the road, from all the enquiries I had made, being reported to be excellent, and a gentle descent. I am sorry to say, however, that I found it, on the contrary, in many parts not only bad, but execrable – by far the very worst I ever travelled. In some places it is certainly very passable, but, in general, it is covered with a multiplicity of large, loose

stones, and the *runners*[1] are absolute destruction to any carriage, going even at a moderate pace. After leaving Sir James Grant's improvements, nothing either beautiful or luxurious is seen for many miles.

The moors, indeed, seem very even, and well adapted for shooting, which may be followed more conveniently here, on horseback, than in any place in Scotland.

‖ As I approached Forres, the road improved, and was crowded with numbers of the country people, both men and women, who adopt the Lowland fashions, the men not retaining the least mark of the Highland dress, which is entirely exploded, except the bonnet, and even that has here a different shape, not near so smart as the Highland; and in their persons they want that lively gait peculiar to a Highlander; nor are the women, in my opinion, better featured.

‖ On my entrance into Forres, found there was a fair, which accounted for the crowd I had met on the road; and, to their credit be it related, I did not see one person intoxicated. The inn I put up at was the Falcon, kept by Barnes, formerly a servant to the Duke of Gordon. I was shown into an extraordinary good room, and, having sent to request the favour of Bailie Forsyth's (my wine merchant) company, I ordered supper, and he passed the evening with me. A very well-served one it was, and I never slept in a more comfortable, plain bedchamber.

SEPTEMBER 27. Morning pleasant, and, in every respect, a very desirable harvest day. I rose early, and took a turn about the town, sending my carriage forward to Elgin. The land, in general, seemed to be in a high state of cultivation, and lets at from three pounds ten shillings to four pounds an acre; but, except close to the town, where its value is determined by conveniency, it is a light, sandy soil. I observed that the fields, to the south-east of the town, were neatly inclosed with good hedges. The town itself is very moderate: it is seated under some little hills, which are prettily divided: there is not any thing in it particularly worth seeing.

‖Proceeded for Elgin, the road most excellent for a horse, and though sandy, not bad for a carriage.

[1] Runner: a small stream. A.J.Y.

Elgin, a town about the size of Forres, has a few good houses in it, which are chiefly built over piazzas; it has little trade excepting its great cattle fairs, but is rich in ecclesiastical antiquities. The people here, as in all the little towns on this coast from Inverness, are employed in making thread and linen, as well as woollen cloth, chiefly for their own use. All these towns, Inverness, Nairn, Forres, and Elgin, have a very dismal appearance, being built of dark stone; nor can they claim the merit of being clean, and Elgin, in filthiness, exceeds them all.

‖ About two miles from Elgin there is a pretty view of the Frith of Murray to the left, and of several corn-fields to the right, some of which were in stook, and others cutting; but, I was sorry to observe, that the crops were stinted and grain small, so that in many parts, it apparently would scarcely pay for the labour of sowing or reaping. The farmers, grasping at too much, plough out more than they can manure and weed. If they would content themselves with fewer acres, and manage them well, I am confident they would find their account in it; but they will not easily be convinced of this.

‖ We came to the ford over our well-known friend the Spey, whom I was happy to see again: she was in good humour; but the strata of gravel and stones, seen for miles, sufficiently testified her powers when enraged. No river can be, at times, more calm, or more rapid than this; and really the ravages and destruction it makes on the Duke of Gordon's property would render it a serious evil, did it not afford sufficient compensation, in a fishery, now let at one thousand five hundred pounds per annum. The seals, or selks, as they are called here, do infinite mischief, by destroying great quantities of salmon.

‖ As the ford was said to be rather dangerous for strangers, I ordered the carriage to be sent over in the boat, and, walking up to some fishermen, who were trying for salmon, I was accosted by Colonel Maxwell, an old college friend, who politely accompanied me to the castle.

GORDON CASTLE. This prodigious, yet elegant, pile of building, stands near some large, well-grown woods, and a considerable one of great hollies. It stands rather low, by which it loses part of its grandeur; but great conveniency, no doubt, is found in its situation, during the cold, windy months.

|| The principal *façade*, to the east, is as magnificent as any in Britain, and the whole edifice is built of the most durable and beautiful stones I ever saw.

The inside is not yet quite finished, but a great number of workmen are employed, not only within the house, but in cultivating the lawn and grounds around it; and, when the whole of the extensive improvements are completed, it will be a most princely residence.

|| SEPTEMBER 29. It was near eleven before I left Castle Gordon, and the day having changed its appearance, I promised myself a pleasant journey, understanding that it was only twenty miles to Grantown, though I think the Book of Roads makes it thirty-five English. It turned very sultry, and, the first six miles being up hill, made it a severe pull; but my carriage horses were very fresh and pretty well in meat.

As there were many cross roads, I enquired my way as often as an opportunity offered; and, having literally gone what I conceived to be eight miles, I was positively assured that it was not four from Gordon Castle. I therefore began to be apprehensive, that, if the future sixteen miles were nearly in the same proportion, I could not possibly reach Grantown that evening, or at least not till very late; and I confess I have no particular *gusto* for travelling unknown, on Highland roads, in the dark. Thus circumstanced, I entertained some thoughts of fishing and amusing myself at the inn at Ballendalloch, and sleeping there; which, after five hours drive, I at length reached.

But for an inn, though I am not very easily distressed with bad accomodations, and as I have travelled where inns cannot be expected to be very capital, I never in my life saw such a one as this; it is really a perfect burlesque on the name: – a house with rooms, indeed, but no windows. I fancy the people, from their extreme poverty, had taken them out, as I observed many other more creditable persons had done, to save Mr Pitt's additional duty: which proves the folly of a heavy tax; for, when severely felt, it will always defeat itself, and be evaded.

I did not expect a sumptuous bill of fare, from the *coup d'oeil* of the place, but I hoped to find eggs: however, they had none. I was thirsty; I asked for porter – they had none; for brandy – they had none; for rum – they had none. This, to many travellers, would have been very distressing; to me, it was of no consequence, accustomed, from my mode of life, to enjoy, or to live without the luxuries, and, sometimes, even the comforts of life: and I have often, in similar situations, reflected on the advantage I had over most of my companions, who cannot exist without their dainties and side dishes; and, even having those, without a good bottle of Pontac,[1] they are still miserable.

However, I expected that my horses would fare pretty well, which was now my only concern; but hay – they had none: that, I thought, might be obviated, by a double portion of corn; but, alas! they had none. Thus I found myself in a charming situation, with the prospect of fifteen English miles to Grantown.

The landlord, indeed, lamented his inability to serve me in terms that softened me much; and, feeling for his unfortunate situation, I soon forgot my own. There was now no other resource but to proceed on my journey; I therefore ordered the carriage to be got ready, and to follow me, while I walked on.

Not far from the inn is a seat of General Grant. The reader may judge that I had no inclination to stop in so inhospitable a country. It appeared to me to be in a pleasant situation. The day was now far advanced – past five o'clock. Following the Spey, I saw some well-cultivated valleys, and a farm in excellent order, under the management, as I found, of Mr M'Gregor, who rents it of Sir James Grant. The state of cultivation every part of this farm appeared to be in, does him great credit. The Spey, I fancy, had received a small flush from the mountains, for I saw a young girl attempting to ford it from the opposite shore under the directions of another on this side of the river. Not seeing me, she made no ceremony, but came forward, till at last it proved so deep, that, had she got a glimpse of my carriage, which I had stopped (only to give my horses their wind) after a severe pull, I am apt to think she would have blushed for her situation. As I had not met above one or two

[1] Pontac: a sweet wine from Pontac in the Basses Pyrénées. A.J.Y.

persons for miles, the animation these females had given to the scenery, I felt with uncommon emotion. Farther on, perceiving two turns in the road, I asked a man, who seemed to be an intelligent person, which was the way to Grantown? He told me that one road led to the bridge over the Spey, and the other to the boat, at which place there was a ford, which he was certain was not deep. This road, which had been represented to me as impassable in a carriage, he likewise assured me, had been mended the week before, and made, in every respect, equal to the other. As I understood it was a mile and a half shorter, I took his advice, but crossed the river at random, for I saw neither boat nor boatmen, nor could any intelligence be had of them. We got across very well, but it was deep enough in all conscience, and followed our directions, but soon found we had been most grossly deceived by our guide, though not intentionally, for the road had the appearance of being newly mended, which exactly corresponded with his account, but though finished in part, the repair stopped short at a descent, and left a very steep fall of at least four feet, extremely dangerous to pass, overhanging a mill-rise on one side, and having, on the other, a bushy, steep bank: but there was no remedy, for it was scarcely possible to turn, otherwise I should certainly have attempted it, and recrossed the Spey, though so far about, to have gained the road by the bridge. Thus circumstanced, I found it necessary to exert my ingenuity, to overcome the difficulty we had got into, which I effected in the following manner: –

I saw a broad plank laid over the mill-rise, which we took up, and placed it in such a manner that one of the wheels should run down it; and the bank, being soft and sandy, we broke down; so that taking one of the horses out, by the servant's leading, and myself retarding the fall, we passed very safely.

We then quickened our pace as much as possible, fearing we should be benighted, and seeing two turnings, we took that we thought the most likely to lead to Grantown; but after travelling about a mile, we were again at a stand, for the road diminished to a horse-track, which obliged me to get on horseback, having been nearly overturned more than once. Riding on to explore the way, I was soon forced to return, and stop the farther progress of the servants, as it was totally impassable for a carriage, being only a sharp path on the side of a steep hill. We then attempted another road, and I flattered myself we should do very well; but our career was again checked, for it led only to a peat-moss.

It was now quite dark, and near eight o'clock: to leave the carriage, seemed, at first, the only plan, and to send people to watch it during the night; but as this would take up some time, I ordered the servants to return, and, if possible, to recross the Spey, at least to attempt it.

In the mean time I pursued my journey on the sharp path, and soon came into a very good road, when seeing a light, I rode up to it. I hallooed, but could obtain no answer, though I heard several people talking. It appeared to me to be a lime-kiln; but I was mistaken; in short I could not conceive what the fire could be made for.

Having asked for the right road, a boy was at last sent to direct me, for I had got quite out of it; and, looking back, I saw the fire moving, which made me enquire into the nature of this strange nocturnal party, and I found that they were poaching for salmon, by *blazing*. This they effect here in the following manner: – They run a net across the stream, and then going up it in a boat, they drive the salmon, which avoid the light, down into the net, having also a spear with which they occasionally strike the fish. By this mode many fish are killed at this time of the year, when they are black, out of season, and spawning; and the fisheries are thereby greatly injured. It would answer their purpose very well, if those who rent these fisheries would employ proper persons to detect and punish the offenders.

Getting now into the main road, I soon reached Grantown, where I had every thing very comfortably prepared for me, and servants sent off to assist mine, if necessary, in bringing on the carriage, which, however, arrived safe, without any further trouble.

|| OCTOBER 4. Morning most heavenly, and the country perfectly dry.

|| The carriage being obliged to wait for some iron work

mending, could not leave Avemore till past three o'clock; in the mean time Mr Mitchell, a very reputable gentleman farmer, calling on me, made me an offer of his house on the side of Loch Laggan, and gave me much reason to hope for excellent sport, both in fishing and shooting. I therefore determined, for a few hours, to proceed thither, keeping our dogs back till we had got on two miles, and were in view of the lake.

The dogs stood, and we got off. I killed some moor-game at one point: on my side one got up; I likewise shot him, and, while I was loading, a brace of old black-cocks rose. Mr M., who had long wished to kill one, had now a fine opportunity, but did not succeed, though an excellent shot: but in this, as in other things, an opportunity once neglected is never after regained.

Soon found some black-game. Lawson killed a brace, and myself one; but do what we could, though we saw numbers, could not get near any more.

The views on the sides of this enchanting lake, Loch Laggan, are far, very far superior to those of any lake I have seen; and, in fact, are beyond all that imagination can paint.

The quantity of hanging woods, some of a mile long, only divided by pendant rocks, or pleasant verdure, and many of them rising in the form of a sugar-loaf, whose tops seem supporting pillars to the clouds, which roll down the summit of these craggy mountains, gave the place a most heavenly appearance.

This lake is about nine miles long and one broad; alive with trout.

The trout here are four kinds, three of which I caught, differing both in colour and taste. The fourth kind, called the *duermain*, I did not catch. They are said to be very large, exceeding twenty pounds. I have heard, above double that weight; but Mr M. assured me, that he has taken them of sixteen pounds.

‖ The road from hence to Moy, where we were engaged to dine, is tolerable. Pass through the forest of Dulnon, and by a neat spot near the new bridge, (the former having been swept away, and the arch being stopt by a float of firs, improperly made, soon blew up the whole), we bid adieu to its charms, with that gratitude, which our having so innocently enjoyed ourselves in it, demanded.

|| Got to Moy about eight o'clock, and found the laird politely ready to receive us.

|| As Messrs M'Intoshes were just returned from the assizes at Inverness, I made particular enquiries, in the course of conversation, concerning the issue of the trial of Kennedy, one of the most daring fellows ever known in this or any other country.

This man having separated from his party, and intelligence being given to M'Kie, a very enterprising constable, who knew, by report, that he was the chief of a gang of robbers; he took him up, I apprehend, on very slight evidence, and he was confined in Inverness gaol.

It seems, when he was brought up for trial, the witnesses were so brow-beaten and threatened by his party, that they durst not appear; by which means he got off, though there is not the least doubt of his guilt; and the whole neighbourhood of Glengary are in continual fear for their lives and property. To such a degree of impudence does the gang carry its villany, that, by common consent, an action is likely to be brought against M'Kie for shooting at Kennedy, who was taken in the following manner:

They attempted to surround the house he was in, but, having got some intelligence of their design, he made his escape, and ran towards an adjoining wood; when M'Kie, not being able to overtake him, shot at him, wounded him, and thus secured him. The gang, however extraordinary it may appear, actually stole no less than between six and seven hundred sheep, in the year 1783, from Mr Butler, steward on the forfeited estate of Locheil. Glengary also has suffered materially.

The gang consists of from twelve to fifteen persons, and they live in the wilds of Glengary.

Returns; black game five.

OCTOBER 5. Morning delightful.

The laird's family do not rise with the lark, but take a comfortable nap; I therefore amused myself, by ordering the nets to be cast into the lake, to try for some char, and we caught a few, very fine; from one of which Mr Gerrard made a beautiful drawing, which was intended to be engraved, but as the colouring is the chief beauty in a char, and as that, together with many other drawings, however desirable, would enhance the price of the work too much, the intention was dropt.

I now adjusted my bullet-gun, by which time the company came down stairs; and at twelve I went out, intending to try for a roebuck, which were said to be more plentiful and better preserved on this estate than in any part of Scotland.

I confess my patience had been so much tried before, that, though I proceeded, I thought my prospect of success very small; but I took all imaginable pains, and saw one, or a brace; yet they were so deep in cover, and sprang so quick, that my eye could scarcely follow them. Determined to go after black game, but, still desirous of succeeding, took one cast more, and got the glimpse of another, at which I shot, and seeing one bound from the place, feared he was only slightly wounded, for I was certain I had not missed him. Reloaded, intending to follow him; when coming up to the rocky, but bushy, ground he was on, found him dead, being shot through the heart, and ordered the Highlander, who was with me, to take him home, after I had thoroughly examined him.

The roebuck is the most timid and innocent of all animals, and about the size of a common two-years-old fallow deer. It differs from them a little in colour, and also in shape, but more particularly in the character and colour of the head and muzzle; the former is very small, and the latter is barred with white. They are always lean, and the only fat found upon them is a small piece on the end of the rump.

Proceeded after black game, but had no success; moved farther up the mountains, and saw some straggling birds, but the eminence I tried was too dry for them.

Returned to the mansion, where the laird added much to the satisfaction my success had given me, by the pleasure it seemed to afford him.

Returns of the day; shot, a roebuck and four moor-game; the falcon, a brace.

O CTOBER 6. – Morning very rainy, which prevented my

taking a ride I had promised myself, before I proceeded for Inverness.

At eleven it cleared up, and, apprehending great falls of rain which are common at this season in these parts, I set out accompanied by my old acquaintance, the Rev. Mr Gordon who, with great goodness of heart, came to meet me at Moy This gentleman has a very mechanical turn, and has made himself a very good electrifying machine. He is a young man remarkably modest in his deportment, and in every respec keeps up the character and decency consistent with his pro fession; but being fond of fishing, his parishioners find fault with him; however, he has the resolution and good sense not to give up so innocent an amusement on account of their bigotry and folly.

I much wished that he would dine with me at Inverness where I had invited several of the citizens; but, being Saturday could not prevail upon him.

If the road was excellent on approaching Moy, in return, i was as bad from thence to Inverness, the ride being over the most dreary, barren country ever beheld.

On approaching the metropolis of the Highlands, the fog dissipated, and I got a good view of the town, where I met with two fellow travellers, Mr O. and Major M. with one of whom I had been acquainted some years.

They had just returned that morning from seal shooting, and were on their way to England. I detained them a few minute to give them some directions that might be serviceable, and then, wishing them a good journey, proceeded to the inn.

INVERNESS

Inverness is a town of considerable magnitude, said to contain about eleven thousand inhabitants. Some of the houses in it are tolerably built, but the streets are narrow and dirty. It i situated on a plain, between the Murray Frith and the River Ness; the first, from the narrow Straight of Ardersier, instantly widens into a fine bay. Ships of four or five hundred tons can ride within a mile of the town, and, at high tide, vessels of two hundred tons can come up to the key, which, though small, is made safe and convenient; and this being the last town of any note in North Britain, is the winter residence of many of the neighbouring gentry, and the present *emporium*, as it was the ancient, of the north of Scotland. The imports are chiefly groceries, haberdasheries, hardware, and other necessaries from London, and of late from six to eight hundred hogsheads are annually brought in.

The principal business carried on by the town's people is the spinning of thread, making linen and woollen cloth for their own consumption, and cording and sacking for exportation. Several large buildings have been erected for those purposes, and much business is carried on in private houses. The rest of their exports are chiefly salmon (those of the Ness being esteemed of more exquisite flavour than any other) and herrings, of an inferior kind, taken in the Frith from August to March. The linen manufacture, however, is the most considerable, and saves the place above three thousand pounds a year, which used to go into Holland for that article. The commerce of this town was at its height a century or two ago, when it engrossed the exports of corn, salmon, and herrings; and had besides a great trade in cured cod-fish, now lost; and in those times very large fortunes were made here.

‖ OCTOBER 7. – Morning, heavy rain.

Rose early; but did not set out till ten o'clock, when the day turned out warm and fine, with only some flying clouds on the mountains, and, the sun shining, gave us every advantage, so that we were highly pleased as we passed along with occasional views of Loch Ness; and were induced to stop and take a drawing of one in particular.

The road between Inverness and the lake, about six miles, is most execrable, being covered with an infinite number of loose stones, which are very dangerous to the rider, and very bad for a carriage. I really could not have supposed so bad a road had been allowed to remain, especially when leading to the principal town in the North, and apprehended we should have a very tedious day's journey, as we could scarcely get on above a gentle trot.

The crops of corn, being half cut down, gave a most luxuriant appearance to the country. Though I am told the grain raised here scarcely suffices for the inhabitants, yet fifty thousand head of black cattle, it is computed, are driven annually from the northern counties of Inverness, Ross, &c. into England. The people do not want industry, as appears from their manufactures, and the cultivated circle of land around them, which would be extended, and add beauty, as well as fertility, to the lower parts of the hills and mountains, if their efforts in agriculture were not damped by an extreme scarcity of fuel, for the mosses are greatly worn out; and when coals, loaded with an impolitic duty, are brought from the Frith of Forth, lime is burnt at a great expence.

The scarcity of corn, in the country around Inverness, is well illustrated by a circumstance, which, to the inhabitants, will doubtless appear somewhat trivial; but which, in the eye of a stranger, is not a little curious. It is common in those spots, that, amidst mosses and hills, are here and there covered with corn, to start a number of domestic fowls, like a covey of partridges. These creatures, which travel many a mile for such a repast, and, like the cattle of the country, do not find sustenance within a narrow compass, being equally lean and vigorous, will spring into the air, and fly over an incredible space, cackling like a parcel of wild-geese.

The large plantations of firs, intermixed with oaks, render the scene here truly magnificent; and, on approaching Loch Ness, a wonderful piece of water, the road runs winding along its shore, in the most fantastic manner imaginable.

Stopped at the inn, called the *General's Hut*. This is but an indifferent house; a few eggs, a mutton-chop, wine and other liquors, are all a traveller must expect; also hay and corn; and, upon the whole, it is only fit simply to bait at: we made use of it for this purpose and then proceeded, as fast as possible, to the *Falls of Fiers*, which we saw to the greatest advantage, as there had been a deluge of rain.

These falls differ very much from each other; the lower one, I fancy, exceeds every thing of the kind in Britain, and, I should think, is equal to the boasted Fall of Tivoli.

|| OCTOBER 10. – Morning most charming, but rather sultry.

We made a hasty breakfast, and Mr Gerrard returned back to Loch Awe, about two miles, to take a view of Kilchurn Castle, which we had much admired the preceding night.

Loch Awe is long and waving; its little isles tufted with trees and just appearing above the water. Its two great feeds of water at each extremity, and its singular lateral discharge near one of them, sufficiently mark this great lake, whose whole extent is supposed to be little less than thirty miles. It is finely indented by promontories, advancing and spreading into it a great way, and joined to the main land only by a narrow isthmus. These, with the islands, form a prospect highly variegated and pleasant.

On the east side there is a great deal of land fit for corn, and some of it is applied to that purpose; but what seems best adapted to the genius of the people is grazing. A great number of black cattle are reared here, and a still greater number of sheep.

At the north end of the loch is the ancient castle of Kilchurn, the most elegant ruins I ever saw. It belongs to the Earl of Breadalbane, whose grand-father inhabited it. The great tower was repaired by his lordship, and garrisoned by him in 1745, for the service of government, in order to prevent the rebels making use of that great pass across the kingdom, but it is now fast falling to decay, having lately been struck by lightning.

This castle, in barbarous times, was the ancient den or stronghold of the family, from which they issued forth at the head of their retainers, like the princes and heroes of Homer, and like those of all uncivilized times and countries, to commit occasional depredations on their neighbours. The present possessor has the happiness to live in a milder age, and one more suited to the natural benignity of his disposition. The sculking place of his remote ancestors is abandoned. The Earl of Breadalbane, following the example of his noble predecessor, while he opens his eyes and his fortune to the general good of every part of the country, exercises an elegant hospitality in his charming residence at Loch Tay, in Perthshire, which shows how much the beauty and magnificence of nature may still be improved by art and cultivated taste.

When I was in this country before, I killed some black game, directly opposite to where Mr Gerrard intended to make his sketch; and had then an extraordinary point at six old black cocks together, a very rare circumstance, as they are a lonely bird, and seldom are seen together, except in crowding, or, as they call it here, belling time, when they fight most furiously.

|| Within four miles of Inverary the country very evidently marks the difference between lands unadorned and uncultivated, and those protected, encouraged, and fostered, under the hands of a judicious master. The road is excellent, and the approach, at every instant, becomes more interesting. The woods, varied in their forms, constantly called off the eye, not half satisfied, from one object to another, and the day, adding fresh lustre to these beauties of nature, made me conceive my horse went too fast.

There never was a spot so judiciously assisted as this has been, nor was nature ever more profuse; she seems here to have exerted all her powers. Hills vie with woods, whether the clothing or the clothes shall have the pre-eminence. The forms being so regularly and pleasantly broken, that the agreeable variety of shade, in general so much wished for, is found here at every angle; nor is the watery element willing to relinquish her magnificence to the terrestrial goddess of the woods, the immensely-noble Loch Fine supports the contest, supplying every species of sea-fish, and adds infinite grandeur to the scene, reflecting the different beauties of the surrounding mountains.

The length of this beautiful expanse of water, from the eastern end to the point of Lomond, is about thirty Scotch miles, though its breadth is scarcely two. Its depth is from sixty to seventy fathom. There are no islands in it, and the mountains are so very high, that they are, in general, covered with clouds. At their bases, near the water, there is a good deal of underwood; and in some spots the land is flat enough to admit of corn and grass for hay. There is a great quantity of sea-weed thrown on the beach, which makes excellent manure, and is applied to that purpose. By these means good crops are produced; but so much rain falls that the poor cottager seldom reaps the fruits of his labour. The culture of potatoes here, as in every part of the country, is an object of great care and attention, and answers very well; but the corn, after it is sown, is greatly neglected, and suffered to be choaked up with weeds, while numbers of people are walking about perfectly idle.

This arm of the sea is noted for the vast shoals of herrings that appear here in July, and continue till January. It likewise produces, in great abundance, cod, haddocks, whitings, and various other kinds of fish; the herrings, however, are the most numerous. The highest season is from September to Christmas, when near six hundred boats, with four men each, are employed. A chain of nets is used (for several are united) of a hundred fathoms in length. 'As the herrings swim at very uncertain depths,' observes a late writer, 'so the nets are sunk to the depth the shoal is found to take: the means, therefore, depends much on the judgment, or good furtune, of the fishers, in taking their due depths; for it often happens that one boat will take multitudes while the next does not catch a single fish, which makes the boatmen perpetually enquire of each other about the depth of their nets. These are kept up by buoys to a proper pitch, the ropes that run through them, fastened with pegs, and, by drawing up or letting out the rope, (after taking out the pegs), they adjust the situation, and then replace them. Sometimes the fish swim in twenty fathoms water, sometimes in fifty, and often times even at the bottom.'

Part of those caught are salted for the use of the neighbouring country, and part sent to Glasgow for exportation, two hundred or three hundred horses being every day brought to the water-side from very distant parts. It is computed that each boat gets about forty pounds in the season. A barrel holds five hundred herrings, if they are of the best kind; at a medium seven hundred; but, if more, they are reckoned very poor. The price is about one pound four shillings per barrel; but there is a drawback of the duty on salt for those that are exported.

The great rendezvous of vessels for the fishery of the Western Isles is at Campbeltown, in Cantyre, where they clear out on the 12th of September, and sometimes three hundred busses are seen there at a time: they must return to their different ports by January the 13th, where they ought to receive the premium of two pounds ten shillings per tun of herrings; but it is said to be very ill paid, which is a great discouragement; for, otherwise, this fishing might be increased, and become a source of great profit to individuals, as well as general advantage to the nation.

‖ As we advanced, the lake by degrees became bolder, and, at its termination, the beautiful woods, through which the road winds with great taste, the lawn, formed most happily into the appearance of the richest English dairy farm, clothed with excellent verdure, and herds of the finest cattle, bursts on the eye: centrically situated, in which luxuriant scene, stands the Castle of Inverary, the Seat of His Grace the Duke of Argyle. This is a very elegant, modern building; but has rather a monastic appearance, from the windows being all turned with a Gothic arch. The Duke of Argyle's castle stands very pleasantly, considering the mountainous country in which it is situated. It forms a square, with four turrets: one story is sunk below the surface of the ground; and round this there is a large area, surrounded by iron rails. The castle has a superstructure issuing from the midst, which is a sort of quadrangular turret, glazed on every side, intended to give light to the central part of the house; but which has rather a heavy appearance on the outside, and is by no means pleasing within. In the attic story are eighteen good bed-chambers, and the house contains many other good rooms, though none of them are very large. This castle, the principal seat of the Duke of Argyle, chief of the Campbells, was built by Duke Archibald. It is composed of a coarse *lapis ollaris*, according to Mr Pennant, brought from the other side of Loch Fine, and is the same kind with that found in Norway, of which the King of Denmark's palace at Copenhagen is built. Near the new castle are some remains of the old.

The woods around are very extensive, as are those near the house. The trees, many of which bear marks of high antiquity, are chiefly beech; there are also some oaks, chesnuts, and ash, with a few others, as the plane and silver fir; these, variegated with thriving plantations, beautifully diversify the rides around this charming spot, some of which extend upwards of twelve miles, regularly formed, and, from this quantity of wood, agreeably shaded.

About three hundred acres of land, clear of wood, is laid down chiefly for hay and grazing land: very little of it is applied to the purpose of raising corn; which, if we may judge from the duke's having a large structure in his park for the purpose of drying grain, the quantity of rain that falls being so great as to render this necessary, would be a very arduous attempt.

|| As for the town of Inverary, it is hardly worth notice, being a small, inconsiderable fishing place, and chiefly dependant upon the castle, from which it is removed about half a mile. It is situated on a point of land that runs into the loch, and consists of about two hundred houses, many of which, though small, are neatly built. The people are chiefly employed in fishing, which sometimes employs near one thousand people. Although the herring be a whimsical as well as migrating animal, I must here contradict the report of the herrings having, in a great measure, forsaken Loch Fine, and gone to other parts of the Scottish coast. About three miles from Inverary, there is a woollen manufactory for cloth and carpets. The person who established it failed, but the business is now conducted by another man, who has met with some success. Coals are nearly as dear here as in London, on account of the additional duty, which is a most impolitic imposition, and operates greatly against all manufactures. The price of labour at Inverary is from ten-pence to one shilling a day. On the whole, the general appearance of the castle, town, and environs of Inverary is such as beseem the head of a great clan, in a strong and mountainous country, who, without losing sight of the origin of his family, in rude and warlike times, adopts the improvements of the present period.

OCTOBER 11. – Sunday, cold and very rainy.

In consequence of the weather, and of the hooping-cough reigning in the vicinity of the castle, we did not go to church, which, I understand, is always most scrupulously attended.

OCTOBER 12. – Day fine. Lord Lorn, a very keen shot, politely attended me to the moors, in order to show me some black-game; and, his lordship being desirous to see my pointers out, we took them. I think I never saw any ground better calculated for black-game: we had several points; but the birds made to the full as good use of their optics as we did, and took care not to be led into any danger from our fire. At one point, though at a considerable distance, no less than eighteen black-cocks arose: we followed them to no purpose, though we found them twice.

We killed, however, three brace of a kind of water-fowl, called *muratts*, with which we had good sport. They dive immediately on the fire, and, being at great distances, are not easily killed.

Returned to dinner, in our way calling and taking a look at Mr Gerrard's sketches.

This day finished my shooting in the Highlands, and, what is seldom found to be the case in schemes on so large a scale as this, every thing, in point of country, weather, game, and sport of every kind, far exceeded my most sanguine expectations.

We soon entered *Glen Crow*, where nature seems to have used her utmost efforts, in collecting as much rock and as little verdure as possible; for, except on the lower parts of the mountains, and in some narrow stripes, not a blade of grass appears. Saw very large herds of oxen and flocks of sheep, absolutely hanging, as it were, down the mountains, and at one time were hemmed in by a large drove, some of them going to Falkirk fair; which, from the conversation I had with one of the drovers, I found, consisted of about five thousand; the great prices they bore at the last market, having induced the High-landers to send every beast that could be spared, or that was in any way marketable. Thus stopt by the cattle of the hills, and the road, which was mending, made it a very long drive to reach Tarbat.

‖ OCTOBER 19. The road . . . to Edinburgh, by Lanark, for want of guide posts, is rather difficult to find, and by no means answered the description given of it, being very stony and hilly; and not near so good as the Kirk of Shotts road; nor are the inns better, if I may be allowed to judge by their external appearance, for I proceeded directly for Edinburgh.

‖ The lands on each side of the road are good sheep pastures.

As I passed, we saw a tribe of gentry, whom I took to be smugglers, and, being in good spirits, I gave them to understand that some custom-house officers were behind, in search of them. They thanked me for my hint, and availed themselves of it by leaving the road instantly, which confirmed my suspicions, and I thought they unloaded their goods on the moors; but the day turning out foggy, we soon lost sight of them.

INDEX OF PLACES

INDEX OF PLACES

Index